EXTREMIST

EXTREMIST

A Response to Geert Wilders &
Terrorists Everywhere

by

QASIM RASHID

EXTREMIST: A Response to Geert Wilders & Terrorists Everywhere
by
Qasim Rashid, Esq.

www.twitter.com/MuslimIQ (@MuslimIQ)
www.facebook.com/TheWrongKindOfMuslim
#StopExtremism
www.qasimrashid.com
bookreply@ahmadiyya.us

Cover Design: Salman Sajid
Editor: Kirkus Reviews

Published in the United States by AyHa Publishing
ISBN: 978-0-9893977-2-8

Follow Qasim Rashid on Twitter @MuslimIQ to stay up to date on
EXTREMIST news. Join the conversation by using the hash-tag
#StopExtremism on social media. Visit www.qasimrashid.com to join
Qasim Rashid's email distribution list.

To Ayesha, Hassan, and Hashim, whom
I love more than words can express.

Critical Acclaim

"In EXTREMIST: A Response to Geert Wilders & Terrorists Everywhere, Qasim Rashid has done a great service to Muslims and non-Muslims alike by challenging the scurrilous attacks on Islam by an influential Islamophobe. The only answer to Islamophobia, which promotes, hatred, fear, and violence, is scholarship and debate. Geert Wilders and his ilk must now respond to EXTREMIST or concede defeat in the field of debate and scholarship."

> **— Professor Akbar Ahmed**
> Ibn Khaldun Chair of Islamic Studies, American University, and author of *The Thistle and the Drone: How America's War on Terror became a Global War on Tribal Islam*

"Qasim Rashid deserves commendation for paying critics of Islam the compliment of responding to their objections in a patient point-by-point manner. There are, of course, multiple traditions of Islam and differences of opinion among Muslims as to the meaning of its authoritative teachings. So Rashid cannot, and does not claim to, speak for all Muslims. (Indeed, Rashid and his fellow Ahmadis have been persecuted by their less tolerant co-religionists in places like Pakistan and Saudi Arabia for being "the wrong kind of Muslim.") But his interpretations of Islamic teaching, here lucidly set forth and rigorously defended, give those of us who are non-Muslims a window into an important school of Islamic thought that eschews extremism, violence, and repression and seeks harmony between Muslims of different traditions and with people of other faiths."

> **— Dr. Robert P. George**
> McCormick Professor of Jurisprudence, Princeton University

Contents

Acknowledgments

Above all, it is by the sheer Grace of Almighty Allah that this project was possible. I thank Him for removing all difficulties, and praise Him for His strength, His protection, and His knowledge.

I am eternally grateful to His Holiness the Khalifa of Islam, Hadhrat Mirza Masroor Ahmad, Khalifatul Masih V^at for his generous prayers, guidance, and support. Without his direction, this project could not have come to fruition. May Allah^swt strengthen his hands.

Likewise, I express my sincere appreciation to Respected Ameer USA Dr. Ahsanullah Zafar and Respected Naib Ameer USA Dr. Nasim Rehmatullah for their generous prayers, guidance, and support.

I'd like to express particular gratitude to the following for their remarkable assistance in scholarly research, writing, editing, and style: Naveed Ahmad Malik, Dr. Kashif Chaudhry, Micah Taair, and Sardar Anees Ahmad, each of whom wrote the initial draft to several chapters in this book. Sardar Anees Ahmad also assisted in editing the original manuscript. While my name is listed as the author, it would be an injustice to ignore the incredible contribution each of the aforementioned writers made to this book. Without their time, sacrifice, and support this project would have been much more difficult. I am grateful for their willingness to support this project and contribute their valuable time. The reader is requested to remember each of them in their special prayers, and to thank them personally should they cross paths with them.

Likewise, Maulana Abdur Rashid Yahya, Maulana Mansoor Ahmad Nuruddin, Humera Malik, and Ayesha Noor assisted in scholarly research, editing, and style. In particular, Maulana Abdur Rashid Yahya and Maulana Mansoor Ahmad Nuruddin provided scholarship into advanced Arabic lexicon, translation, interpretation, and Qur'anic hermeneutics. Naveed Ahmad Malik also assisted in this regard. Humera Malik and Ayesha Noor provided valuable research and editing support. I'd also like to express my appreciation to Munir-ud-Din Shams, Additional Wakil-ut-Tasnif, London, for his helpful edits to both style and substance. Likewise, Salman Sajid graciously provided his time and expertise in cover design, layout, and formatting. I am grateful to both Dr. Robert George and Dr. Akbar Ahmed for their generous endorsements.

I hope this "jihad of the pen" sheds light on Islam's actual teachings of peace, pluralism, and human progress. Likewise, I hope this effort again demonstrates what Prophet Muhammad[sa] demonstrated fourteen hundred years ago—that Islam champions universal religious freedom, universal human rights, intellectual investigation, and interfaith harmony.

In the end, we praise Allah and send blessings on His Noble Messenger[sa]. Ameen.

Qasim Rashid, Esq.
Richmond, Virginia
March 23, 2014

Publisher's Note

In this book the name of Muhammad[sa], the holy prophet[sa] of Islam, has been followed by the symbol [sa], which is an abbreviation for the salutation *sallallahu 'alaihi wasallam* ("may peace and blessings of Allah be upon him"). The names of other prophets and messengers are followed by the symbol [as], an abbreviation for *'alaihissalam/'alaihimussalam* ("on whom be peace"). The salutations have generally not been set out in full for the sake of brevity, but they should nevertheless be understood as being repeated in full in each case. The symbol [ra] is used with the name of the companions of the holy prophet[sa] and those of the promised messiah[as]. It stands for r*adi allahu 'anhu/'anha/'anhum* ("may Allah be pleased with him/with her/with them"). Likewise, [rm] stands for *rahimahullahu ta'ala* ("may Allah's mercy be on him") and [aba] stands for *ayyadahullahu ta'ala* ("may Allah, the almighty, help him").

Hadhrat is an Islamic title of respect translatable to "His Holiness."

In transliterating Arabic words, we have followed the following system adopted by the Royal Asiatic Society.

ا   at the beginning of a word, pronounced as *a, i, u*, preceded by a very slight aspiration, like *h* in the English word *honor*.

ث   *th*, pronounced like *th* in the English word *thing*.

ح   *h*, a guttural aspirate, stronger than *h*.

خ   *kh*, pronounced like the Scotch *ch* in *loch*.

ذ   *dh*, pronounced like the English *th* in that.

ص   *s*, strongly articulated *s*.

ض   *d*, similar to the English *th* in *this*.

ط   *t*, strongly articulated palatal *t*.

ظ   *z*, strongly articulated *z*.

ع   ', a strong guttural, the pronunciation of which must be learned by the ear.

غ *gh*, a sound approached very nearly in the *r* in *grasseye* in French, and in the German *r*. It requires the muscles of the throat to be in the "gargling" position while pronouncing.

ق *q*, a deep, guttural *k* sound.

ى ', a sort of catch in the voice.

Please note that in transliterated words, the letter *e* is to be pronounced as in *prey*, which rhymes with *day*; however, the pronunciation is flat without the element of the English diphthong. If in Urdu and Persian words *e* is lengthened a bit more, it is transliterated as *ei*, to be pronounced as *ei* in *feign* without the element of diphthong. For the nasal sound of *n* we have used the symbol *ń*, to be pronounced as *mein*.

The consonants not included in the above list have the same phonetic value as in the principal languages of Europe.

We have not transliterated Arabic words that have become part of English language, e.g., Islam, Mahdi, Qur'an, Hijra, Ramadan, hadith, ulema, *ummah*, sunna, *kafir*, etc.

Qur'an Citations

In our system of Qur'anic references, we have counted *bismillah hirahman niraheem* ("in the name of God, the gracious, the merciful) as the first verse of each chapter in which it appears. Therefore, our references may seem one verse off from some references found elsewhere. This is not an error. We ask our readers to keep this slight adjustment in mind when researching any Qur'anic reference.

Introduction

"Faith is restraint against all violence. Let no believer commit violence."
— PROPHET MUHAMMAD[SA]

Everyone has a 9/11 story. Where they were, whom they were with, what went through their minds as they watched television. I was nineteen, a sophomore in college, and lived in Lombard—a suburb seventeen miles due west of Chicago. I remember not immediately realizing the scope of what was happening. We've grown so accustomed to smartphones and social media, it is easy to forget how much slower information travelled just ten or fifteen years ago. In fact, even my car back then, an old, beat-up Nissan, didn't have a radio. As I arrived at work that morning, I saw a crowd gathered in front of the big-screen television in the lobby. Nothing attracts a crowd like a crowd, so naturally I wandered over to catch up on what I'd missed during my twenty-minute commute.

Right then, on live television, I saw the second plane strike.

A gasp went through the crowd as some covered their mouths while others literally pulled their hair out. What was happening? Who was to blame? No one quite knew, but we remained glued to the screen, waiting for answers. It wasn't long before we began to hear names like Osama bin Laden and Al Qaeda and words like *jihad* and *mujahideen*—all for the first time. It wasn't long before I felt eyes turn to me with a strange look. My heart tore in two. Here my nation had been hijacked, my fellow citizens murdered in cold blood—and now my faith was being hijacked and blamed. I quickly went from being a proud American with a brother in the United States Marine Corps on September 10 to a "for-

1

eigner Muzlum" who was a prime suspect at every traffic stop and airport by September 12.

President Bush insisted during a speech just six days after 9/11 that:

> The face of terrorist [sic] is not the true faith of Islam. That's not what Islam is all about. Islam is peace. These terrorists don't represent peace, they represent evil and war. When we think of Islam, we think of a faith that brings comfort to a billion people around the world. Billions of people find comfort and solace and peace. And that's made brothers and sisters out of every race, out of every race. America counts millions of Muslims amongst our citizens, and Muslims make an incredibly valuable contribution to our country.[1]

Three days later, on September 20, 2001, President Bush added,

> I also want to speak tonight directly to Muslims throughout the world. We respect your faith. It's practiced freely by many millions of Americans, and by millions more in countries that America counts as friends. Its teachings are good and peaceful, and those who commit evil in the name of Allah blaspheme the name of Allah. The terrorists are traitors to their own faith, trying, in effect, to hijack Islam itself. The enemy of America is not our many Muslim friends; it is not our many Arab friends.[2]

---

1. "9/11 10th anniversary: Bush statement recalled, 'Islam is peace,'" MassLive.com,

2. "George W. Bush Addresses Muslims in the Aftermath of the 9/11 Attacks," Georgetown University Berkley Center for Religion, Peace and World Affairs, accessed December 14, 2013,
    http://berkleycenter.georgetown.edu/resources/quotes/george-w-bush-addresses-muslims-in-the-aftermath-of-the-9-11-attacks.

But sadly, President Bush's words could not drown out the increasing voices of anti-Muslim personalities decisively bent on driving a wedge between Muslims and non-Muslims. And sadly, it is a wedge that seems to drive itself deeper every year. Since 9/11, anti-Muslim organizations have spent more than $42 million to advance an agenda that demonizes and creates fear of Muslims.[3]

And it has worked.

For starters, only a fool denies the devastation and barbarity of 9/11. Only a coldhearted person remains callous to the horrific loss of life. Every aspect of 9/11 is condemnable. And for the record, as an American Muslim, I condemn every aspect of 9/11—as does the *overwhelming* majority of Muslims worldwide of all sects and all backgrounds.

Still, dozens of American states have tried to pass nonsensical "anti-Shariah" laws, and numerous European nations have passed laws banning the veil, minarets, or Islamic religious symbols. Hate crimes against Muslims and anyone who "looks" Muslim (Sikhs and Hindus, for example) have increased. And even police forces, such as the New York Police Department, have engaged in illegal surveillance of their local mosques. Indeed, Norwegian terrorist Anders Breivik cited multiple American anti-Muslim personalities in his fifteen-hundred-page, hate-filled manifesto as the inspiration for his mass murder. The Center for American Progress has compiled an outstanding report titled: *Fear, Inc.* which well illustrates just how systematic the anti-Muslim campaign actually is and how quickly it is spreading.

But to what avail does this anti-Muslim campaign exist? I assure you, it is no different than the anti-Catholic, anti-Jew, and anti-Mormon

---

3.   Faiz Shakir, "REPORT: $42 Million From Seven Foundations Helped Fuel The Rise Of Islamophobia In America," Think Progress, accessed December 14, 2013, http://thinkprogress.org/politics/2011/08/26/304306/islamophobia-network/. (Original report: http://www.americanprogress.org/wp-content/uploads/issues/2011/08/pdf/islamophobia_intro.pdf.)

campaigns of yesteryear in America. Yet, the anti-Muslim campaign grows.

And thus, to ensure we stop the wedge being driven between Muslims and non-Muslims, the conversation needs to go beyond mere condemnation and into the realm of understanding and dialogue—and that is where this book advances the relationship between Muslims and non-Muslims. It arms Muslims and non-Muslims alike with the world's most powerful weapon—knowledge—to combat the false narrative against Islam. As we've seen in the devastating wars since 9/11, maintaining fear and ignorance of one another only ensures a higher likelihood of more violence and disorder. Nations and peoples do not go to war because they were too civil with each other or because they maintained too much open and honest dialogue. War begins when communication ceases. Fear begins where education ends.

And such is the greatest intellectual tragedy of 9/11—that millions of Americans, and indeed Westerners as a whole, received their first introduction to what they were told was Islam when the Twin Towers fell. It is important for non-Muslims to grasp the gravity of this fact. No intelligent Christian would approve of non-Christians learning about Christianity from the Ku Klux Klan, the Irish Republican Army, or the Lord's Resistance Army. Likewise, no intelligent Muslim approves of the learning of Islam from extremists like the Taliban or Al Qaeda, or from anti-Muslim extremists presenting a false narrative. This false narrative continues to drive the wedge between Muslims and non-Muslims, in America and internationally. This vicious cycle of misinformation and fear must stop.

And it will stop when we do enough to share the right narrative on Islam—one that has not been heard enough just yet. As anti-Islam extremists and extremists ascribing to Islam continue to present their false narrative, this book presents a response to both. Perhaps America's greatest characteristic is its undying support for freedom of conscience and expression. And it is in that spirit that I respond to these false narratives on Islam and provide a candid and clear example, to all non-

4

Muslims (and Muslims) of all backgrounds, of what Islam actually means. What does the right kind of Muslim look like? What are his or her views on apostasy, blasphemy, gender equity, and of other faiths?

It is critically important to note that the anti-Muslim sentiment is not just some "American" issue. Indeed, this book primarily tackles and thoroughly addresses one such international anti-Muslim personality: Dutch politician Geert Wilders. But my response here should not be viewed as just a response to him, as the answers I provide are just as applicable to any number of anti-Islam critics worldwide. Indeed, much of Wilders's rhetoric echoes verbatim the rhetoric that accelerated immediately after 9/11, and it certainly copies that of several of his anti-Muslim cohorts in years prior. I respond to allegations Wilders has made simply because his polemic, "Marked for Death," is one of the more recent books to spread a false narrative of Islam. I can complete a similar analysis of the propaganda any number of anti-Muslim personalities has published over the years. Perhaps in the future I will. But for now, while my case analysis is of Wilders's book, I promise my readers that my analysis offers a wide application.

I present here a true narrative of Islam, and my intent is to make this a worldwide conversation. Why do I believe I can speak for Islam? Well, if anti-Muslim personalities can spend $42 million to present their false narratives, and if terrorists can propagandize their extreme narratives, then surely I—as a practicing Muslim—have an inherent right and obligation in this free country and world to present a factual narrative.

Life is more than mere survival. For us to thrive as humanity, we must learn about each other from each other—not from those with ulterior motives and agendas. Yes, everyone has a 9/11 story, and mine isn't over yet. I have much more to say. I thank you for listening, and I thank you for arming yourself with the knowledge presented here.

So, to write the right narrative on Islam, I begin with a most simple, yet most important question: Who is the right kind of Muslim? To answer, I turn your attention to the first Muslim and the most righteous Muslim who ever was or ever will be: Prophet Muhammad[sa].

The Prophet Muhammad[sa]

At the dawn of the seventh century in Arabia, a lone voice of light emerged from an era of utter darkness. That voice came to proclaim the unity of God and the unity of humankind. That voice taught absolute justice in interpersonal and international affairs, equity between men and women, and an uncompromising zeal to establish universal freedom of conscience. By the age of eight, that young voice from the tribe of Quraish lost both parents and his grandfather—yet he managed to find some comfort in his uncle's home. During the next three decades, he established himself among his people as a beacon of integrity, earning the nicknames of As-Sádiq and Al-Amín, the Truthful and the Trustworthy.

In 610 AD, he was informed, through divine revelation, that he was the long-awaited prophet foretold in the Old Testament, the New Testament, the Bhagavad Gita, and the Vedas, and various other ancient and noble religious traditions. Though he began weak and alone with every hand against him, he won the hearts of virtually all those around him and established a universal religion based on the tenets of justice, equality, and compassion. That lone voice emerged to be none other than the Unlettered One, the Seal of the Prophets, the Prince of Peace, the King of Arabia, the Paraclete, the Comforter, the Chief among ten thousand, the Mercy for the entire Universe, the Orphan who adopted the world, the Chosen One, the Holy Founder of Islam, the Messenger of Allah, grandson of Abdul Muttalib, son of Abdullah, father of Qasim—none other than the altogether lovely Muhammad Mustafa[sa].

Dr. Michael Hart ranks him as "the most influential person in history" and "a secular and religious leader," writing:

I find in his character such diverse and manifold qualities, as it would be impossible to find in any other man whose biography has been preserved by history. He is a king having a whole country under his control, but never claiming mastery even on his own self, ever taking pride in his being the serf of God.[4]

Nearly two centuries prior to Dr. Hart, French poet and statesman Alphonse de Lamartine wrote:

Philosopher, orator, apostle, legislator, warrior, conqueror of ideas, restorer of rational dogmas, of a cult without images; the founder of twenty terrestrial empires and of one spiritual empire, that is Muhammad[sa]. As regards all standards by which human greatness may be measured, we may well ask, is there any man greater than he?[5]

Annie Besant, a prominent British theosophist, women's rights activist, and feminist wrote her own tribute to Prophet Muhammad[sa] in the early twentieth century:

It is impossible for anyone who studies the life and character of the great Prophet of Arabia, who knew how he taught and how he lived, to feel anything but reverence for that mighty Prophet, one of the great messengers of the Supreme. And although in what I put to you I shall say many things which may be familiar to many, yet I myself feel, whenever I reread them, a new way of ad-

---

4. Michael Hart, The 100: A Ranking of the Most Influential Persons in History (1978), 33.

5. Alphonse de Lamartine, *Histoire de la Turquie*, vol. 2.

miration, a new sense of reverence for that mighty Arabian teach-er.[6]

Likewise, Nobel laureate Sir George Bernard Shaw states:

> I have always held the religion of Muhammad in high estimation because of its wonderful vitality. It is the only religion, which appears to me to possess that assimilating capacity to the changing phase of existence, which can make itself appeal to every age. I have studied him—the wonderful man and in my opinion far from being an anti-Christ, he must be called the Saviour of Humanity.[7]

These tributes form but a snapshot of the volumes of unmatched praise heaped on Prophet Muhammad[sa] for his unmatched contributions to humanity. Nobel laureates, Oscar winners, scientists, physicians, professors, statesmen, poets, philosophers, feminists, and historians; friends, foes, Muslims, non-Muslims, Eastern scholars, and Western academics—all testify to Muhammad's[sa] greatness.

Yet, with one blind swipe of the pen, contemporary critics ignorantly and unfairly ignore these great individuals who came decades, even centuries before, and attribute the most vicious propaganda to that mighty Arabian teacher[sa].

One such critic is Mr. Geert Wilders, author of the recent polemic against Prophet Muhammad[sa] and Islam entitled *Marked for Death: Islam's War Against the West and Me*. The researched testimony of the aforementioned scholars collectively demonstrates a fact Wilders attempts to subvert throughout his book: that throughout history, Prophet Muhammad[sa] has consistently been regarded as nothing less than the

---

6.   Annie Besant, The Life and Teachings of Mohammad (Madras: 1932), 4.

7.   Sir George Bernard Shaw, *The Genuine Islam* 1, no. 8 (1936).

greatest man that ever lived. But this is but one of many facts Wilders censors from his readers. Indeed, this is a fact that all anti-Muslim personalities censor from their audience.

But scholars and supporters aside, perhaps the strongest rebuttal of critical allegations against Prophet Muhammad[sa] is one that the Qur'an revealed fourteen hundred years ago. This argument is so simple that any child can understand it. Yet it is simultaneously so profound that no person on Earth—layman or scholar—has ever managed to refute it. In his polemic, Wilders, too, is unable to refute this argument that testifies to Prophet Muhammad's[sa] perfection and greatness. Indeed, it is one of many powerful arguments Wilders ignores altogether.

When questioned whether he was the recipient of divine revelation, God commanded Prophet Muhammad[sa] to declare, "I have indeed lived among you a whole lifetime before this. Will you not then understand?"[8] In this verse, Prophet Muhammad's[sa] critics are reminded to reflect upon his entire life and cite a single flaw in his character, a single injustice he committed, or a single lie that he told. History records that not a single contemporary—friend or foe, ally or adversary—could cite a flaw in Muhammad's[sa] life prior to his claim to prophethood. Accordingly, history records that the criticism he received after his claim to prophethood was not of his character, but of the claim itself. The argument concludes, therefore, that if Prophet Muhammad[sa] lived a demonstrably flawless and truthful life before his claim to prophethood, how could he suddenly lie about God?

Despite the numerous absurd allegations anti-Islam critics like Wilders launch against Prophet Muhammad[sa], not even one addresses Prophet Muhammad's[sa] character *prior* to his claim to prophethood. Had Wilders demonstrated that Prophet Muhammad[sa] had lived an imperfect life before claiming prophethood, no other argument would be necessary. But Wilders knows he cannot do this, because no flaw exists

---

8.   Qur'an 10:17.

and history records no flaw—indeed, even Prophet Muhammad's[sa] most vehement critics of that time could not cite a single one. Instead, Wilders's blind objection to Muhammad's[sa] prophethood itself provides no credence to Wilders's arguments. After all, why is it surprising that Wilders—a self-described atheist—finds objection to a man claiming prophethood? Wilders may just as well levy this objection against Jesus Christ[as], Moses[as], Abraham[as], Krishna[as], or any other claimant of divine guidance—and his objection would be baseless just the same.

Indeed, Prophet Muhammad[sa] is a model for all of humankind. The countless endorsements from countless non-Muslim historians and scholars demonstrate that even those who did not accept Islam still recognized Prophet Muhammad[sa] as a truthful and compassionate person. Thus, by attempting to promote a false narrative, anti-Islam critics not only deceive contemporary society, they shamelessly undermine centuries of history from a limitless list of prolific theologians, historians, scholars, and world leaders. As I write the truthful narrative on Islam, I will present to you, the reader, with what those scholars and historians saw in Prophet Muhammad[sa] and why they fell in love with him. I will arm you with the knowledge that convinced them.

And though Wilders may never be convinced of Prophet Muhammad's[sa] truthful character, he is not my concern. In a world where information is freely exchanged, the best ideas win out. Unlike Wilders, who wants to censor the Qur'an and physically prevent Muslims from migrating, I welcome open dialogue and discussion. I believe that the best antidote for false narratives, like the one anti-Islam extremists like Wilders and extremists ascribing to Islam both espouse, are truthful narratives like that of Prophet Muhammad[sa]. Indeed, my book also repudiates extremists ascribing to Islam who, like anti-Islam extremists, miss Prophet Muhammad's[sa] true nature of compassion, justice, and service to humanity. Such extremists are a cancer to humanity, undoubtedly the worst creatures on Earth.

Prophet Muhammad[sa] is the right kind of Muslim, and it is his narrative we must study to understand Islam. As Hadhrat Ayesha[ra] once declared, "Muhammad^{sa} is the walking Qur'an." But let us pause for a moment. Before we can delve too substantively into Wilders's polemic, it is necessary to review some crucial preliminary guidelines. These guidelines will help the reader form the proper scope and expectation of what this book, *EXTREMIST*, offers.

Preliminary Guidelines

I have titled this book *EXTREMIST: A Response to Geert Wilders & Terrorists Everywhere*. Merriam-Webster defines an extremist as "a person who holds extreme or fanatical political or religious views, especially one who resorts to or advocates extreme action." Geert Wilders has well established his reputation as a fanatical politician demanding extreme actions: banning the Qur'an, forcibly stopping Islam from spreading, ceasing all immigration from Muslim majority nations—and the list goes on. My book takes the lead in providing a point-by-point refutation of Geert Wilders's extremist polemic, *Marked for Death: Islam's War Against the West and Me*. Likewise, my book adds to the plethora of scholarship already available to repudiate terrorists ascribing to Islam.

My book promotes a movement in society of intellectual dialogue. It is a "jihad of the pen" that shields against the antipluralism vitriol those like Wilders spew. Prophet Muhammad^{sa} imbibed this intellectual movement throughout his life with his multiple letters imploring peace to world leaders and his interfaith dialogue with, for example, Christians of Najran and of Abyssinia. The Qur'an champions this movement, constantly exhorting Muslims to ponder, reflect, investigate, and educate. This book once again demonstrates that the best, and indeed only, means to defend Islam is with the pen, with scholarship, and with intellect. This is the Islam for which Prophet Muhammad^{sa} stood, and this is the Islam for which billions of Muslims stand today.

As you read *EXTREMIST*, I ask you to keep a few matters in mind.

First, nothing in this book should be construed to endorse, approve, or legitimize the death threats and violence that Wilders faces. Those who threaten or intimidate Wilders or any critic of Islam with violence are cowards behaving contrary to Islamic teachings, and their actions are condemnable without exception. Furthermore, such cowards do more to harm Islam than Wilders ever could, because they provide the examples that Wilders needs to allege that Islam is a violent religion. My sincere hope and prayer is that Wilders remains unharmed, and I condemn anyone who intends or advocates worldly force or worldly harm against him. As a Muslim, I intend to disprove Wilders's allegations through reason, thereby challenging Wilders's assertion that Muslims avoid debate and scholarship. Thus, in presenting this response, I send Wilders a message of peaceful dialogue and exchange while categorically condemning any and all worldly force against him.

Next, it is necessary to recognize this book's scope. Though Wilders insists that he is some sort of groundbreaking, anti-Islam champion, the fact is that he is no pioneer of anti-Islam rhetoric. Like his predecessors, Wilders presents the same baseless arguments as all other anti-Islam critics against Islam, Prophet Muhammad[sa], the Qur'an, the first four khalifas (generally known as the *khulafa rashidin*, the "rightly guided khalifas"), historical Islamic governments, contemporary Islamic governments, and against individual Muslims contemporarily and throughout world history. This book responds specifically to Wilders's allegations against Islam, Prophet Muhammad[sa], the Qur'an, and the *khulafa rashidin*. This book neither excuses nor answers for Muslim political regimes or for the criminal and violent acts of individual Muslims throughout history or today.

The reason for this is simple. If Islam is to be judged, it must be judged according to the life of its holy founder—Prophet Muhammad[sa] and the *khulafa rashidin*, who were Prophet Muhammad's[sa] closest companions. For example, to hold Prophet Muhammad[sa] or the Qur'an accountable for 9/11 is tantamount to holding Jesus Christ[as] and the Bible accountable for Joseph Kony and the Lord's Resistance Army

(LRA). The LRA has, for example, murdered thousands and maimed tens of thousands—all in the name of Christ—and with the stated mission of establishing a theocratic state based on the Ten Commandments. According to Wilders's logic, Christ must also be held liable for the four-hundred-year African slave trade that resulted in upward of twenty million deaths, the Spanish Inquisition in which not even infants were spared, the European witch hunt in which thousands of innocent women were burned at the stake, the destruction of the Native Americans by Christian imperialists, and the conquests of Africa and Australia.

Likewise, by Wilders's logic, Moses and the Old Testament should be held accountable for Baruch Goldstein, an American Israeli doctor who committed the 1994 Cave of the Patriarchs massacre, mercilessly murdering twenty-nine Muslim worshipers and injuring one hundred twenty-five more. Geert Wilders, a self-proclaimed atheist/agnostic, should himself be accountable for the human rights atrocities in atheist/agnostic China—in which more than fifty million were brutally murdered. If this line of argumentation sounds ridiculous—it should. Yet this is precisely the line of argumentation Wilders espouses, citing violent actions of certain Muslims in his attack against Islam and the Prophet Muhammad[sa].

But Wilders has a ready response to the present argument:

Most people today, even most Christians, will acknowledge that many Christians throughout history committed terrible crimes in the name of Christ. [President John Quincy] Adams, however, rightly observed that such actions actually violate Christian doctrine. This is not the case with Islam, since the Koran plainly sanctions violence in the name of Allah.[9]

9.   Geert Wilders, Marked for Death: Islam's War Against the West and Me (2012), 19–20.

In this instance, among many others, Wilders presents no reference for his assertion that "the Koran plainly sanctions violence in the name of Allah."[10] Instead, he relies solely on President Adams's opinion. President Adams also offers nothing from the Qur'an to legitimize his own opinion.

But herein lies a classic example of the double standard Wilders employs when judging Islam and Christianity. Wilders still passionately defends the God of Christianity and Judaism—insisting that He is a different God from the God of Islam. Not only is such an assertion meritless, this assertion does far more to harm Wilders's argument than help it. After all, Judeo-Christian histories, even up through contemporary times, present no shortage of religious violence. By Wilders's logic against Islam, we must ignorantly and blindly also condemn all Jews and Christians and their respective faiths.

For example, the transatlantic slave trade thrived for more than four centuries under the assumption of Christian dominance. The Bible was commonly used both as the justification for slavery and to ensure that slaves did not revolt.[11] Ephesians 6:5 was a Christian slave owner favorite for pushing this agenda: "Servants be obedient to them that are your masters according to the flesh, with fear and trembling, in singleness of your heart, as unto Christ."[12]

Christopher Columbus and the Catholic Church together laid the groundwork for this indoctrination and enabled the foundation for the transatlantic slave trade. Columbus wrote to King Ferdinand and Queen Isabella:

> Your Highnesses, as Catholic Christians and Princes who love the holy Christian faith, and the propagation of it, and who are

---

10. Ibid.

11. Gayraud S. Wilmore, *Black Religion and Black Radicalism*, 2nd ed. (1983), 24.

12. Ibid.

enemies to the sect of Mahomet and to all idolatries and heresies, resolved to send me, Cristobal Colon, to the said parts of India to see the said princes...with a view that they might be converted to our holy faith...Thus, after having turned out all the Jews from all your kingdoms and lordships...your Highnesses gave orders to me that with a sufficient fleet I should go to the said parts of India...I shall forget sleep, and shall work at the business of navigation, so that the service is performed.[13]

Pope Alexander, too, blessed Columbus's actions, issuing an *inter cetera* document that articulated his desire that the "discovered" people be "subjugated and brought to the [Christian] faith itself,"[14] hoping that this would propagate the "Christian Empire."[15] Upon hearing of this endorsement, Portugal complained to the pope that his edict permitted conquer of even Christian lands. The pope issued another edict on May 4, 1493, that Spain shall not try to establish dominion over lands already "[in] the possession of any Christian lords."[16] According to Wilders, these state policies by Christian leaders and Christian generals in the name of Christ do not represent Christianity. Yet a rogue band of Muslims acting violently somehow directly represents Islam.

Lest Wilders claim that the slave trade, among the others provided, is an ancient example, perhaps a contemporary one will suffice. After decades in which Black Americans were brutally persecuted, on November 20, 1962, John F. Kennedy became America's first president to issue an

13. E. G. Borne, The Northmen, Columbus and Cabot, 985–1503: The Voyages of the Northmen, The Voyages of Columbus and of John Cabot (1906), 76.

14. Frances Gardiner Davenport, *European Treaties Bearing on the History of the United States and Its Dependencies to 1648*, vol. 1, (Washington, D.C.: Carnegie Institution of Washington, 1917), 68.

15. John Boyd Thacher, *Christopher Columbus*, vol. 11 (New York: G.P. Putnam's Sons, 1903), 127.

16. Davenport, *European Treaties*, 68.

executive order barring racial and religious discrimination in federally financed housing. This executive order was necessary because Black Americans continued to suffer through perpetual and increasing discrimination and violence from certain Christian organizations in the United States.[17] Thus, it was civil law, not Christianity, that protected Black Americans from terrorism even in the latter half of the twentieth century.

Wilders's attempt to paint Islam exclusively as a religion that justifies extremism ignores the atrocities committed in the name not just of Christianity, but also of Hinduism,[18] Judaism,[19] and especially secularism.

Yes, secularist terrorism not only exists, but also has unleashed unprecedented carnage in the modern era. In fact, University of Chicago Professor Robert Pape, who serves as director of the Chicago Project on Suicide Terrorism, reports that the Tamil Tigers of Sri Lanka have

---

17. Ibid., 432.

18. Examples of Hindu terrorism: see Zubair Ahmed, "'Hindu terrorism' debate grips India," BBC News, last updated November 27, 2008, accessed May 26, 2012, http://news.bbc.co.uk/2/hi/7739541.stm; and Simon Denyer and Rama Lakshmi, "Hindu terrorism charges for India to reflect on prejudices against Muslims," The Washington Post, March 14, 2011, accessed May 26, 2012, http://www.washingtonpost.com/wp-dyn/content/article/2011/03/12/AR2011031202421.html.

19. Examples of Jewish religious terrorism: The Gush Emunim Underground (1979–84) was formed by members of the Isra'eli political movement Gush Emunim. This group is most well known for two actions: first, the bomb attacks on the mayors of West Bank cities on June 2, 1980, and second, an abandoned plot to blow up the Temple Mount mosques. The Isra'eli judge Zvi Cohen, heading the sentencing panel at the group's trial, stated that they had three motives "not necessarily shared by all the defendants. The first motive, at the heart of the Temple Mount conspiracy, is religious." See also the "Bat Ayin Underground" (or Bat Ayin group). In 2002, four people from Bat Ayin and Hebron were arrested outside of Abu Tor School, a Palestinian girls' school in East Jerusalem, with a trailer filled with explosives. Three of the men were convicted for the attempted bombing. Likewise, Eden Natan-Zada killed four Isra'eli Arab civilians on August 4, 2005. Author Ami Pedhzer describes his motivations as religious.

committed more suicide bombings over the past three decades than "Al Qaeda, Hamas or Islamic Jihad," and more than seventy thousand individuals have died in these acts of terrorism.[20] According to Professor Pape, the Tamil Tigers are "a purely secularist terrorist group."[21] If we apply Wilders's logic, Wilders himself must be expelled from Europe and America, because the terrorist group that has committed the most acts of terror during the past thirty years is, like Wilders, secularist. (As a side, Wilders does not ascribe to any faith. He explains he was a radical atheist but is now *more so* agnostic. For the purposes of this book, I take a broad approach to avoid misidentifying).

The purpose of this exercise is not to debate whether the Bible justifies or condemns slavery—nor is it to attack Christianity. Muslims revere Christ[as] and all the Old Testament prophets as God's perfect and beloved messengers. Indeed, one of Islam's Six Articles of Faith is to believe in *all* of God's prophets. This exercise in revisiting dark chapters of history demonstrates that extremism exists in every religion and secular ideology and that broad-brush strokes condemning an entire population for the acts of a few are absurd.

This absurdity *should* be of no surprise to Wilders. In fact, Wilders's polemic becomes even more bizarre because he repeatedly admits that the vast majority of Muslims are moderate.[22] For example, during a BBC *Hardtalk* interview, Wilders explained, "I don't believe that the majority of Muslims are terrorists. I acknowledge the fact that the majority of Muslims are not terrorists, I have a problem with Islam."[23] His statement, however, contradicts his book's repeated focus on individual Muslims, political regimes, and terrorists acting in Islam's name. Still, I

---

20. Lynn Neary, "Tamil Tigers: Suicide Bombing Innovators," May 21, 2009, accessed May 26, 2012, http://www.npr.org/templates/story/story.php?storyId=104391493.

21. Ibid.

22. Geert Wilders, interview by Stephen Sackur, Hardtalk, BBC, August 2008, accessed August 21, 2012, http://www.youtube.com/watch?v=o6cFKQNBH3s.

23. Ibid.

embrace his statement that the majority of Muslims are not terrorists and therefore exclusively address his allegations against Islam—where his "problem" resides. Should Wilders object that I've ignored his complaints about individual Muslims, I merely direct his attention to his own statement.

Accordingly, the reader will note that my response to Wilders is "front heavy." That is, the vast majority of his arguments are addressed in chapters 1 through 6, while chapters 7 through 13 remain largely empty. This is for two reasons.

First, Wilders repeats himself numerous times. For example, his allegation that Islam prescribes death for apostasy appears in his chapter 2, chapter 4, chapter 7, and in chapter 10. Rather than address Wilders's allegation about Islam and apostasy four separate times, I thoroughly address it in my chapter 2. As a rule, I have addressed each of his arguments in full according to the chapter in which they first appear.

Second, Wilders spends the lion's share of the second half of his book complaining about acts of terrorism that Muslims have committed and about corrupt political practices prevalent in several Muslim-majority nations. Both of these matters are outside the scope of my response for reasons already mentioned. That is, Islam must be judged based on the Qur'an and Prophet Muhammad[sa], not on the acts of politicians and terrorists claiming to act in the name of Islam. Despite claiming that he has no problems with Muslims, Wilders spends the vast majority of the latter chapters of his polemic explaining his problems with Muslims. Wilders ignores the fact that Muslims worldwide have condemned unjust Muslim political regimes long before Wilders ever heard the word *Islam*, and we continue to do so despite his baseless belief to the contrary.

Furthermore, one significant purpose of my book is to again condemn extremists who ascribe their acts to Islam and to do so by referencing the correct application of Islam as Prophet Muhammad[sa] taught. My book is not just about repudiating Wilders, it is also about demonstrating that the Islam of terrorist organizations like the Taliban or Jamaat-e-

Islaami having nothing to do with the true Islam of Prophet Muhammadˢᵃ. Therefore, it makes little sense to address individual acts of terrorism that Muslims have committed, or discuss corrupt political practices prevalent in several Muslim-majority nations, when one driving purpose of my book is to write the narrative *against* such acts of extremism. The overriding principles my book espouses discuss what Islam actually teaches as Prophet Muhammadˢᵃ taught. This approach effectively demonstrates that the acts of terror and corruption Wilders objects to are a reflection only of those committing the acts—not something Islam endorses, much less teaches.

Unfortunately, and finally, while I have worked diligently to write this comprehensive response, it became difficult to respond to many of Wilders's allegations because of his citations—or lack thereof. Wilders exercises extreme liberty in formulating his arguments and commits the following three cardinal errors that any student of legitimate scholarship would find untenable. I found it necessary to address these errors directly.

Logistical Issues in Responding to Wilders's Allegations

First, Wilders all too often does not provide citations in support of his arguments. For example, early in his book, Wilders states while referring to fellow atheist and known anti-Islam personality Ayaan Hirsi Ali, "[by] renouncing her Islamic faith, [Ali] had committed apostasy, the ultimate crime in Islam, for which the Koran prescribes the death penalty; once you are Islamic, you are never allowed to leave."[24] Wilders proposes four outlandish allegations against Islam: that apostasy is crime in Islam, that it is not just a crime but the *ultimate* crime in Islam, that the Qur'an prescribes the death penalty for apostates, and that "Islamics" are

---

24. Wilders, Marked for Death, 8.

never allowed to leave Islam. Remarkably, Wilders does not offer a *single* reference for any of these allegations.

This begs the question: Is it necessary to respond to such baseless statements? Wilders's lack of citation demonstrates that his book is anything but legitimate nonfiction. Yet I found myself compelled to respond to such allegations, because failure to respond might be incorrectly interpreted as an inability to respond. Still, I hope the reader recognizes that by refusing to cite his arguments, Wilders exercises gross disregard for legitimate scholarship practices.

Moreover, such a tactic is abhorrent to free speech and honest dialogue. As I demonstrate numerous times in my response, Wilders repeatedly censors crucial information from his readers to twist arguments his way. His "death for apostasy" allegation is but one of many such examples. While Wilders fancies himself a "champion of free speech," his repeated and deliberate censorship proves quite the contrary.

Second, when Wilders manages to offer some reference to support an assertion, he all too often cites anti-Islam websites, recognized hatemongers, and/or those who do not have a shred of peer-reviewed academic credentials on Islam. In his book, Wilders cites hatemongers as alleged authorities—and those same hatemongers then cite Wilders as an authority. This is not research, but the very definition of propaganda.

For perspective, I do not use the term *hatemongers* lightly; it is in fact not even my term. Rather, it is employed by the Southern Poverty Law Center (SPLC), an American-based, nonpartisan, nonprofit civil rights organization dedicated to monitoring hate groups.[25] The SPLC reserves the hatemonger label for the most bigoted of groups, such as the KKK, neo-Nazi, and Black Panther organizations—and report that "[an anti-

---

25. "The Southern Poverty Law Center is a nonprofit civil rights organization dedicated to fighting hate and bigotry, and to seeking justice for the most vulnerable members of our society [...] the SPLC is internationally known for tracking and exposing the activities of hate groups." Southern Poverty Law Center, "Who We Are," accessed May 27, 2012, http://www.splcenter.org/who-we-are.

Islam hatemonger that Wilders often cites] has been known to fraternize with European racists and neo-fascists." [26] Likewise, the Anti-Defamation League (ADL) has also warned that Wilders, and [his] associates "promote a conspiratorial anti-Muslim agenda under the guise of fighting radical Islam...and seeks to rouse public fears by consistently vilifying the Islamic faith."[27] These are the individuals Wilders regularly cites throughout his book as "experts" on Islam. Again, by citing known hatemongers, none of whom have even a single peer-reviewed publication on Islam to their names, let alone a university level degree on Islam of any sort, Wilders ignores legitimate scholarship practices.

Wilders also cites news articles every so often. These news articles, however, are cited as complaints about some contemporary act of terrorism for which he claims Islam is to blame. Wilders does not actually trouble himself to explain a direct or even plausible connection between the violent act and Islam but simply and unreservedly ascribes blame to Islam. As discussed earlier, I do not address or recognize as legitimate arguments against Islam that follow this line of reasoning.

Third and finally, for those rare circumstances in which Wilders cites a specific Qur'anic verse or hadith, I gladly provide a detailed response to the verses or hadith in question. But herein lies the third issue with Wilders's polemic: his glaringly obvious refusal to apply proper hermeneutic principles.

As a legislator, Wilders must be aware of the importance of reading a law in full—not in excerpt—to appreciate its full intent. Judges and legal scholars, liberals and conservatives, and anyone with a mind for objectiv-

---

26. Robert Steinback, "The Anti-Muslim Inner Circle," *Southern Poverty Law Center Intelligence Report* 42 (Summer 2011), accessed August 15, 2012, http://www.splcenter.org/get-informed/intelligence-report/browse-all-issues/2011/summer/the-anti-muslim-inner-circle.

27. Anti-Defamation League, "Stop Islamization of America (SIOA)," September 19, 2012, accesssed August 15, 2012, http://www.adl.org/civil-rights/discrimination/c/stop-islamization-of-america.html.

ity are loath to draw legal conclusions from partial interpretation. Yet Wilders repeatedly employs this tactic in Qur'anic and hadith interpretation. Several references Wilders cites as "violent" or "discriminatory" are actually incomplete renderings and tenuously related stories.

In addition, Wilders violates every tenet of Qur'anic hermeneutics, or scriptural interpretation, when he takes the authority of an Islamic historian or a hadith as superior to that of the Qur'an. The Qur'an is the primary and uncontested authority on Islam because it is considered the word of God Himself. Prophet Muhammad[sa] himself clarified, "Whenever a Hadith is presented to you in my name, verify it with the Qur'an. If it agrees with the Qur'an, accept it, and if it is in conflict, discard it."[28] Likewise, "There is no doubt that, there will be Ahadith coming after me, claiming that I have said things. So you *must* test those Ahadith from the Qur'an. If it is really according to the Qur'an only then accept it, otherwise reject it."[29] Likewise, Salama relates, ""I heard the Prophet saying, "Whoever (intentionally) ascribes to me what I have not said then (surely) let him occupy his seat in Hell-fire.""[30]

Wilders ignores these clear injunctions altogether. For example, he repeatedly and unfairly references Ibn-e-Ishaq as a leading Islamic authority. Ibn-e-Ishaq, a historian, lived from 704 to 761 (while some sources say 767). He is largely credited for writing Prophet Muhammad's[sa] first biography. Still, no legitimate Islamic scholar throughout history has accepted his work as more authoritative than authentic ahadith, and certainly not more authoritative than the Qur'an.

Wilders, instead, takes the status "first biography" as an unwarranted badge of absolute authenticity. In taking every word of Ibn-e-Ishaq as undisputed gospel, Wilders ignores the Qur'an and hadith, as well as several facts that call to question Ibn-e-Ishaq's reliability.

---

28. Al-Tibiyan wat Tabayyen, vol. 2, 28.

29. Sanan Dar Qatni, vol. 2, 513, Book – Imrani Abee Musa, Matba Farooqi.

30. Sahih Jami' Bukhari, vol. 1, Book 3, #109.

For example, Ibn-e-Ishaq's original writings do not exist—a fact Wilders does not share with his readers (or perhaps one he does not know). Instead, one of Ibn-e-Ishaq's students, al-Bakki, ultimately pieced together an edited copy of Ibn-e-Ishaq's work. Likewise, Salamah bin Fadl al-Ansári, too, recorded Ibn-e-Ishaq's work. Today, none of al-Bakki's works exist, and al-Ansári's work only exists in random and sparing fragments. Thus, what remains today of Ibn-e-Ishaq's original work are a twice-removed and further edited biography by Ibn-e-Hishám, who was al-Bakki's student. Ibn-e-Hishám never met Ibn-e-Ishaq. Wilders shares none of this with his readers.

But Ibn-e-Ishaq's unreliability and inconsistencies do not stop here. The Asmaa ur Rijál books are a well-known and respected series, reporting the biographies of the six authentic recorders of hadith—Bukhari, Muslim, Tirmidhi, Ibn Majah, Abu Dawud, and Masnad Ahmad bin Hambal, respectively. According to every book of Asmaa ur Rijál, Ibn-e-Ishaq often borrowed from completely unreliable sources. Thus, Ibn-e-Ishaq's contemporaries unanimously agree that Ibn-e-Ishaq used unreliable sources when recording Prophet Muhammad's[sa] life. Yet, despite these concerns with accuracy and authenticity, Wilders repeatedly ignores more authoritative sources and gives preference instead to Ibn-e-Ishaq's much less reliable and fragmented work.

Ibn-e-Ishaq's work provides some historical value on Islam, so Muslim scholars and historians do not entirely dismiss him. But to rely on him as the primary source while ignoring the serious authenticity issues that accompany his writing is inappropriate at best and malicious at worst. An objective seeker of truth recognizes these facts, but Wilders ignores them altogether.

Islamic jurisprudence requires that the Qur'an remain the primary and uncontested authority, all other authorities being understood within Qur'anic context—never vice versa. Wilders ignores this crucial Islamic jurisprudential principle and thus commits grave error upon error in his attempts to criticize Islam.

In sum, Wilders's three grave errors are that he does not cite his allegations, cites individuals unqualified to speak academically about Islam who are often known hatemongers, and ignores basic hermeneutics when interpreting Islamic teachings. All this points to an individual focused solely on his own preconceived agenda and not on the truth about what Islam and Prophet Muhammad[sa] actually teach. This brings us to the next subsection of the introduction: What scholarship or authority does Wilders actually have to speak about Islam?

Is Wilders Qualified to Speak with Authority?

Earning the right to speak with authority on issues like religious history, hermeneutics, and Islamic jurisprudence requires years of undergraduate, graduate, doctoral, and even postdoctoral studies. The scholars cited in this book to refute Wilders's allegations meet this standard. The scholars who helped research and write this book meet this standard. Wilders, however, does not even come close to meeting this standard.

This burden of authority is yet further compounded in Wilders's case, because in addition to claiming a scholarly work of nonfiction, Wilders claims that he can demonstrate "how the West can defend itself against an existential enemy [Islam] determined to conquer the globe."[31]

This is a tall order. Because Wilders presents himself as an authority on the aforementioned complex matters, the reader ought to be aware of his educational background and credentials. In fact, throughout his book, Wilders compares himself to the likes of British prime minister Winston Churchill and United States president Teddy Roosevelt. It is only fitting for the reader to see how legitimate is this comparison.

Here are Wilders's credentials.

---

31. Wilders, *Marked for Death*, inside front cover.

Wilders's educational background consists of a high school degree and a course in health insurance at Stichting Opleiding Sociale Verzekeringen in Amsterdam. He also has some law certificates from Dutch Open University—an online institution. Dutch Open University's stated goal is to "make higher education accessible to anyone with the necessary aptitudes and interests, *regardless of formal qualifications.*"[32] And, true to his quasi alma mater, Wilders entirely disregards formal qualifications when writing his polemic—which is convenient, because he has none.

Had Wilders merely related his life experiences, no level of scholarship would have been necessary. But Wilders presents himself as the legitimate authority on Islam. On the contrary, Wilders has no training in world history, no training in Islam or Islamic history, no training in Arabic, and no training in Qur'anic hermeneutics or hadith interpretation. His entire understanding of Islam is summed up in his own testimony: "I myself am a fervent reader of the Koran" and "I have read the Koran several times."[33]

In other words, Geert Wilders is a high school graduate with a few online certifications reserved for the most select members of society—those with Internet access (pardon: *regular* Internet access). Remarkably, no one can even call Wilders a college dropout, because he never actually attended a legitimate university. Yet, this is the man who will educate and save the West from an alleged existential threat of Islam.

But lest I be accused of proverbially shooting the messenger, Wilders's allegations against Islam are not baseless only because of his grotesquely unqualified resume. Let us say that Wilders had numerous degrees and doctorates from actual universities. Even then, his allegations against Islam would remain baseless because of his insistence on

---

32. See http://www.eadtu.nl/usbm/files/guide/ounlvirtualenvironment.htm (accessed August 12, 2012). (Emphasis added.)

33. Wilders, Marked for Death, 20.

citing extremists and hatemongers and, in many cases, his avoidance of citations altogether. How ironic that Wilders attempts to fight extremism by citing extremists! When Wilders finally cites Islamic sources, he violates even the most basic tenets of Islamic jurisprudence, often holding an ambiguous historical event as an authority while ignoring clear Qur'anic guidance. While such a strategy is many things, scholarship it is not. Likewise, while I condemn "Muslims" who threaten Wilders, being the recipient of death threats hardly qualifies one as an expert.

Thus, it is painstakingly clear that Wilders speaks with little, if any, authority on Islam. As you read through EXTREMIST, I hope you see the painstaking measures my research team and I took to respond to Wilders's propagandized arguments with legitimate scholarship. And this brings me to the final introductory note.

Final Introductory Note

I have worked diligently to refute every substantive allegation Wilders puts forth against Islam, the Qur'an, the Prophet Muhammad[sa], and the *khulafa-e-rashidin*. Each argument is organized into a series of parts: allegation, reference, and response. The *allegation* section cites and reproduces Wilders's specific allegation. The *reference* records the source Wilders cites (if any) to support his allegation. Finally, the *response* provides a detailed analysis and refutation of Wilders's allegation.

Next, due to Wilders's incessant condemnation of everything Islam and unmitigated endorsement of everything Judeo-Christian, I was forced to delve deeper into the Torah and Gospels to determine if his allegations had merit. I found myself performing extensive research into Christian and Jewish history and, in some cases, unearthing religious violence done in the name of Christ and the Bible. I report these historical and scriptural matters not to condemn any religion or ideology; far from it. Indeed, one purpose my book serves is to clearly demonstrate that Islam respects all faiths and champions universal freedom of conscience.

However, it is important that my readers know that my book's criticisms of extreme acts done in the name of Christianity, Judaism, or of any other faith are not criticisms of Christ or Old Testament prophets. Rather, they are demonstrations that every faith has extremists, that such extremists can twist any scripture to serve their purposes, and that throughout history, some Christians and some Jews have unfortunately committed horrific atrocities in the name of their faiths.

I cite these examples to demonstrate to those like Wilders what Shakespeare recognized many centuries ago: "The devil can cite scripture for his purpose." All faiths have extremists, and it is up to us moderates to write the true narratives of our respective faiths—that of tolerance, compassion, service to humanity, and civility. Any belief that *only* Islam has extremists—historically or contemporarily—is contrary to the easily observable world around us. Thus, this book's criticism of violent acts in the name of Christianity, Judaism, etc. are only that, a criticism of violent acts in the name of Christianity, Judaism, etc.—not a criticism of the religion, or of that religion's holy founder, or of the millions or billions of moderate adherents to the particular faith or ideology. Most people get this; Wilders unfortunately doesn't.

Finally, as mentioned, I have generally ignored those allegations not specifically against Islam, the Qur'an, Prophet Muhammad[sa], or the *khulafa-e-rashidin* because such allegations are outside this book's scope. Moreover, one purpose of my book is to condemn those violent acts as well. Therefore, no ambiguity should exist on this matter—Islam categorically condemns terrorism and religious violence.

That said, it is possible that I have simply missed an allegation within this book's stated scope. If you, the reader, feel I have missed an in-scope allegation, kindly send it to me at bookreply@ahmadiyya.us and advise which page in Wilders's polemic lists the missed allegation. I shall respond to those allegations within this book's scope. Likewise, I welcome and encourage all general thoughts, questions, and inquiries either via email or on Twitter @MuslimIQ.

With this background, I present to you *EXTREMIST: A Response to Geert Wilders & Terrorists Everywhere.*

Chapter 1

Wilders's First Fabrication

"A lie cannot live."

— DR. MARTIN LUTHER KING, JR.

In his Chapter 1, Wilders makes only a few allegations directly against Islam, instead spending the lion's share of his space relating Kurt Westergaard's story. Westergaard, a Danish cartoonist, infamously drew an offensive image of Prophet Muhammad[sa] in 2005. That cartoon angered extremists, ultimately resulting in rioting, violence, and even death. Wilders tactfully avoids mentioning that significantly more Muslims publicly, unequivocally, and peacefully condemned the violence.[34]

---

34. Hadrat Mirza Masroor Ahmad, The Blessed Model of the Holy Prophet Muhammad and the Caricatures: Friday Sermons Delivered by Hadrat Mirza Masroor Ahmad, Khalifatul Masih V, Imam Jama'at-e-Ahmadiyya (Islam International Publications 2006), pp.97-98.

　　See also, "Freedom of Conscience and Expression in Islam, Review of Religions, Siddiq, Nadeem Ahmad, available at

It is, however, still remarkable that Wilders begins his book with Kurt Westergaard. Westergaard has clearly and publicly renounced Wilders's extremist ideology, stating, "Wilders has an overly generalized perception of Muslims as potential terrorists, it is not like that at all. I know a lot of Muslims here in Denmark who accept democracy completely and who live their religion as a private matter."[35] Furthermore, when presented with Westergaard's repudiation during a BBC Hardtalk interview, Wilders replied, "I don't disagree [with Westergaard]. I don't believe that the majority of Muslims are terrorists. I acknowledge the fact that the majority of Muslims are not terrorists, I have a problem with Islam."[36]

Why Wilders finds it necessary to cite a man who has repudiated him to explain his "problem with Islam" is beyond me. In any case, Wilders openly acknowledges that "the majority of Muslims" are peaceful; I agree. Wilders condemns those Muslims who engage in violence, and I welcome him to the club. The Qur'an and Prophet Muhammad[sa] have been at the forefront of condemning violence and disorder in the name of Islam—or of any religion—since Islam's founding fourteen hundred years ago.[37] Thus, I will continue to

---

http://www.reviewofreligions.org/2342/freedom-of-conscience-and-expression-in-islam/ (Last Visited May 14, 2014).

35. Wilders, interview by Stephen Sackur, BBC Hardtalk. (Emphasis added).

36. Ibid.

37. Qur'an 7:57. "And create not disorder in the earth after it has been set in order, and call upon Him in fear and hope. Surely, the mercy of Allah is nigh unto those who do good." Likewise, Prophet Muhammad declared, "A Muslim is one from whose tongue and hands other Muslims are safe. A Mu'min (true believer) is one in whom

address Wilders's trouble with Islam. Below is the only substantive allegation Wilders makes in his Chapter 1 that is within my book's scope.

all mankind has a sanctuary for life and property" (Sahih Jami' Muslim #6721, #6631).

ALLEGATION 1

Islam Demands Unjust Retribution

Wilders writes, "Though some pretend Islam is an Abrahamic faith like Judaism and Christianity, Islam does not restrict revenge and retribution. It does not retaliate against a cartoon with another cartoon; it demands a head for a cartoon—a head for every drawing, book, speech, or movie that it deems to be "insulting."[38]

REFERENCE: Thomas Landen, "Heeere's Muhammed!," Gatestone Institute, January 4, 2010, www.gatestoneinstitute.org/980/heeeres-muhammed.

RESPONSE: Wilders actually makes two allegations here. First, that Islam requires a harsher retaliation than the original injury. Second, that Islam requires physical and violent retaliation for insults.

First, Wilders does not reference any Islamic source for either of these allegations. His source for the allegation that "Islam does not restrict revenge and retribution" is an opinion editorial from an anti-Islam website—a website that itself offers no citations. To be fair, the blame rests on Wilders, as opinion editorials typically do not have citations—they are, by definition, opinions. But this is Wilders's habit throughout his book—he gives weight to random opinions instead of to verifiable facts to the contrary.

For example, the Qur'an specifically refutes Wilders's allegation that Islam prescribes inequitable retaliation:

---

38.   Wilders, *Marked for Death*, 5.

O ye who believe! *Equitable retaliation in the matter of the slain is prescribed for you:* the free man for the free man, and the slave for the slave, and the female for the female. But if one is granted any remission by one's brother, then pursuing the matter for the realization of the blood money shall be done with fairness and the murderer shall pay him the blood money in a handsome manner. This is an alleviation from your Lord and a mercy. And whoso transgresses thereafter, for him there shall be a grievous punishment.[39]

The verse clarifies that even regarding murder, Islam holds equity as the upper limit of retaliation. Furthermore, even with murder, Islam permits and encourages remission. This remission is known as "blood money." Blood money—or as it is known and practiced in the West, a civil settlement—compensates the murder victim's family. Finally, the verse warns that God will hold transgressors accountable, again ensuring that the victim does not demand excessive retribution.

The Qur'an further states, "And the recompense of an injury is an injury the like thereof; but whoso forgives and his act brings about reformation, his reward is with Allah. Surely, He loves not the wrongdoers."[40]

This verse applies to any injury a Muslim might suffer at the hands of another, and demonstrates that whatever the recompense, it must never exceed the initial injury. Again, the Qur'an implores Muslims to "forgive to bring about reformation" rather than demand a harsher retribution as Wilders's unreferenced allegation asserts. Thus, those extremists who claimed the offensive cartoons somehow "injured" them, the Qur'an allows no violent response and instead implores forgiveness and mercy.

Combined, these verses demonstrate that the Islamic concept of retribution is neither absolute punishment nor absolute forgiveness, but

---

39. Qur'an 2:179. (Emphasis added.)

40. Qur'an 42:41.

reformation. Islam argues that if an individual is a repeat offender, forgiving him or her invites more crime and therefore punishment is necessary to protect potential victims. Likewise, if a person commits an innocent or even deliberate but isolated error and forgiveness would realistically result in reformation, a Muslim should lean toward forgiveness. The decision process requires compassion and assessing each situation individually—not applying a cookie-cutter, black-and-white rule.

Second, Wilders claims that Islam requires "a head for every drawing, book, speech, or movie that it deems insulting." Basically, Wilders is alleging that Islam mandates punishing blasphemy. He repeats this allegation in Chapter 7[41], Chapter 10[42], and Chapter 12[43] of his book. This allegation is false. Throughout his "many" readings of the Qur'an, Wilders unfortunately missed the following verse:

> And when thou seest those who engage in vain discourse concerning Our Signs, then turn thou away from them until they engage in a discourse other than that.[44]

Or this verse:

> We will, surely, suffice thee against those who mock.[45]

Or this verse:

---

41.   Wilders, *Marked for Death*, 123, 125.
42.   Ibid., 167.
43.   Ibid., 188, 191, 194.
44.   Qur'an 6:69.
45.   Qur'an 15:96.

> And the servants of the Gracious God are those who walk on the
> earth in a dignified manner, and when the ignorant address them,
> they say, "Peace!"[46]

Or this verse:

> And those who bear not false witness, and when they pass by any-
> thing vain, they pass on with dignity.[47]

Far from endorsing any form of violence in response to insults, the
Qur'an specifically commands Muslims to simply "pass on with dignity"
or "turn away" or "say peace." Likewise, the Qur'an does not advocate or
allow Muslims to isolate themselves permanently, but instead encourages Muslims to only turn away until "they engage in a discourse other
than that."

In fact, the Qur'an, in addition to forbidding Muslims from retaliat-
ing for insults, specifically commands Muslims never to insult others: "O
ye who believe! Let not one people deride another people, who may be
better than they, nor let women deride other women, who may be better
than they. And defame not your own people, nor call one another by
nicknames."[48]

In short, Wilders ignores—or is wholly ignorant—that the Qur'an
sanctions no punishment for blasphemy. The Qur'an addresses blasphemy on seven occasions but only instructs that Muslims avoid the

---

46.   Qur'an 25:64.
47.   Qur'an 25:73.
48.   Qur'an 49:12.

blasphemer's company as a response.[49] The Qur'an, on more than forty occasions, recognizes and protects freedom of speech and expression.[50]

Prophet Muhammad's[sa] example echoes this teaching. As Medina's ruler Muhammad[sa] patiently tolerated his enemies' abuse. For example, Abdullah bin Ubay bin Salul was guilty of sedition,[51] and also spread the cruel lie that Prophet Muhammad's[sa] wife, Hadhrat Ayesha[ra], was not chaste.[52] In response, Prophet Muhammad[sa] forgave Abdullah Salul and also led his funeral prayer.[53] On another occasion, a group of Jews walked past Prophet Muhammad[sa] and said, "Death be upon you." As the ruler of Medina, Prophet Muhammad[sa] had the power to order any form of punishment or impose any form of restriction of speech.[54] History records that he ordered neither punishment nor restricted their speech. Non-Muslims clearly enjoyed free speech under Prophet Muhammad's[sa] rule—so much so that they knew they could even wish death upon the Prophet[sa] to his face without fear of reprisal.

Islam's limits on free speech echo the same premise upon which the United States Supreme Court has also banned the utterance of inflammatory speech.[55] In such instances, punishment is not only warranted, but also mandated if an individual is a threat to the state due to, for example, advocacy for or incitement to terrorism. It is upon this premise that citizens were punished in Prophet Muhammad's[sa] state—be they Muslim or non-Muslim. In addition to America, at least fifteen "progres-

---

49. Qur'an 4:141, 157; 6:69, 109; 18:5; 60:3; 63:9.

50. Qur'an 2:5, 112, 257, 273; 3:21; 4:56, 80–81, 138; 5:91–93, 99–100; 6:67, 105–108, 112–113; 10:100–101; 11:29; 13:41; 16:83; 17:54–55; 21:25, 42; 22:68; 24:55; 25:32, 42–44; 27:108–110; 28:76; 29:19; 36:8, 17–18, 31; 37:157–158; 39:40–42; 42:7–8, 48–49; 43:8; 50:46; 64:9–13; 67:26–27; 76:30; 88:22–25; 109:2–7.

51. Ibn-e-Hisham, Kitab Sirat Rasul Allah, 995.

52. Sahih Jami' Bukhari, vol. 3, Book 48, #829.

53. Sahih Jami' Muslim, Book 38, #6680.

54. Sahih Jami' Bukhari, vol. 4, Book 52, #186.

55. Chaplinsky v. State of New Hampshire, 315 U.S. 568 (1942).

sive" European nations have laws punishing certain types of blasphemy—something Islam has not endorsed. Accordingly, Muslim majority nations that impose blasphemy laws do so in opposition to Islamic teachings.

Islam aside, Wilders repeatedly contrasts the allegedly violent Qur'an with what he deems is a far more progressive Bible. He ignores—or is wholly ignorant—that the Bible sanctions capital punishment for blasphemy in no uncertain terms.[56] He cannot argue that the New Testament does not sanction punishment for apostasy, as critics can just as easily point out that Jesus Christ[as] stated that nothing of the Old Testament is abrogated.[57] Prominent Church theologians such as Saint Thomas Aquinas, no doubt, justified capital punishment for blasphemy on such grounds.

In sum, Wilders provides no evidence for his claim that Islam demands harsher retaliation for an offensive act or that Islam punishes for blasphemy. On the contrary, the Qur'an and ahadith demonstrate that Islam promotes forgiveness, justice, and freedom of speech.

---

56. Leviticus 24:16 states, "Anyone who blasphemes the name of the Lord is to be put to death. The entire assembly must stone them. Whether foreigner or native-born, when they blaspheme the Name they are to be put to death." Deuteronomy 13:6–11 states, "6 If your very own brother, or your son or daughter, or the wife you love, or your closest friend secretly entices you, saying, 'Let us go and worship other gods' (gods that neither you nor your ancestors have known, 7 gods of the peoples around you, whether near or far, from one end of the land to the other), 8 do not yield to them or listen to them. Show them no pity. Do not spare them or shield them. 9 You must certainly put them to death. Your hand must be the first in putting them to death, and then the hands of all the people. 10 Stone them to death, because they tried to turn you away from the Lord your God, who brought you out of Egypt, out of the land of slavery. 11 Then all Isra'el will hear and be afraid, and no one among you will do such an evil thing again."

57. Matthew 5:17–18; 23:1–3.

Conclusion

In his Chapter 1, Wilders immediately attempts to separate Islam from its Abrahamic predecessors—Christianity and Judaism. This act is deliberate but unsuccessful. Though non-religious himself, Wilders remarkably and repeatedly tries to defend Jews and Christians. Perhaps he recognizes that his financial motives are best served by siding with anti-Islamic critics who subscribe to Christianity and Judaism. For example, even his publisher, Regnery Publishing, is a known conservative publishing company that caters to known anti-Islam hatemongers. Rather than be averse to leading American hatemongers, Wilders cites and sides with them throughout his book. Still, his attempts in Chapter 1 are relatively mild compared to the vitriol he spews going forward.

Chapter 2

Freedom from Wilders's Propaganda

"The future must not belong to those who slander the prophet of Islam. Yet to be credible, those who condemn that slander must also condemn the hate we see when the image of Jesus Christ is desecrated, churches are destroyed, or the holocaust is denied."

— PRESIDENT BARACK OBAMA

Like his approach in Chapter 1, Wilders spends most of his Chapter 2 complaining about things other than Islam. Specifically, Wilders complains about Muslims, whom—I remind the reader—he considers mostly peaceful. Wilders begins with an explanation of how his propaganda film *Fitna* offended Muslims, when he received his first death threats, and his bemused reaction to President Obama's 2009 Cairo address.

Wilders concludes the Chapter with the sensation-alist and unreferenced allegation that Islam only offers non-Muslims death, conversion, or enslavement.

ALLEGATION 2

Islam Teaches Death for Apostasy

As mentioned in the introduction, Wilders cites Ayaan Hirsi Ali, not any Islamic reference, to allege that Islam prescribes death for apostasy. He writes, "In fact, [Ayaan Hirsi Ali] was subject to far more threats than I was. By renouncing her Islamic faith, she had committed apostasy, the ultimate crime in Islam, for which the Koran prescribes the death penalty; once you are Islamic, you are never allowed to leave."[58] Wilders repeats the "death for apostasy" allegation again in his Chapter 4,[59] Chapter 7,[60] and in Chapter 10.[61]

REFERENCE: None.

RESPONSE: In one sentence, Wilders makes four unsubstantiated allegations.

First, that apostasy is both a crime and the "ultimate crime" in Islam. These false allegations are based on the incorrect assumption that apostasy is some crime that humans can punish. Yes, Islam admonishes Muslims to remain Muslims. But what faith encourages its adherents to leave? Even then, Islam is quite liberal. Certain Christians declare eternal hell for those who leave Christianity. Certain Jews consider themselves the chosen people, to the exclusion of all others. Certain Hindus believe in the caste system, forbidding anyone from joining or leaving a

---

58.   Wilders, *Marked for Death*, 8.

59.   Ibid., 58.

60.   Ibid., 124.

61.   Ibid., 160.

caste. Therefore, it is surprising that Wilders objects to the Islamic admonition not to forsake Islam.

In any case, Islam defines the "ultimate crime" against humanity as murder and treason—not apostasy. In fact, murder and treason are the only reasons for which a person may receive capital punishment in Islam.[62] Some theologians have argued that those who engage in unconscionably violent acts such as rape may be deserving of the death penalty (i.e. the rapist, not the victim of rape). The Qur'an, however, does not allow capital punishment for any other reason other than murder or treason—certainly not for apostasy. And, as mentioned earlier, even when capital punishment is a possibility, it is by permission, never by commandment.

Second, Wilders claims that "the Koran prescribes death [for apostates]" but provides no reference to validate this claim. Let alone that Islam does not prescribe death for apostates, the Qur'an was the first religious scripture to categorically declare, "There shall be no compulsion in religion."[63] Likewise, the Qur'an repeatedly states that Muslims, including Prophet Muhammad[sa], can only admonish non-Muslims regarding religious matters.[64] The Qur'an addresses disbelief more than 150 times, yet no human being is ever given authority to punish the disbeliever. If Islam did sanction death for apostasy, why does the Qur'an never sanction worldly punishment for the apostate who repeatedly believes and disbelieves?[65] As the majority of these verses were revealed in

---

62. Qur'an 5:33. "On account of this, We prescribed for the children of Isra'el that who-soever killed a person—*unless it be for killing a person or for creating disorder in the land*—it shall be as if he had killed all mankind; and whoso gave life to one, it shall be as if he had given life to all mankind. And Our Messengers came to them with clear Signs, yet even after that, many of them commit excesses in the land." (Emphasis added.)

63. Qur'an 2:257.

64. Qur'an 4:64; 6:70–71; 10:109; 11:47; 50:46; 88:22–23.

65. Qur'an 2:218; 3:21, 73, 91; 4:138; 5:55, 62, 93, 100; 9:3, 66–68, 74; 16:107; 47:26–27; 63:2–7.

Medina, not Mecca, Wilders cannot resort to the lame "argument" of abrogation of Qur'anic verses—an issue I thoroughly address in Chapter 3.

Prophet Muhammad's[sa] example corroborates the view that no punishment for apostasy exists in Islam. Once, a Bedouin convert to Islam suffered a fever while in Medina. He asked to be released from his pledge three times and was refused three times. Still, he left Medina unharmed.[66] The reader may question if a single incident during Prophet Muhammad's[sa] life is sufficient to prove that Islam does not punish an apostate. The problem is that Wilders could not even do this much to support his allegation that Islam requires death for apostates. In fact, I challenge Wilders to produce a single instance when Prophet Muhammad[sa] punished an individual specifically because he or she apostatized. No such incident exists.

Wilders's meritless allegations against Islam aside, he ignores—or is wholly ignorant of—the Bible's views on apostasy. This is significant, because Wilders repeatedly defends the Bible as a progressive book compared to the Qur'an. Instead, Wilders claims the Qur'an sanctions death for apostasy—while no such Qur'anic verse exists—and simultaneously ignores the biblical verses that clearly demand death for apostasy. For example, the Bible states:

> If your very own brother, or your son or daughter, or the wife you love, or your closest friend secretly entices you, saying, "Let us go and worship other gods", do not yield to him or listen to him. Show him no pity. Do not spare him or shield him. You must certainly put him to death. Your hand must be the first in putting him to death, and then the hands of all the people. Stone him to

---

66. Sahih Jami' Bukhari, vol. 1, Book 3, #28.

death, because he tried to turn you away from the LORD your God, who brought you out of Egypt, out of the land of slavery.[67]

Arguing that the New Testament sanctions no punishment for apostasy is useless, as Jesus Christ[as] stated that nothing of the Old Testament is abrogated.[68] Accordingly, prominent Christian theologians such as Saint Thomas Aquinas have endorsed death for apostasy:

> Heretics and apostates can be compelled, even physically, to fulfill their promises and hold to do what they once pro-fessed...adopting the faith is voluntary, but sticking to it once adopted is obligatory. About heretics there are two things to say. Their sin deserves banishment not only from the church by ex-communication but also from the world by death. [69]

It is remarkable that while Wilders approves of such teachings, he finds fault with the Qur'an for vociferously restricting any worldly punish-ment for apostasy.

Finally, contrary to Wilders's claim, Islam does not restrict aposta-sy.[70] Any "punishment" an apostate incurs is a matter between that per-son and God. On what grounds Wilders made the above allegations, I am unaware. The Qur'an, however, is clear: apostasy is not a worldly crime; it is certainly not the "ultimate" crime, and apostates are not to be harmed, let alone put to death—and those who choose to leave Islam have every right to do so.

---

67. Deuteronomy 13:6–10.

68. Matthew 5:17–18; 23:1–3.

69. Saint Thomas Aquinas, *Summa Theologiae: A Concise Translation*, ed. Timothy McDermott (Westminster, MD: Christian Classics, 1997), 339–40.

70. Qur'an 4:138; 10:100; 18:30.

Before closing this section, I felt compelled to address Wilders's reference to Ayaan Hirsi Ali. Wilders and Ali are good friends and worked together in Dutch Parliament before Ali's Dutch citizenship was revoked when the public discovered she lied about her immigration. In my original draft of EXTREMIST I concluded this present section by writing the following:

> Though Ayaan Hirsi Ali and I have ideological disagreements on religion, I do not in any way dismiss the barbaric experiences through which Ms. Ali suffered. Instead, I categorically condemn them. No woman deserves what she has suffered through. Indeed, the extremists who physically and psychologically harmed Ms. Ali are criminals and their acts condemnable without exception. Islam emphatically rejects their acts of violence and terrorism and offers them no refuge and no excuse.

I wrote this for no other reason than what is obvious from the text itself. But after reflecting on Zembla's 2006 interview-documentary of Ayaan Hirsi Magan, which is available on YouTube, I felt it necessary to provide my readers greater context. Magan, as both I and most of humanity were initially unaware, is Ayaan Hirsi's actual last name. To complete this documentary, Zembla, a well-respected European news agency, sent investigative journalists to Somalia and Kenya to determine the veracity of Ayaan Hirsi Magan's claims. When they found inconsistencies in her story as compared to documented evidence, they confronted Magan in an interview. What Ayaan Hirsi Magan confirms in that interview, and what the interview uncovers, is an entirely different picture of what the world believed about her.

First, Ayaan Hirsi Magan did not flee horrific civil war in Somalia. In fact, let alone witnessing five civil wars as the story went, she has never seen any war whatsoever. Her family left for Kenya well before any civil war began. In Kenya she lived in peace, relative luxury with running water and electricity, and attained free UN-funded education for over a decade.

Second, the interview casts serious doubt as to whether Ayaan Hirsi Magan fled an honor killing or forced marriage. In the Zembla interview she admits that her ex-husband was a "good man" and she found "nothing wrong with him." After going to the Netherlands she contacted him to come see her and asked him to stay with her in the Netherlands. When he declined to stay—wanting to return to his home in Canada instead—she sought divorce. Ali/Magan's ex-husband immediately granted divorce without delay or intimidation. It is worth noting, however, that Canada is one of the world's most peaceful and progressive nations. Surely she was not asked to live in some draconian backwards or extremist nation. And the alleged violent father who Ali/Magan claims would have "honor killed" her had he found her? She kept in regular contact with him with ongoing letters while she was in "hiding." Why would a woman in hiding, fearing for her life, keep in regular contact and meet with the men who are trying to find and kill her?

Third, Ayaan Hirsi Magan lied about the above and changed her last name to Ali for the purpose of gaining asylum in the Netherlands. She knew that the Dutch would send her back to Kenya—which was and is a peaceful and stable nation—so she concocted a fabricated story and changed her name. Ayaan Hirsi Magan thus stole an asylum seat from some persecuted person who actually deserved asylum. (Remarkably, years later as MP she passed strict laws to deport immigrants who attempted exactly what she succeeded to do—lie to gain asylum).

Fourth, Ayaan Hirsi Magan used this fabricated platform to run for—and win—a seat in Dutch parliament. More remarkably, however, is that her colleagues knew she was lying and consciously chose to move forward with her campaign—knowing it was on fraudulent terms. In other words, Ayaan Hirsi Magan consciously lied to those not of her circle to help advance her political agenda. Later in his book, Wilders pathetically introduces a meritless argument known as *taqiyya*, the alleged permission Islam gives Muslims to lie to "infidels" to gain a tactical advantage. While Islam offers no such permission, the irony here would make Shakespeare himself envious he didn't write it himself. While baselessly accusing Muslims of lying to gain a tactical advantage, Geert Wilders's own close colleague Ayaan Hirsi Magan admittedly lied to those not of her party to gain a tactical advantage. Wilders, of course, does not bother pointing this out.

Yet these are the individuals that will save the West from the alleged threat of Islam? Ayaan Hirsi Magan has even proposed military action to crush and destroy Islam. Yet, as fate would have it, her own words now condemn her as an admitted and confirmed liar.

The forty-minute long Zembla interview-documentary does not, however, touch on one element of Ayaan Hirsi Magan's story—whether she actually suffered FGM. Considering she lied about every other aspect of her asylum claim, is it wise to accept her claim of FGM at face value without any doctor's corroboration, testimony from the "surgeon", or a shred of actual evidence? Whatever the case, I give Ayaan Hirsi Magan the benefit of the doubt. Let my earlier condemnation of what she suffered through apply here and condemn the FGM through which she claims she suffered. After all, even a stopped clock tells the truth twice a day.

To be clear, all of the above is based on Ayaan Hirsi Magan's own testimony—not my opinion. In short, it seems that Ayaan Hirsi Magan dismisses just about everything we know about her. This is the company Geert Wilders keeps and after all, birds of a feather...

As a final reiteration, Islam categorically condemns religious compulsion and strongly forbids any worldly punishment for those who choose to leave Islam. The Qur'an is clear, no person can interfere in another's faith—freedom of conscience must remain free.

ALLEGATION 3

The Qur'an Sanctions Violence

Having dealt with the question of apostasy, I turn now to the allegation that the Qur'an sanctions violence. Wilders writes, "The Koran plainly sanctions violence in the name of Allah. A Christian who proclaims hatred to any group of people violates Christian principles. Not so with Muslims."[71]

REFERENCE: None.

RESPONSE: Wilders cites the late United States president John Quincy Adams's opinion of Islam as his reference. In other words, this allegation is based on a non-Muslim's views—not that of any Islamic resource. Therefore, I record Wilders as having no actual reference to support his claim.

I note, however, a disturbing fact about Wilders's decision to cite President Adams. For as much as Wilders objects (rightfully) to threats of violence against himself, he remarkably cites President Adams's desire to use force and violence to destroy Islam: "It is only by force, that [Prophet Muhammad's] false doctrines can be dispelled, and his power annihilated."[72] This statement is significant for a number of reasons.

First, it demonstrates Wilders's clear desire to use force against Muslims. Wilders is an elected politician, expressing his desire to forcibly destroy a minority religious group in Europe. Such rhetoric has had real consequences. Norwegian "Christian" terrorist Anders Breivik—who

---

71. Wilders, *Marked for Death*, 19–20.

72. Ibid., 20.

brutally murdered seventy-seven civilians on July 22, 2011—cites Wilders (and his ilk) dozens of times in his anti-Islam manifesto, praising Wilders for his anti-Islamic platform. While Wilders dismisses Breivik's praise—incredibly somehow blaming Al Qaeda—Wilders's own words now condemn him. Wilders takes no remediating measures to qualify or denounce President Adams's desire that force be used to dispel Islam. Rather, he continues to praise Adams for his comments.

Wilders not only demonstrates his tacit approval of Breivik's actions, but also, according to Wilders's own words, Breivik did exactly what Wilders endorsed—use force to dispel Islam. And now, Wilders claims that Breivik acted on his own and that he, Wilders, does not advocate violence?

As far as the unreferenced allegation that the Qur'an sanctions violence, any fair-minded person can see that the Qur'an repeatedly condemns those who create disorder and violence:

Eat and drink of what Allah has provided, and commit not iniquity in the earth, creating disorder.[73]

And they strive to create disorder in the earth, and Allah loves not those who create disorder. [74]

And create not disorder in the earth after it has been set in order... [75]

...create not disorder in the earth after it has been set in order. This is better for you, if you are believers.[76]

---

73. Qur'an 2:61.

74. Qur'an 5:65.

75. Qur'an 7:57.

76. Qur'an 7:86.

In contrast, Wilders does not cite a single example to validate his claim that the Qur'an sanctions violence. This is simply because no such example exists.

In sum, while Wilders claims to promote peace and alleges the Qur'an promotes violence, the exact opposite is true. By his own admission, Wilders seeks to dispel Islam by force yet does not cite a single example to substantiate his allegation that the Qur'an sanctions violence.

ALLEGATION 4

Islam Forbids Protection to Non-Muslim Dwellings

Wilders claims that non-Muslims living under Prophet Muhammad's[sa] rule were stripped of all privacy rights: "...privacy does not apply to non-Muslims. Infidels have no rights in Islam. Their 'dwellings' are not protected, as Muhammad himself made clear—he had five of his followers break into the house of Abu Ráfi, a chief of the Jewish-Arab Banu Nádir tribe, and murder him."[77]

REFERENCE: Alfred Guillaume, Life of Muhammad: A Translation of Ibn-e-Ishaq's Sirat Rasul Allah (Oxford University Press, 1955), 482–84.

RESPONSE: Wilders mischaracterizes Abu Ráfi's death as a murder instead of as a consequence for his wanton and malicious actions. But before proceeding, it is necessary to appreciate the status that Jews enjoyed under Prophet Muhammad's[sa] rule.

First, Islam does not consider Jews as "infidels." They are referred to as the "People of the Book" and have been afforded a position of equality.[78] When Prophet Muhammad[sa] arrived in Medina, he promulgated the Charter of Medina. This mutually developed charter served as the constitution to govern Medina and forge an alliance between Jews and

---

77. Wilders, *Marked for Death*, 23.

78. Qur'an 3:65, for example, says while referring to Jews and Christians: "Say, 'O People of the Book! come to a word equal between us and you—that we worship none but Allah, and that we associate no partner with Him, and that some of us take not others for Lords beside Allah.' But if they turn away, then say, 'Bear witness that we have submitted to God.'"

Muslims.[79] Among its numerous progressive articles, articles 16 through 19 explain Prophet Muhammad's[sa] stance regarding Jews and their rights in Medina:

16. Those Jews who follow the Believers will be helped and will be treated with equality. [Social, legal and economic equality is promised to all loyal citizens of the State].

17. No Jew will be wronged for being a Jew.

18. The enemies of the Jews who follow us [i.e., us Muslims] will not be helped.

19. The peace of the Believers (of the State of Medina) cannot be divided. (It is either peace or war for all. It cannot be that a part of the population is at war with the outsiders and a part is at peace). [80]

Thus, not only did Prophet Muhammad[sa] establish religious freedom and equality for Jews, but he also ensured that Muslims were forbidden from supporting any enemy of the Jews. The Charter of Medina further added in articles 21, 30, and 31, respectively:

---

79. Charter of Medina article 1 states, "This is a document from Muhammad the Prophet (may peace and blessings of Allah be upon him), governing relations between the Believers i.e. Muslims of Quraysh and Yathrib and those who followed them and worked hard with them. They form one nation—Ummah."

   http://www.constitution.org/cons/medina/macharter.htm (via the Constitution Society, a nonprofit organization established in 1994 dedicated to research and publication of constitutional republican government)

80. Ibid.

21. Conditions of peace and war and the accompanying ease or hardships must be fair and equitable to all citizens alike.

30. The Jews of Bani Awf will be treated as one community with the Believers. The Jews have their religion. This will also apply to their freedmen. The exception will be those who act unjustly and sinfully. By so doing they wrong themselves and their families.

31. The same applies to Jews of Bani An-Nájjar, Bani Al-Hárith, Bani Saeeda, Bani Jushám, Bani Al-Aws, Thaalba, and the Jaffna, (a clan of the Bani Thaalba) and the Bani Ash-Shutayba. [81]

These articles are clear—Jews are to be treated as one community and will enjoy religious freedom, except those individuals who act against the tenets of justice. The charter elaborates further rights and responsibilities in articles 38 through 42:

38. If anyone attacks anyone who is a party to this Pact the other must come to his help.

39. They (parties to this Pact) must seek mutual advice and consultation.

40. Loyalty gives protection against treachery. Those who avoid mutual consultation do so because of lack of sincerity and loyalty.

41. A man will not be made liable for misdeeds of his ally.

42. Anyone (any individual or party) who is wronged must be helped. [82]

---

81. Ibid.

Clearly, Prophet Muhammad[sa] established a unified sovereign nation based on religious freedom, mutual respect, and trust. As Medina's ruler, he ensured the charter included article 39—a requirement to seek mutual advice and consultation from the Jews—lest any party accuse the other of unjust or unilateral actions. This article also refutes the notion that Prophet Muhammad[sa] ruled as a dictator—far from it, as he obliged himself to seek mutual advice and consultation from all parties of Medina. Finally, articles 44 and 49 hold both the Muslims and the Jews accountable for not fulfilling their obligation of loyalty to one another.

> 44. Yathrib [i.e., Medina] will be Sanctuary for the people of this Pact.

> 49. The parties to this Pact are bound to help each other in the event of an attack on Yathrib.

Thus, the Muslims and Jews mutually agreed to protect one another from attack and to operate as citizens of one sovereign state. Rebellion against this democratic pact was treason. Even today, virtually every sovereign nation, including the United States and in most of Europe, prescribes capital punishment for treason. Keeping in mind the Charter of Medina, the equality it afforded all citizens Muslims and Jewish, and the punishment for treason, I return to Wilders's allegation.

Wilders claims that Prophet Muhammad[sa] had Abu Ráfi, chief of the Banu Nádir tribe, killed because "infidels have no rights in Islam and their dwellings are not protected."[83] He cites Ibn-e-Ishaq to validate his claim but censors the full story from his readers. The full reference in Ibn-e-Ishaq explains why Prophet Muhammad[sa] ordered that Abu Ráfi, chief of the Banu Nádir tribe, receive capital punishment:

---

82.   Ibid.

83.   Wilders, *Marked for Death*, 23.

When the fight at the trench and the affair of the Banu Qurayzah were over, the matter of Salaam bin Abu'l-Huqayq known as Abu Ráfi came up in connection with those who had collected the mixed tribes together against Prophet Muhammad.[84]

As historians have established, two Jewish tribes in Medina, the Banu Nádir and the Banu Qurayzah, revolted against Prophet Muhammad[sa] and the Muslims while Medina was being attacked.[85] These tribes were eventually exiled for treason. And, as Ibn-e-Ishaq reports, Abu Ráfi was the tribe leader who ordered the treasonous act in direct violation to the Charter of Medina's articles 19, 30, 31, 38, 42, 44, and 49. These articles bound Muslims and Jews to help one another should Medina be attacked. Likewise, Bukhari records, "Abu Ráfi used to hurt Allah's Apostle and help his enemies against him."[86]

Therefore, Abu Ráfi was not executed because "he was an Infidel whose home was not protected." Abu Ráfi was executed because he encouraged treason and actually rebelled against the state of Medina, despite willingly signing and ratifying the Charter of Medina. Innocent people lost their lives because of Abu Ráfi's treason. What government today would tolerate any citizen who willingly helps the enemy harm the state?

Also, Ibn-e-Ishaq reports the following about Abu Ráfi's punishment:

84. Alfred Guillaume, Life of Muhammad: A Translation of Ibn-e-Ishaq's Sirat Rasul Allah (Oxford University Press, 1955), 482.

85. PBS, "Muhammad: Legacy of a Prophet. Muhammand and...the Jews of Medina," accessed August 12, 2012, http://www.pbs.org/muhammad/ma_jews.shtml.

86. Sahih Jami' Bukhari, vol. 5, Book 59, #371.

"As they left [to kill Abu Ráfi for his treason] the [Prophet Muhammad] appointed Abdullah bin Atik as their leader, and he forbade them to kill women or children."[87]

True to orders, the men did not harm Abu Ráfi's wife, even though she nearly foiled their attempt on him. Contrast this to the injuries Osama bin Laden's wife sustained in the raid to kill him, simply to understand the high level of responsibility Prophet Muhammad[sa] bestowed upon his followers to be aware of their actions.

If Wilders has an objection to capital punishment for treason, I suggest he first repudiate the United States, which currently applies capital punishment for treason, and Israel, which applied capital punishment for treason as late as the twentieth century. Regardless, Wilders is wholly incorrect to paint Abu Ráfi's punishment as a preemptive attack. Abu Ráfi's punishment was the just, previously signed-to, and agreed-upon consequence of treason against a sovereign and unified state of Muslims and Jews.

---

87.   Guillaume, *Life of Muhammad*, 482.

ALLEGATION 5

Islam Forbids Privacy to Non-Muslims

I could have addressed Wilders's allegations that Islam does not afford privacy to non-Muslims in the previous section, but I chose to address it here as a more thorough repudiation. Wilders claims, "The Koran tells all sorts of similar stories and issues myriad instructions indicating a total lack of respect for the privacy and even the lives of non-Muslims. Referring to apostates, the Koran says, "If they desert you, seize them and put them to death wherever you find them." The death penalty is to be taken literally, as is the phrase, "wherever you find them." Clearly no permission is needed to enter the dwellings of these renegades."[88]

REFERENCE: Qur'an 4:90.

RESPONSE: I have already responded in Allegation 2 to Wilders's claim that Islam prescribes death for apostasy. Here, I respond to Wilders's misrepresentation of Chapter 4, verse 90, and his allegation that Islam does not respect privacy rights of non-Muslims.

First, Wilders is ignorant to the immense emphasis Islam places on privacy rights for all people. Not only did the Qur'an champion privacy rights centuries before any modern constitution, but also, perhaps no law in history preserves the right to privacy as thoroughly and emphatically as does the Qur'an. It declares:

> O ye who believe! Enter not houses other than your own until you have asked leave and saluted the inmates thereof. That is bet-

---

88. Wilders, *Marked for Death*, 23.

ter for you, that you may be heedful. And if you find no one therein, do not enter them until you are given permission. And if it be said to you, 'Go back' then go back; that is purer for you. And God knows well what you do.[89]

In an era of NSA surveillance and warrantless wiretaps, this Qur'anic teaching's immense value should become crystal clear. The Qur'an forbids entering any home of another person, inhabited or uninhabited, without the owner's permission. The Qur'an further commands people to retreat immediately when they are told to retreat from the home in question—all in the name of protecting a person's privacy. The Qur'an makes no exception for "non-Muslim" homes but specifically commands Muslims to "enter not houses other than your own until you have asked leave." In fact, Prophet Muhammad's[sa] hadith details how important privacy is in Islam:

> A man peeped through a hole in the door of God's Apostle's house, and at that time, God's Apostle had a Midri (an iron comb or bar) with which he was rubbing his head. So when God's Apostle saw him, he said (to him), "If I had been sure that you were looking at me (through the door), I would have poked your eye with this (sharp iron bar)." God's Apostle added, "The asking for permission to enter has been enjoined so that one may not look unlawfully (at what there is in the house without the permission of its people)."[90]

Some might allege that poking an eye is a cruel punishment. On the contrary, this hadith further emphasizes Islam's ardent protection of an individual's privacy. Privacy, particularly for women and minors—two

---

89.   Qur'an 24:28–29.

90.   Sahih Jami' Bukhari, vol. 9, Book 83, #38.

classes that are most victim to sexual abuse—cannot be emphasized enough.

First, consider the ease with which a person can simply not take the unauthorized liberty of peering into another's home without permission. Contrast that with the massive potential and actual threat that exists for those who are victim to such voyeurism. Based on the ease of compliance and the potentially devastating harm to a victim of privacy violations, an active deterrent is necessary to ensure that privacy—for all people of all faiths—remains protected. Thus, Islam places immense emphasis on privacy in ways that Western governments today have only begun to match with privacy laws. And with the recent NSA spying revelations, it seems that even Western governments' efforts in the modern era pale in comparison to the unmatched privacy laws Prophet Muhammad[sa] established fourteen hundred years ago.

Next, Wilders claims that the Qur'an 4:90 passage, "if they desert you, seize them and put them to death wherever you find them," refers to apostates. The reader will see shortly that nothing in this verse refers to apostates. Rather, it refers to hypocrites who first signed a peace treaty with the Muslims and then violated that treaty. In my introduction, I noted that Wilders consistently cites only part of a verse to argue some asinine point—this is one such example. The verse is presented below in proper context. It is easy to see how emphatically this verse promotes justice.

> What has happened to you that you are divided into two parties regarding the hypocrites? And Allah has overthrown them because of what they earned. Desire ye to guide him whom Allah has caused to perish? And for him whom Allah causes to perish thou shalt not find a way.

> They wish that you should disbelieve as they have disbelieved, so that you may become all alike. Take not, therefore, friends from among them, until they emigrate in the way of Allah. And if they

turn away, then seize them and kill them wherever you find them; and take no friend nor helper from among them;

Except those who are connected with a people between whom and you there is a pact, or those who come to you, while their hearts shrink from fighting you or fighting their own people. And if Allah had so pleased, He would have given them power over you, then they would have surely fought you. So, if they keep aloof from you and fight you not, and make you an offer of peace, then remember that Allah has allowed you no way of aggression against them. [91]

By reading 4:90 with honesty, it becomes difficult to understand what Wilders finds objectionable. In 4:89, God admonishes Muslims not to trust hypocrites, because they are, well, hypocrites.

Next, verse 4:90 has nothing to do with privacy—which is protected—and instead further admonishes Muslims not to befriend hypocrites because they may deceive Muslims at any moment. Due to the constraints of war, it prescribes capital punishment for treason—a concept explained earlier. Finally, 4:91 specifically qualifies the guidance provided in the previous two verses to forbid Muslims from fighting three groups of people:

"Those who are connected with a people between whom and you there is a pact, or those who come to you, while their hearts shrink from fighting you, or fighting their own people."

Thus, Muslims are forbidden from fighting those with whom the Muslims have an established mutual relationship, those with whom a pact has been signed, and those who shy away from fighting. Commenting on

---

91.   Qur'an 4:89–4:91.

this principle, Prophet Muhammad[sa] declared, "Whoever killed a person protected by a treaty shall not smell the fragrance of Paradise though its fragrance can be found at a distance of forty years (of traveling)."[92]

Likewise, 4:92 further clarifies, "if they do not keep aloof from you nor offer you peace nor restrain their hands, then seize them and kill them." Thus, Muslims may only fight those who fight them first, and are absolutely forbidden from any aggression against those who do not fight Muslims, or make an offer of peace to Muslims.

Notice that the Qur'an makes no conditions on that peace offering other than a cease of fighting. Non-Muslims need not "submit" to Islamic authority, or convert to Islam, or relinquish their sovereignty. They need only to "keep aloof, not fight, or make an offer of peace."

Therefore, Wilders not only deceptively and incorrectly claims that 4:90 refers to apostates—indeed this verse has nothing to do with apostates—but he also altogether misses this just Qur'anic guidance to promote peace.

---

92.   Sahih Jami' Bukhari, vol. 9, Book 83, #49.

ALLEGATION 6

Islam Requires Either Death, Enslavement, or Conversion

Later in this book—in Chapter 6 specifically—I thoroughly address Wilders's allegation that Islam promotes slavery. Here, I respond generally to his obscure assertion that Islam only offers death, enslavement, or conversion. Wilders writes, "We should not allow total freedom to an ideology that intends to force on us the grim choice of death, enslavement, or conversion to Islam—which is the fate of all non-Muslims as prescribed by Muhammad himself."[93]

REFERENCE: Robert Spencer, *The Truth About Muhammad: Founder of the World's Most Intolerant Religion* (Regnery, 2006), 153.

RESPONSE: Aside from supporting his claim based on a reference from a hatemonger, on page 26 of his book Wilders writes, "I wish to emphasize, I am talking about the ideology of Islam, not about individual Muslim people. There are many moderate Muslims." The jump Wilders makes from "there are many moderate Muslims" to Muslims forcing the world to make a "grim choice of death, enslavement, or conversion" is nonsensical and laughable at best. If, as Wilders admits, the vast majority of Muslims are moderate, then what threat exists for Muslims to suddenly force people into Islam? Likewise, how did the vast majority of Muslims become moderate if Islam is not a moderate religion? Wilders would have us believe that while the vast majority of Muslims are mod-

---

93. Geert Wilders, *Marked for Death*, 27.

erate, the religion of Islam they follow is somehow immoderate, and therefore we should fear Islam because...it produces so many moderate Muslims?

As mentioned in the introduction, it becomes increasingly difficult to take Wilders seriously. This difficulty is further exasperated when his "authentic" references for such a wild allegation against Islam are hate-mongers. Robert Spencer is one such hatemonger. The Southern Poverty Law Center describes him as a member of the "Anti-Muslim Inner Circle." [94] The SPLC explains that "a close look at their rhetoric reveals how doggedly this group works to provoke and guide populist anger over what is seen as the threat posed by the 0.6% of Americans who are Muslim—an agenda that goes beyond reasonable concern about terrorism into the realm of demonization."[95] Furthermore, like Wilders, Spencer has absolutely no training in Islam, Arabic, Qur'anic hermeneutics, or Islamic world history. While Spencer holds a master's degree in Christian studies, how that qualifies him to speak on Islam is a mystery to us all. Indeed, citing Spencer to discuss Islam is akin to citing the Ku Klux Klan to discuss the equality of Africans.

In short, Wilders refuses to cite any Islamic authority to support his allegation or the claim that Prophet Muhammad[sa] himself acted to enforce "death, conversion, or enslavement." I have already demonstrated in my explanation of 4:90 that Islam implores Muslims to seek out peace treaties and to actively avoid aggression. The Charter of Medina further demonstrates how Muslims treated non-Muslims—with equality and absolute justice. These facts alone refute Wilders's allegation that Islam demands death. Likewise, I have mentioned 2:257, which states, "There shall be no compulsion in religion," thus refuting Wilders's allegation of forced conversion. Again, I thoroughly address his allegation about Islam and slavery in Chapter 6.

---

94.   Steinback, "The Anti-Muslim Inner Circle."

95.   Ibid.

Conclusion

Wilders aggressively criticizes Islam and Prophet Muhammad[sa] in his Chapter 2. His most egregious allegations, however, such as death for apostasy, are offered without any references. Likewise, Wilders's allegations that Prophet Muhammad[sa] dealt harshly with non-Muslims (i.e., invading their privacy and homes) is the exact opposite of what history records and of what Islam teaches.

By now Wilders has already demonstrated his lack of even a rudimentary understanding of the most basic Qur'anic interpretation—or reading—setting a tone that remains consistent throughout his book. In his Chapter 3, Wilders presents probably his most aggressive series of attacks against Islam and Prophet Muhammad[sa]. My book's discussion of these is one of its longest because many of the allegations Wilders makes in his Chapter 3 are repeated throughout his book. Accordingly, I have condensed those responses into my Chapter 3, presented next.

Chapter 3

Wilders Rewrites History

"No other religion in history spread so rapidly as Islam. The West has widely believed that this surge of religion was made possible by the sword. But no modern scholar accepts this idea, and the Qur'an is explicit in the support of the freedom of conscience."

— JAMES MICHENER
READER'S DIGEST (MAY 1955)

This is one of the most comprehensive Chapters in response to Wilders's polemic. Wilders begins his Chapter 3 with a brief biography of his life, where he explains his decision to become an atheist, and how his "radical atheism" has now transformed into some form of agnosticism, though the reader remains unsure of where exactly he stands. This is why at certain points in my book I refer to Wilders as an atheist, at other times non-religious, and at other times as an agnostic. One thing is for sure that Wilders does not actually subscribe to any religious belief and maintains a healthy dose of skepticism.

Wilders then spends most of Chapter 3 inventing a biography of Prophet Muhammad[sa], complete with new facts and new events never before heard or recorded. He paints a preposterous picture of a man bent on worldly domination by any means necessary—and claims he is describing Prophet Muhammad[sa]. But, true to Wilders's style of scholarship, he avoids even the most basic references or a shred of objectivity to substantiate his claims. In refuting his allegations, the difficulty arose not in responding to his logic but in trying to understand how he concocted such wild allegations in the first place. In them, Wilders demonstrates his mudslinging skills and has no problem launching attacks against Prophet Muhammad's[sa] family. Wilders begins his series of bizarre allegations by fabricating an incident about Prophet Muhammad's[sa] honorable wife, Hadhrat Khadija[ra].

ALLEGATION 7

Khadija^ra Consummated with Muhammad^sa in Front of Gabriel

Wilders writes, "Muhammad wanted to know if the man [he was seeing visions of] was truly the archangel [Gabriel]. Fortunately, Khadija knew how to determine this. During Gabriel's next visit, she told Muhammad to have sex with her. Lo and behold, as soon as Muhammad penetrated his wife, the visitor disappeared. Surely he must have been an angel, Khadija concluded, since the devil would have stayed to watch their sexual escapades."[96]

REFERENCE: Alfred Guillaume, Life of Muhammad: A Translation of Ibn-e-Ishaq's Sirat Rasul Allah (Oxford University Press, 1955), 107.

RESPONSE: In Chapter 2, I refuted Wilders's allegation that Prophet Muhammad^sa unjustly killed Abu Ráfi. I referenced the same page in Ibn-e-Ishaq's writings that Wilders uses to demonstrate that Abu Ráfi committed treason. Regarding Abu Ráfi: should someone read only one paragraph and not the full account (as Wilders deceptively does), Wilders's conclusion is plausible, though inaccurate. To refute Wilders's accusation regarding Abu Ráfi, I merely expanded the scope of Ibn-e-Ishaq's writings and saw that Abu Ráfi was guilty of treason against the state of Medina—a fact Wilders censors from his readers. In this allegation against Khadija, however, Wilders not only selectively quotes and

---

96. Wilders, *Marked for Death*, 34.

censors history from his readers, but he also invents an entirely new story—committing four major errors.

First, Wilders ignores several *sahih* (authentic) ahadith that long predate Ibn-e-Ishaq's work and do not make the slightest indication of Wilders's aforementioned shameless allegation against Hadhrat Khadija^{ra}. These ahadith record that Hadhrat Khadija^{ra} required no validation from her husband beyond Prophet Muhammad's^{sa} testimony alone before she believed his claim. For example, Bukhari records:

> Allah's Apostle returned with the Inspiration, his neck muscles twitching with terror till he entered upon Khadija and said, "Cover me! Cover me!" They covered him till his fear was over and then he said, "O Khadija, what is wrong with me?" Then he told her everything that had happened and said, "I fear that something may happen to me." Khadija said, "Never! But have the glad tidings, for by Allah, Allah will never disgrace you as you keep good relations with your Kith and kin, speak the truth, help the poor and the destitute, serve your guest generously and assist the deserving, calamity-afflicted ones."[97]

Second, Wilders does not actually cite Ibn-e-Ishaq's words. Rather, because Wilders does not bother to look at the original Arabic—or perhaps he purposely ignored facts unfavorable to him—the paragraph he cites is not made up of Ibn-e-Ishaq's own words, but the words of a third party recording what he *thought* Ibn-e-Ishaq said. Recall that in the introduction, I clarified that none of Ibn-e-Ishaq's original works have survived. Wilders's present baseless allegation is a clear example of the danger in relying solely on Ibn-e-Ishaq. In doing so, Wilders attributes something to Ibn-e-Ishaq that Ibn-e-Ishaq never actually said.

---

97. Sahih Jami' Bukhari, vol. 1, Book 1, #3.

Third, while all the books of ahadith unanimously agree with the story as related in the Bukhari hadith above, Wilders presents an unprecedented angle. Any fair-minded researcher would accept unanimous agreement from more authentic sources well before tolerating a wayward recording known for historical inaccuracies.

Fourth, and perhaps most remarkable, the original Arabic of what Wilders cites provides absolutely no indication that consummation took place. What Wilders presents as consummation is actually—at most—Hadhrat Khadija^ra removing her niqaab or veil in Gabriel's presence. Ibn-e-Ishaq's text, as unreliable as it is, still does not even remotely support Wilders's allegation. Wilders literally fabricates history.

I wonder what motivated Wilders to fabricate this story? I leave judgment to you, the reader. In any case, nothing supports Wilders's shameless allegation. Meanwhile, numerous authentic historical references prove Khadija's^ra honorable and immediate recognition of her husband's truthful claim to prophethood.

ALLEGATION 8

The Meccans Were Multicultural and Pluralistic

Wilders exceeds all bounds of historical integrity with the assertion that the Meccans were multicultural and pluralistic. He writes, "The Meccans were multiculturalists *avant la lettre*.[98] They were pluralistic and tolerant, willing to accommodate new religious groups."[99]

REFERENCE: None.

RESPONSE: On the surface, this may not seem like an allegation against Islam or Prophet Muhammad[sa], but I felt compelled to address this statement for two reasons.

First, this unsupported opinion is historically and factually false in every sense. Therefore, I needed to call it out. Second, Wilders makes this statement as a premise for later arguing that Prophet Muhammad[sa] instigated discord and violence in an allegedly tolerant and pluralistic society—another false allegation. For now, I merely focus on Wilders's allegation that the Meccans were multiculturalists, pluralistic, and tolerant.

Islamic scholar Sufi Mutiur Rahman Bengalee writes about the pre-Islamic Arabs:

---

98. Avant la lettre means "before a concept was invented or before a term was coined" (for example, such as a philosopher explaining the concept of gravity before it was a widely accepted scientific principle).

99. Wilders, *Marked for Death*, 34.

The women of pagan Arabia occupied a very low position. The birth of a female child was regarded as a calamity... The barbarous custom of burying infant girls alive was prevalent. Women were deprived of the right of inheritance, but often were the inherited property of their stepsons, who could make them their wives and dispose of them at their will... Drinking and gambling were rampant... Slavery was the basis of the whole social structure. Bloodshed was a daily occurrence. With the pagan Arabs, blood revenge was a necessity based on their code of honor, and warfare raged incessantly and continued for centuries, so that *the pre-Islamic history of Arabia is a record of deadly tribal feuds and constant guerrilla warfare. The pre-Islamic Arabs had no government worthy of name. By the time of Muhammad, the peninsula was in a state of hopeless political disunity.*[100]

Additionally, though a known critic of Islam and Prophet Muhammad[sa], Sir William Muir is compelled to admit:

...the tide of indigenous idolatry and Ishmaelite superstition, settling strongly from every quarter toward Ka'aba, gave ample evidence that the faith and worship of Mecca held the Arab mind in rigorous and undisputed thralldom... *The prospects of Arabia before the rise of Mahomet were as unfavorable to religious reform as they were to political union or national regeneration.*[101]

Ignoring the established history, Wilders believes that a society that treated women like slaves and slaves like animals, where tribes engaged in

---

100. Sufi Mutiur Rahman Bengalee, The Life of Muhammad (Kessinger Publishing, 2010), 25–26. (Emphasis added.)

101. Sir William Muir, "Introduction to Chapter II," in The Life of Mahomet (1878). (Emphasis added.)

regular warfare, where religious, political, or national regeneration was alien, a society "unfavorable to religious reform"—was a multicultural and pluralistic society.

Ironically, the society Wilders alleges as pluralistic was actually a society that well reflects current Taliban ideology—misogynistic, discriminatory, and violent. In fact, Prophet Muhammad[sa] was sent to this society steeped in ignorance and treachery to peacefully reform them. And since Wilders is partial to Christian theologians, I cite the testimony of one of Arabia's foremost Christian scholars of the time.

Prophet Muhammad[sa] related his divine experience to one of his contemporaries, Waraqa ibn Nawfal, a Christian Nazarene priest and Bible scholar. While Wilders dismissively mentions Waraqa, upon hearing Prophet Muhammad's[sa] testimony, Waraqa responded without hesitation:

> This is the same angel who appeared in times long past to Moses. Would that I might still be alive when you will be turned out of your native city. I could then help you to my heart's content." Prophet Muhammad responded, "Shall I be banished from my native city?" Waraqa replied, "Any man who came with something similar to what you have brought was treated with hostility; and if I should remain alive till the day when you will be turned out then I would support you strongly.[102]

Sadly, Waraqa bin Nawfal died soon thereafter. But the point of this information is to demonstrate that a contemporary Christian scholar of sound mind and body immediately recognized Prophet Muhammad's[sa] claim as truthful. Moreover, he foretold the persecution that Prophet Muhammad[sa] would face at Meccan hands, likening him to Prophet Moses[as] and other past prophets who faced similar persecution and exile.

---

102. Sahih Jami' Bukhari, vol. 4, Book 55, #605.

Waraqa bin Nawfal unambiguously acknowledged Prophet Muhammad's[sa] noble pre-prophethood character. Yet, for as much as Wilders quotes contemporary Christian pseudo-scholars, he completely ignores Waraqa bin Nawfal's testimony—a man who was Prophet Muhammad's[sa] contemporary, who studied the Bible in Hebrew and Arabic, and was one of the leading Christian scholars of ancient Arabia.

Moreover, contrary to Wilders's claim that the Meccans were "willing to accommodate new religious groups," Waraqa—a Meccan and scholar—declares precisely the opposite. Waraqa's foresight was correct—Prophet Muhammad[sa] was persecuted like Prophet Moses[as], precisely because he brought the message of God to the Arabs just like Prophet Moses[as] did to Pharaoh. Far from being pluralistic, the Meccans treated Prophet Muhammad[sa] just as Pharaoh and his people treated Prophet Moses[as]—with hatred, contempt, and persecution. History demonstrates that Wilders's claim that the pre-Islamic Arabs were "multiculturalists *avant la lettre*" is nothing more than a figment of his own imagination.

ALLEGATION 9

Muhammad[sa] Initially Permitted Idol Worship

While Wilders concocts some new allegations, several others he makes are allegations that new-age critics of Islam incessantly repeat despite clear evidence to the contrary. The allegation that Prophet Muhammad[sa] initially permitted idolatry is one such example. Wilders writes, "Since Muhammad was not powerful enough to impose his will on everyone, the Islamic prophet initially agreed to a *modus vivendi* with the Meccan Quraishi establishment. He thus produced Koranic verses allowing Muslims to pray to Mecca's female deities as intercessors before Allah. Later Muhammad revoked these verses, claiming they had been inspired by the devil."[103]

REFERENCE: None.

RESPONSE: Addressing this fabricated incident, esteemed historian and Islamic scholar Hadhrat Mirza Bashir Ahmad[ra] cites accepted and ancient scholars, concluding:[104]

> ...this story is entirely a fabrication, and its forgery is clearly evident from every rational aspect. Hence, the great Muhaddithin and leaders of Hadith, such as 'Allamah 'Ainī, Qazi 'Ayad and 'Allamah Nawawi have expounded with conclusive argumentation that this occurrence is false and nothing more than a fabri-

---

103. Geert Wilders, *Marked for Death*, 35.

104. Mirza Bashir Ahmad, The Life and Character of the Seal of Prophets, vol. 1 (2011), 209–11. http://www.alislam.org/holyprophet/Seal-of-Prophets-Vol-1.pdf.

cated Hadith. Thus, 'Allamah 'Aini writes in debate of this issue: "This story is evidently negated, both in light of narration and common sense."[105]

Then, Qazi 'Ayad writes:

"Prudent and reliable individuals have not accepted this narration due to the fact that the narration of this story is confusing, and its authenticity is very weak. Moreover, the manner of its narration is also weak and feeble. In addition, *no narrator has successfully traced this narration to the Holy Prophet*[sa] *or any of his companions.*"[106]

Furthermore, 'Allamah Nawawi writes:

"Nothing of this narration is correct, neither in the aspect of narration nor in the aspect of common sense.'[107]

On the other hand, many a'immah-e-hadith (scholars of Hadith) have not even made mention of this occurrence. For example, the Sihah Sittah has not even hinted towards it, though mention of the recitation of Surah An-Najm and the prostration of the Quraish is present in it. It is apparent that this narration passed the eyes of the Muhaddithin, who rejected it with belief of its forgery and unreliability.

---

105. 'Umdatul-Qārī Sharḥu Ṣaḥīḥil-Bukhārī, vol. 19, 313: Kitābu Tafsīril-Qur'ān, Sūratul-Qamar, Under the verse "Fasjudū lillāhi wa'budūhu" [An-Najm (53:63)], Dārul-Iḥyā'it-Turāthil-'Arabī, (Beirut, Lebanon, Edition 2003).

106. Muḥammad bin 'Abdul-Bāqī Az-Zarqānī, Sharḥul-'Allāmatiz-Zarqānī 'alal-Mawāhibil-Ladunniyyah, vol. 2 (Beirut: Bābu Dukhūlish-Sha'bi wa Khabriṣ-Ṣaḥīfah, Dārul-Kutubil-'Ilmiyyah, 1996), 25. (Emphasis added.)

107. Al-Minhāju bi-Sharḥi Ṣaḥīḥ Muslim bin Al-Ḥajjāj, Kitābul-Masājid wa Mawāḍi'iṣ-Ṣalāh, Bābu Sujūdit-Tilāwah, Dāru Ibni Hazam (2002), 533.

In the same manner, many great Mufassirin [commentators of the Holy Qur'an], such as Imam Razi have declared this instance vain and devoid of truth.[108] Moreover, among the mystics, sagacious ones, the like of Ibni 'Arabi, have stated, "There exists no truth in this occurrence."[109]

Thus, no such verse was revealed that compromised the worship of one God. I remind the reader to consider that while I have offered several references from throughout Islamic history to prove my point, Wilders does not offer a single reference to support his baseless opinion. This only serves as further validation that Wilders's allegations are fabricated.

---

108. Imām Muḥammad bin 'Umar bin Al-Ḥusain Fakhr-ud-Dīn Ar-Rāzī, "Tafsīru Sūratil-Ḥajj," Verse 53, in At-Tafsīrul-Kabīr, vol. 23 (Beirut: Dārul-Kutubil-'Ilmiyyah , 2004), 44–48

109. Muḥammad bin 'Abdul-Bāqī Az-Zarqānī, Sharḥul-'Allāmatiz-Zarqānī 'alal-Mawāhibil-Ladunniyyah, vol. 2, Bābu Dukhūlish-Sha'bi wa Khabriṣ-Ṣaḥīfah (Beirut: Dārul-Kutubil-'Ilmiyyah, 1996), 25

ALLEGATION 10

Muhammad^sa Demanded Slaughter of the Pluralistic Meccans

Earlier I refuted Wilders's assertion that the Meccans were pluralistic. Here, Wilders employs that same unfounded assertion to argue that "as Muhammad's following grew, he became intolerant and demanding, and the controversy between Mecca's pluralist polytheists and Muhammad became ever more virulent. One day, Muhammad entered the *Kaaba* shrine and addressed the Meccans with a menacing threat: 'By Him who holds my life in His hand: I bring you slaughter.'"[110] Wilders's claim that Prophet Muhammad^sa instigated discord is once again contrary to historical fact.

REFERENCE: Alfred Guillaume, Life of Muhammad: A Translation of Ibn-e-Ishaq's Sirat Rasul Allah (Oxford University Press, 1955), 131.

RESPONSE: This logic is baffling. On one hand the Meccans are allegedly tolerant and pluralistic, and on the other hand they're being drawn to a man who is allegedly intolerant and violent? If anything the "tolerant" Meccans should have never been drawn to such an intolerant person. Moreover, I ask the reader again to take a cautioned approach regarding Ibn-e-Ishaq. In painting this incident as an example of Prophet Muhammad's^sa alleged attempts to instigate against "pluralistic" Meccans, Wilders is caught in yet another lie. To demonstrate this point, I simply present the reader with the full paragraph of Alfred Guillaume's transla-

---

110. Wilders, *Marked for Death*, 35.

tion of Ibn-e-Ishaq's work, not just the isolated fragment that Wilders reports to his readers. I, in the spirit of Islam and free speech, instead believe in full disclosure and condemn Wilders's censored "research."

The writings attributed to Ibn-e-Ishaq record the full background surrounding this allegation as follows:

> When the Quraysh became distressed by the trouble caused by the enmity between them and the apostle and those of their people who accepted his teaching, they stirred up against him foolish men who called him a liar, insulted him, and accused him of being a poet, a sorcerer, a diviner, and of being possessed. However, the apostle continued to proclaim what God had ordered him to proclaim, concealing nothing, and exciting their dislike by contemning their religion, forsaking their ideals, and leaving them to their unbelief.[111]

Already we see that Prophet Muhammad's[sa] only "crime" was openly preaching his faith. No complaints are made against him for being violent or instigating violence—rather, complaints of enmity are raised because Prophet Muhammad[sa] disavowed idol worship. Wilders, a self-proclaimed champion of free speech, remarkably condemns Prophet Muhammad[sa] for exercising his own right to free speech. That Wilders further objects to Prophet Muhammad's[sa] "offensive" preaching against idolatry is also perplexing, as he is at the forefront in demanding Muslims tolerate those who make offensive remarks against Islam. Likewise, Ibn-e-Ishaq records that "foolish men" were stirred up to call Prophet Muhammad[sa] a liar—clearly demonstrating that the wise and educated understood well that Prophet Muhammad[sa] was quite the opposite. Adding to Wilders's deception and hypocrisy is the rest of this incident, which he also censors from his readers.

---

111. Guillaume, Life of Muhammad, 131. (Emphasis ours.)

Yahya b. Urwa b. az-Zubayr on the authority of his father from Abdullah b. Amr b. Al-As then relates:

> While they [the Meccans] were discussing him [Muhammad], the apostle came towards them and kissed the black stone, then he passed them as he walked round the temple [Ka'aba]. As he passed they said some injurious things about him. This I could see from his expression. He went on and as he passed them the second time they attacked him similarly. This I could see from his expression. Then he passed the third time, and they did the same. He stopped and said, "Will you listen to me O Quraysh? By him who holds my life in His hand, I bring you *Dhabh* [slaughter]." This word so struck the people that not one of them but stood silent and still; even one who had hitherto been most violent spoke to him in the kindest way possible saying, "Depart, O Abu'l-Qasim,[112] for by God you are not violent." So the apostle went away...[113]

While Wilders paints the story as Prophet Muhammad's[sa] uninstigated threat, the facts instead demonstrate Prophet Muhammad[sa] patiently bore repeated insults while he peacefully worshiped. His allegedly violent statement was, instead, a reaction. Moreover, it was merely a reflection of what prophets are wont to do: warn their people to stop their abuse. In fact, Prophet Muhammad's[sa] statement is no different from that of Prophet Moses[as] who declared, "On that same night I will pass through Egypt and strike down every firstborn—both men and animals—and I

---

112. Per Arab tradition, a man was referred to as the father of his son. Muhammad was called Abu'l Qasim (Father of Qasim) on account of his young son Qasim, who passed away in infancy.

113. Guillaume, Life of Muhammad, 131.

will bring judgment on all the gods of Egypt. I am the LORD."[114] Wilders does not object to Prophet Moses[as] in the least, but instead argues that the Bible has been revived and reformed in the New Testament. Perhaps Wilders missed Jesus Christ's[as] proclamation: "Do not think that I came to bring peace on Earth; I did not come to bring peace, but a sword."[115] Whether or not Wilders recognizes that Prophet Muhammad[sa] said nothing different from what previous prophets declared, the most telling testimony is that of the very people insulting Prophet Muhammad[sa], who declared, "O [Muhammad], by God you are not violent!"

What remarkable testimony! The same people that Wilders claims as victims of Prophet Muhammad's[sa] alleged tyranny not only openly insult Prophet Muhammad[sa] without fear of reprisal, but recognized that whatever he meant in using the word *slaughter*, one thing was for sure—by God, Prophet Muhammad[sa] was *not* violent. People who fear a tyrant do not repeatedly insult him to his face. They certainly do not swear by God that the alleged tyrant is not violent. Rather, we see a people that aggressively engaged Prophet Muhammad[sa], insulted him repeatedly only for his faith, yet recognized that he was, above all and by God, a peaceful man.

Another portion of this story remains that Wilders censors from his readers, perhaps hoping the lay reader will ignore it. Yahya b. Urwa b. az-Zubayr further reports that after Prophet Muhammad[sa] peacefully left the company of those insulting him, the next day the Meccan idol worshipers—unprovoked—tried to murder Prophet Muhammad[sa]:

> ...[The Meccan leaders] assembled in the Hijr, I being there too, and they asked one another if they remembered what had taken place between them and the apostle so that when he openly said

---

114. Exodus 12:12.

115. Matthew 10:34.

something unpleasant they let him alone. While they were talking thus the apostle appeared, and they leaped upon him as one man and encircled him, saying, "Are you the one who said so-and-so against our gods and our religion?" The apostle said, "Yes I am the one who has said that." And I saw one of them seize his robe. Then Abu Bakr interposed himself weeping and saying, "Would you kill a man for saying Allah is my Lord?" Then they left him... Abu Bakr returned that day with the hair of his head torn [because] they had dragged him along by his beard.[116]

Thus, Wilders censors the fact that the Meccans—unprovoked—attacked and attempted to assassinate Prophet Muhammad[sa], even after they swore by God that he was not a violent man. The attack was so vicious that even Hadhrat Abu Bakr[ra], companion and first khalifa of Prophet Muhammad[sa], literally had his hair and beard ripped from his face as he tried to protect Prophet Muhammad[sa] from certain death.

More telling, perhaps, is that Hadhrat Abu Bakr[ra] proclaimed Prophet Muhammad's[sa] "crime," for which they tried to kill him—simply declaring that Allah is his Lord. That is—Prophet Muhammad's[sa] crime, for which the Meccans tried to murder him, was exercising his freedom of speech and freedom of religion. At no point did any of Prophet Muhammad's[sa] enemies allege that their desire to kill him was due to an injustice he had committed, any wrong he had done, or any harm he had caused a person, or due to any act of violence or terrorism. While Wilders constantly reminds his readers of the bounty upon his own head for his desire to exercise free speech, he shamelessly ignores the brutal attacks and assassination attempts on Prophet Muhammad[sa] for exercising *his* right to free speech. But Wilders's hypocrisy continues.

Later in his book, Wilders pathetically introduces a meritless argument known as *taqiyya*, the alleged permission Islam gives Muslims to lie

116. Guillaume, Life of Muhammad, 131.

to "infidels" to gain a tactical advantage. (When you, the reader, reach my response in Chapter 5, I request you to reflect back to the this incident.) In this incident, Prophet Muhammad[sa] was afforded the perfect opportunity to lie to the "infidels" and spare himself from an assassination attempt. He was alone, without any military, sovereignty, or weaponry. When asked if he was the one speaking against idolatry, it would have been easy to lie and escape unscathed. On the contrary, even in the face of certain death, he spoke the truth and said that yes, he was the person who had spoken against their idols. Wilders altogether ignores this incident when he propagandizes taqiyya. Despite all the nonsense that taqiyya-theory proponents espouse, Prophet Muhammad's[sa] truthful example in the face of assassination undercuts their entire platform.

Contrary to Wilders's assertion, Prophet Muhammad[sa] was anything but a persecutor. Rather, he was a model of compassion on such a profound level that even his most hardened enemies—even those that sought to murder him—could not help but swear by God that he was not a violent man. Prophet Muhammad's[sa] contemporaries—critics and friends alike—unreservedly proclaimed this fact. Yet, we are asked to believe that a man who lives fourteen hundred years later and thousands of miles away, with the qualifications of an online certification and a course in health insurance regulation, knows better.

ALLEGATION 11

Muhammad^{sa} Became
Proactively Hostile to Jews and Christians

Wilders alleges that Prophet Muhammad became proactively hostile against Jews and Christians once he saw that they refused to give him favor. He writes, "When it became clear, however, that the Jewish tribes distrusted him and that Jewish poets even mocked him in verse and song, the Koran became extremely hostile toward Jews. Later still, when Muhammad realized that many Christians would not support him either the Koran began to predict hell and damnation for Christians as well."[117]

REFERENCE: Regarding alleged hostility toward Jews: Koran 2:62, 3:111, 4:161–162, 5:13, 5:52, 5:58, 5:64–67, 9:31, etc. [sic]. Regarding alleged damnation for Christians: Koran 3:111, 5:15, 5:52, 5:58–61, 5:67, 5:76, etc. [sic]

RESPONSE: Wilders's repeated attempts to claim that he has made a substantive argument just because he refers to a few verses is illogical. A substantive argument would require that he explain how those verses support his allegation. He does not do this for any of the verses cited. Therefore, I do not intend to delve into a lengthy commentary on each of the aforementioned verses to "prove" that they are not anti-Jewish or anti-Christian. Should readers care to see thorough exegeses on these verses, however, I encourage them to visit www.alislam.org/quran.

---

117. Wilders, *Marked for Death*, 35.

There, one may enjoy the massive and free online Qur'an translation and commentary—in as many as seventy different languages—and personally study the verses in question. For now, I'll debunk the broad allegations Wilders asserts—the myths that the Qur'an is anti-Jew, or that it somehow automatically relegates Christians to hell.

Dr. Philip Jenkins, a foremost scholar of the Bible, professor at Pennsylvania State and Baylor Universities, author of numerous books on Christianity, and himself a non-Muslim, writes:

> The Myth of Jew Hatred: None of the Qur'an's alleged manifestations of 'Jew hatred' are convincing as expressions of systematic racial hatred. Critics of the Qur'an cite verse 2:62 [which Wilders cites above] as a foundational text for Islamic anti-Semitism, and some later Islamic commentators did indeed take the words in this sense. [But] the passage does not contemplate the damnation or denigration of any race. This is scarcely a charter for 'Jew hatred.'[118]

In *Laying Down the Sword*, Dr. Jenkins performs a thorough and excellent analysis of virtually every verse Wilders lists as examples of the Qur'an's alleged anti-Jew stance. He concludes:

> In order to make such texts look vicious, anti-Islamic critics systematically exaggerate the Jewish element in the passage...[119] The Qur'an offers nothing vaguely as explicit as the New Testament passages in which Jesus himself, who is for Christians the incarnation of the Divine, speaks so furiously against 'the Jews.' It is the Jesus of the New Testament who calls his enemies the children

---

118. Philip Jenkins, Laying Down the Sword: Why We Can't Ignore the Bible's Violent Verses (2011), 87–88. (Emphasis added.)

119. Ibid., 89.

not of Abraham but of the Devil, the Father of Lies. That same Jesus denounces the Jews of his day, warning that 'this generation will be held responsible for the blood of all the prophets that has been shed since the beginning of the world.' He was not condemning all Jews in any racial sense, but was rather attacking rival factions and leaders in his day. And that is the model we find in the Qur'an.[120] In reality, the Qur'an has nothing that need be taken as a condemnation of Jews, or of any ethnic group.[121]

This is but a snippet of Dr. Jenkins's detailed analysis, debunking the myth that the Qur'an teaches anti-Semitic or anti-Christian ideology or violence. Unlike the unqualified anti-Islam critics Wilders repeatedly cites, Dr. Jenkins is a prolific religion scholar, a disinterested party in Islam, and presents objective and peer reviewed information. His books are certainly worth the read for those seeking facts. This is one topic, however, that I revisit later in this book.

Finally, in response to the allegation that the Qur'an condemns Christians to hell, Wilders foolishly ignores the fact that the Qur'an is the only ancient religious scripture that explicitly declares that non-Muslims can and shall attain paradise. Ironically, verse 2:63, the verse subsequent to the alleged anti-Jew verse that Wilders cites, presents this teaching: "Surely, the Believers, and the Jews, and the Christians and those of other paths—whichever party from among these truly believes in Allah and the Last Day and does good deeds—shall have their reward with their Lord, and no fear shall come upon them, nor shall they grieve."[122] The Qur'an lumps Muslims, Jews, Christians, and those of other paths into one group, demonstrating that Islam teaches no monopoly on paradise.

---

120. Ibid., 91.

121. Ibid., 94. (Emphasis added.)

122. Qur'an 2:63.

Why Wilders, a former "radical" atheist, even cares where Islam may or may not send a person to a place that according to him does not exist is beyond comprehension. Regardless, despite Wilders alleged "many, many" readings of the Qur'an, he continues to miss these basic Qur'anic principles. Contrary to Wilders's allegations, no such "Jew-hatred" and no such blanket condemnation of Christians exists in the Qur'an or in Islam in general.

ALLEGATION 12

The Qur'an Has Been Abrogated

Numerous anti-Islam critics cite the "theory" of abrogation and Wilders follows suit. He writes, "Muslims later became embarrassed by these contradictions between earlier and later Koranic verse. Islamic theologians solved this problem with the concept of *an-Nasikh wal mansukh* ("the abrogating and the abrogated"). According to this concept, whenever there are contradictions in the Koran, later verses overrule earlier ones; in other words, Allah revoked what he had earlier revealed. This means, in effect, that the earlier verses speaking favorably of Jews and Christians are overruled by later, hostile verses, and that tolerant verses are overruled by intolerant ones. Speaking about the often-quoted tolerant verses, "There shall be no compulsion in religion, Pope Benedict XVI observed, "According to some of the experts, this is probably one of the suras of the early period, when Muhammad was still powerless and under threat." It is contradicted, as the Pope pointed out, by "the instructions, developed later and recorded in the Koran, concerning holy war.""[123]

REFERENCE: None.

RESPONSE: Not surprisingly, Wilders, who has no training in Qur'anic hermeneutics, does not cite any reference to substantiate his allegation. In short, the theory of Qur'anic abrogation is nonsense without a shred

---

123. Wilders, *Marked For Death*, 35. Also, on page 37 Wilders makes a similar allegation: "Muhammad presented his personal tyranny as a theocracy, exploiting his ability to abrogate Koranic verses and fabricate new ones on the spot according to whatever the situation demanded."

of merit. The Qur'an itself explains how it is to be interpreted. The Qur'an contains verses that are "firm and decisive in meaning" (*muhkamat*) which are used to interpret those verses susceptible of different interpretations (*mutashaabihat*).[124] Thus, if a *muhkamat* verse contradicts an interpretation of a *mutashaabihat* verse, that particular *interpretation* is rejected—never the actual verse. This method is in harmony with the spirit of the Qur'an, which repeatedly urges the exercise of reason and reflection.[125] In teaching Muslims about proper hermeneutics, Prophet Muhammad[sa] states:

> Thus were ruined those who have gone before you. They interpreted certain parts of their scriptures in such a manner as to make them contradict other parts. But the Qur'an has been so revealed that different parts of it should corroborate one another. So do not reject any truth by making one part contradict the other. Act on what you understand thereof and refer that which you do not understand to those who know and understand it.[126]

Indeed, no consensus exists on even a single verse being abrogated. Likewise, among extremists who promulgate the abrogation theory, the range of abrogated verses is as few as five verses to as many as eleven hundred. As Prophet Muhammad[sa] clarified long before abrogation theorists espoused their arguments, "contradictions" lay only in the eye of an ignorant few. The facts are that no such "embarrassment" existed regarding Qur'anic "contradictions," as Wilders baselessly claims.

The former pope incorrectly suggests that verses revealed later in Prophet Muhammad's[sa] life—such as those calling for war—abrogate

---

124. Qur'an 3:8.

125. Qur'an 2:257; 3:191–192; 38:30.

126. *Musnad Ahmad bin Hanbal*, "Hadith no. 6741," in.Musnad Abdullah bin amar bin al-Aas. (Beirut: Alim ul Kutab, 1998)

those emphasizing tolerance and steadfastness. (The footnotes link a thorough refutation of the pope's remarks.[127]) Contrary to the pope's assertion, the verse "There is no compulsion in religion" was revealed after Prophet Muhammad[sa] migrated to Medina and thus after he gained political and worldly power—it was not revealed at the onset of Muhammad's[sa] ministry. This historical fact demonstrates not only the pope's and Wilders's erroneous understanding of Islamic history, but more important, it further refutes their abrogation theory.

Notably, Wilders fails to cite a single pair of verses illustrative of the abrogation theory. Assess Wilders's allegation, therefore, based on my explanation of Qur'anic verses: limiting retaliation in Chapter 1, treatment of apostates in Chapter 2, addressing Jews and Christians in this Chapter, addressing jihad in Chapter 5, addressing jizya in Chapter 6, and so on. These concepts are not contradictory, but work in perfect harmony when looked at objectively and contextually.

---

127. Imam Mukhtar Cheema, "A Rejoinder to the Pope's Allegations Against Islam," http://www.alislam.org/topics/response-to-pope/A_Rejoinder_to_Popes_Allegations_Against_Islam.pdf.

ALLEGATION 13

Muhammad[sa] Rejected
Meccan Efforts to Establish Peace

Wilders repeatedly proffers his unsubstantiated claim that the Meccans were pluralistic and peace loving. He writes, "Muhammad showed in word and deed his rejection of the Meccans' pluralism. In 619, Abu Talib, the highly respected clan leader of the Hashemites and Muhammad's uncle and foster father, lay on his deathbed. The other Quraishi leaders used the occasion to try to reconcile with Prophet Muhammad[sa] and establish peaceful coexistence between Muslims and non-Muslims. The prophet, however, rejected all their proposals and demanded that Mecca unconditionally submit to Allah—in other words, submit to him."[128]

REFERENCE: None.

RESPONSE: As I have already demonstrated earlier in this Chapter, nothing about the Meccans' worldview indicated that they embraced pluralism in the least. Yet, Wilders insists that the same Meccans who earlier tried to kill Prophet Muhammad[sa] for exercising his right to free speech were pluralistic.

Wilders correctly notes, thankfully, that Abu Talib was a highly respected clan leader and Prophet Muhammad's[sa] uncle and foster father. However, Wilders's allegation that while the Quraish attempted to use the occasion to reconcile, Prophet Muhammad[sa] worked to the contrary, is fabricated. This might also be why Wilders doesn't bother to offer a

---

128. Wilders, *Marked For Death*, 35.

94

reference: none exists to support his claim. In reality and in exact contrast to Wilders's allegation, the Meccans were hell-bent on murdering Prophet Muhammad[sa] due to his preaching the unity of God. And this intent to murder existed despite Abu Talib's intense efforts to encourage the Meccans to avoid violence. At a meeting at Abu Talib's home between Prophet Muhammad[sa] and the Meccans, history records that it was in fact the Meccans who left with the intent to kill Prophet Muhammad[sa]:

> The chiefs got up without achieving any result, and 'Uqbah bin Abi Mu'it began saying loudly: "Leave him alone. Advice is of no use. He [Muhammad] should be assassinated; he should be finished off."[129]

Abu Talib was naturally disturbed at the thought of his nephew's assassination. When he heard of a secret meeting to execute this plan, he attended it and proclaimed:

> "Yesterday Muhammad disappeared from us for some time. I thought that you had acted upon what 'Uqbah had said and had killed him. Hence, I decided to come to Masjidul Haram along with these men. I had also instructed them that each one of them should sit by the side of each one of you and as soon as they heard me speak aloud they should get up and attack you with their concealed weapons. However, luckily I found Muhammad alive and safe from any harm from you." Then he asked his men to take out their concealed weapons and ended his speech with these words: "By Allah! If you had killed him I would not have spared even one of you and would have fought with you to the last."[130]

---

129. Tara'if, 85 and al-Hujjah, 59–61.

130. Tara'if, 85 and al-Hujjah, 61.

Thus, Abu Talib—whom Wilders admits was a highly respected clan leader—saw the Meccans' violent tendencies for what they were and worked proactively to ensure his nephew remained safe. As Sir William Muir also admits:

> The sacrifices to which Abu Talib exposed himself and his family for the sake of his nephew, while yet incredulous of his mission, stamp his character as singularly noble and unselfish. They afford at the same time strong proof of the sincerity of Mohammad. Abu Talib would not have acted thus for an interested deceiver; and he had ample means of scrutiny.[131]

Finally, contrary to the false picture Wilders paints about Abu Talib's death, Abu Talib's dying words were as follows, demonstrating that it was the Meccans, not Prophet Muhammad[sa], who refused to reconcile:

> I recommend Muhammad to you, because he is the trusted one of Quraish and the truthful one of Arabia and possesses all the virtues. He has brought a religion, which has been accepted by the hearts, but the tongues have chosen to deny it on account of fear of taunts. I can see that the weak and the helpless of Arabia have got up to support Muhammad and believe in him, and he has also risen to help them breaking the ranks of Quraish. He has humiliated the chiefs of Quraish and devastated their homes and has made the helpless strong and given them status." He concluded his remarks with these words: "O my kinsmen! Become the friends and supporters of his faith (Islam). Whoever follows him becomes prosperous. If death had given me some more time, I would have warded off all the dangers that came to him.[132]

---

131. Sir William Muir, Life of Mahomet, 105.

132. Seerah-i Halabi, vol. 1, 390.

In another record, Abu Talib said:

> O Party of the Quraish! Among the creation of Allāh, you are a chosen people. God has given you great reverence. I advise that you treat Muhammad well, because amongst you, he is a man of the highest morals. He possesses distinction among the Arabs on account of his truthfulness and straightforwardness. If you ask the truth, he has brought a message to us which the tongue rejects but the heart accepts. I have stood by Muhammad a lifetime and have stepped forward to protect him in all times of difficulty, and if I receive more time, I shall continue to do so in the future as well. And O Quraish! I also advise you not to insist upon causing him grief, but help him and support him, for your betterment lies in this.[133]

Yet, while praising Abu Talib on one hand, Wilders censors his powerful testimony from readers. Indeed, if anyone's statement could be construed as requiring "unconditional submission," it was that of Abu Talib—and even that would take a word-twisting artist like Wilders to misconstrue. The facts demonstrate that Abu Talib admired Prophet Muhammad's[sa] virtuous example immensely and wanted nothing more than to protect him so that Prophet Muhammad[sa] could continue to raise the status of the weak and helpless.

Likewise, contrary to Wilders's assertions that the Meccans were pluralists, Ibn-e-Ishaq well records the danger that Prophet Muhammad[sa] and the Muslims faced at Meccan hands:

> The Polytheists Persecute the Muslims of The Lower Classes: Then the Quraish showed their enmity to all those who followed the apostle; every clan which contained Muslims, attacked them,

---

133. Az-Zarqānī, Sharḥul-'Allāmatiz-Zarqānī 'alal-Mawāhibil-Ladunniyyah, 46–48.

imprisoning them, and beating them, allowing them no food or drink, and exposing them to the burning heat of Mecca, so as to seduce them from their religion. Some gave way under pressure of persecution, and others resisted them, being protected by God. Khalaf b. Wahb b. Hudhaifa b. Jumah used to bring [Bilal] (a slave who had accepted Islam) out at the hottest part of the day and throw him on his back in the open valley and have a great rock put on his chest; then he would say to him, 'You will stay here till you die or deny Muhammad and worship Al-Lat and al-Uzza.' [Bilal] used to say while he was enduring this, 'One, one!'[134]

Yet, Wilders shares none of these incidents. He instead paints the Meccans as innocent bystanders suffering through some terrible ordeal while Muslims persecuted them. History records the exact opposite scenario. Abu Talib's dying words described his desire to "ward off all dangers that came to [Muhammad[sa]]." He describes Prophet Muhammad[sa] as a champion for the poor, a truthful and just person, and a person destined to prosper. He likewise warns the Meccans that he is ready to fight them should they dare harm his nephew.

Common sense shows Prophet Muhammad[sa] relentlessly strove for peace, while Meccans attempted to thwart every effort. Abu Talib's testimony is clear: in Mecca, the danger did not emanate from Prophet Muhammad[sa] but was viciously directed *at* him by Meccans. The scars on Hadhrat Bilal's[ra] back long served as the reminder. In short, the Meccans—not Prophet Muhammad[sa]—rejected peace efforts.

---

134. Guillaume, Life of Muhammad, 143–44.

ALLEGATION 14

Muhammad[sa] Left Mecca
Due to Losing Abu Talib's[ra] Protection

Wilders claims that "by 622, after the deaths of both Abu Talib and Khadija, Muhammad realized he had lost his most influential protectors. Consequently, the Muslims slipped out of Mecca and began their hijra, or 'emigration,' to the oasis of Yathrib, 210 miles to the north."[135]

REFERENCE: None.

RESPONSE: Prophet Muhammad's[sa] reason for emigration was not because he "lost his most influential protectors." Indeed, Hadhrat Khadija[ra] was not a Meccan chief who could grant him protection. Prophet Muhammad[sa] left under divine guidance, as God informed him that the Meccans were plotting to assassinate him once again. After suffering for more than twelve years the most brutal persecution ever witnessed in history, Prophet Muhammad[sa] and the Muslims did not raise a single sword or pick a single fight. Rather, they left under cover of darkness and fled for their lives. As Sufi Mutiur Rahman Bengalee writes:

> When the Meccans came to know that the cause of the Prophet was making rapid and steady progress, they now resorted to a new plan to put an end to the Prophet's life and cause. They selected one man from each tribe who pledged himself to assist in making a united assault in order to assassinate the Prophet at night when

---

135. Wilders, *Marked for Death*, 36.

he was asleep so that the guilt of the crime would be evenly distributed. If they could kill the Prophet, they believed it would be impossible for the Prophet's people to stand against the combined tribes of Mecca.[136]

Muhammad, however, received a revelation, which warned him of the danger; he was commanded by God to leave town and seek refuge in Medina. A substitution had to be made, so his cousin Ali volunteered to lie down upon the prophet's bed. With tears in his eyes he gazed at the Ka'aba and said: 'Oh, Mecca, thou hast been to me the dearest spot in all the world, but thy sons would not let me live here.'[137] The Prophet's enemies found Ali in Muhammad's bed. They were so angry that they put Ali in confinement, but finding such procedure useless, they soon released him. A bounty of 100 camels was placed on Muhammad's head, dead or alive.[138]

Thus, what Wilders describes as a casual decision to leave was a painful event in Prophet Muhammad's[sa] life, when he was forced to leave his homeland to escape assassination. Prophet Muhammad[sa] left to flee persecution—precisely as the Christian scholar Waraqa bin Nawfal had foretold twelve years prior.

Wilders also ignores that Prophet Muhammad's[sa] decision to preach or migrate was not based on whether he had Abu Talib's protection. It was in fact Abu Talib who insisted that he wanted to protect his nephew, and thus, that protection remained. Prophet Muhammad[sa], however, made clear that his protection was not from any man, but from God alone—as per God's promise to him in the Qur'an: "O Messenger! Convey to the people what has been revealed to thee from thy Lord; and if thou do it not, thou hast not conveyed His Message at all. *And Allah*

---

136. Bengalee, Life of Muhammad, 67.

137. Ibid.

138. Ibid., 68–70.

will protect thee from men. Surely, Allah guides not the disbelieving people."[139]

In short, Wilders ignores well-recorded history in alleging that Prophet Muhammad[sa] migrated due to a lack of protection from other men. His migration, in fact, was based upon divine guidance to escape assassination from the violent and intolerant Meccans.

139. Qur'an 5:68.

ALLEGATION 15

Muhammad^sa Established
Political Dictatorship in Medina

Wilders writes, "The *Muhajirun*, or 'immigrants,' as the Tayyibians called Muhammad and his gang, were welcome to stay, and the Jewish tribes even asked Muhammad to mediate their quarrels. It was a foolish request with devastating consequences, for Muhammad used the opportunity to establish a political dictatorship based on his Koranic revelations...Yathrib also became the site of the Muslims' first mosque, a symbol of their political domination over the town."[140] Wilders repeats these allegations in Chapter 10, claiming that the Hijra was a means to stealthily and forcefully spread Islam,[141] and in his Chapter 11.[142] I respond to each of these allegations here.

REFERENCE: None.

RESPONSE: I responded earlier to Wilders's fabrication that "Muhammad established political authority based on his Koranic revelations" by introducing the reader to the Charter of Medina. In short, Prophet Muhammad^sa established the Charter of Medina, a secular constitution, to govern Yathrib's affairs. Every Jewish and Muslim community in Yathrib participated in its development, and each signed and ratified it without coercion. Wilders's argument about a political dicta-

---

140. Wilders, *Marked for Death*, 36–37.

141. Ibid., 163.

142. Ibid., 176.

torship finds zero historical merit. Not surprisingly, he hopes his readers do not bother with details, facts, and reality, and instead remain, like him, lost in the wilderness. (The reader may refer back to the thorough aforementioned description of the Charter of Medina in Chapter 2 for a refutation of Wilders's present baseless—and yet again unreferenced—claim.)

Furthermore, Wilders insults the Jewish tribes' intelligence, deeming them so foolish that they asked an allegedly violent man to mediate their disputes and become their leader. After all, Mecca and Medina—though a month's journey apart—maintained regular trade and communication with each other. Surely a man with the allegedly unjust personality Wilders paints would have had a reputation that preceded him. Wilders in fact unwittingly admits that even after his claim to prophethood, Prophet Muhammad[sa] was so well respected and revered outside of Mecca that the Jewish tribes of Medina willingly asked him to become their leader.

Finally, Wilders's statement about the Muslims' first mosque is confusing. On one hand, he claims Yathrib was just as tolerant as Mecca (which itself is a lie, as Mecca's intolerance and Yathrib's tolerance is why Muslims fled Mecca and flourished in Yathrib). On the other hand, when Muslims exercise their freedom of worship in Yathrib—it suddenly becomes, according to Wilders, "a symbol of their political domination." Evidently, while Wilders claims he promotes pluralism and wants Muslims to promote pluralism, he does not want Muslims to benefit from pluralism themselves by exercising even basic freedom of worship.

ALLEGATION 16

Muhammad[sa] Married Ayesha[ra] When She Was Underage

Contemporary critics have repeatedly claimed, without merit, that Prophet Muhammad[sa] married Hadhrat Ayesha[ra] when she was not of age. Wilders is no different. He writes, "...Jibreel suddenly announced that Muslims were allowed to take several wives, thus permitting the prophet, then in his late fifties, to marry the 6-year-old Ayesha... Before long, Muhammad had eleven wives, including the child Ayesha."[143]

REFERENCE: None.

RESPONSE: Wilders presents no facts or references—yet again—to support his claim that Hadhrat Ayesha[ra] was six upon her marriage to Prophet Muhammad[sa]. The facts instead indicate that Hadhrat Ayesha[ra] was no younger than twelve or thirteen at the time of her willing marriage with parental consent, and she may have been as old as nineteen or twenty. Most likely, Hadhrat Ayesha[ra] was between the two ages: around fifteen or sixteen. A variety of authentic historical references substantiate this conclusion—none of which Wilders consults.

Before I delve into Islamic history, consider that the age deemed "acceptable" for girls to marry is not some objective standard across time, culture, and religion—but a subjective standard based on social construct. For example, the Catholic Encyclopedia reports regarding Mary[as], mother of Jesus[as]:

---

143. Ibid., 37.

...the priests announced through Judea that they wished to find in Juda a respectable man to espouse Mary, then twelve to fourteen years of age. Joseph, who was at the time ninety years old, went up to Jerusalem among the candidates; a miracle manifested the choice God had made of Joseph, and two years later the Annunciation took place.[144]

Likewise, the Talmud recommends "marrying off one's daughter as soon after she reaches adulthood as possible, even to one's Slave."[145] In fact, the Talmud presents some peculiar guidance on marriage, also stating, "A maiden aged three years and a day may be acquired in marriage by coition, and if her deceased husband's brother cohabits with her, she becomes his."[146] So while the Catholic Encyclopedia tells us that Mary and Joseph were married at the ages of about twelve to fourteen and ninety, respectively, the Talmud permits marrying girls as young as three years and one day. Lest this seem like an attack on Christianity and Judaism— which it is not—I present marriage laws in the West.

For centuries in Scotland, the age of consent for girls was twelve— and parental consent was unnecessary.[147] Only in 1929 was the age raised to sixteen for girls.[148] In America even today, Hadhrat Ayesha's[ra] consenting marriage to Prophet Muhammad[sa] would be considered valid. For example, in New Hampshire, the legal age for girls is thirteen with parental consent.[149] In Massachusetts, the legal age for girls is twelve with

---

144. The Catholic Encyclopedia: An International Reference of Work on the Constitution, Doctrine, Discipline, and History of the Catholic Church, vol 8. (New York: Robert Appleton Company), 505.

145. Talmud, Pesachim 113a.

146. Talmud, Sanhedrin 55b.

147. E. Ewen, "The early modern family" in T. M. Devine and J. Wormald, eds, The Oxford Handbook of Modern Scottish History (Oxford: Oxford University Press, 2012), 271.

148. Ibid.

149. Entry for New Hampshire at http://topics.law.cornell.edu/wex/table_marriage#g.

parental consent.[150] In Mississippi, there is no age minimum for girls, as long as there is parental consent.[151] In California, there is no age minimum for girls, as long as there is parental consent.[152]

Granted, the American state laws were passed in the nineteenth and twentieth centuries—not today. And granted, Americans aged twelve or thirteen do not typically get married today. The point is, however, that even in recent American history, Americans found value—not objection—in girls marrying at twelve or thirteen (or even younger), and passed laws through their respective state legislatures to affirm that value. This exercise in no way argues for a return to such marrying ages. Rather, it merely establishes the point that "appropriate" marriage ages are based on ever-changing social constructs—not some supposed objective, advanced contemporary standard. Therefore, if we are to accuse Prophet Muhammad[sa] of any impropriety in marrying Hadhrat Ayesha[ra] even if she was twelve or thirteen, then we must also condemn the Old Testament, New Testament, Europe, and numerous American states.

Next, Wilders's assertion that Prophet Muhammad[sa] was in his "late fifties" upon his marriage to Hadhrat Ayesha[ra] is also inaccurate. Their marriage took place in 624 AD—the year after migration from Mecca to Medina—placing Prophet Muhammad's[sa] age at fifty-four or fifty-five. Though this is not a major point of contention, I present it as just another example of Wilders's disregard for detail and facts.

So far, I have demonstrated that Hadhrat Ayesha's[ra] marriage to Prophet Muhammad[sa], even if she was twelve or thirteen, was not by any means unusual when compared across time and culture—even to contemporary standards. Now I shall demonstrate that Wilders's assertion that Hadhrat Ayesha[ra] was only six is meritless, and also demonstrate Hadhrat Ayesha's[ra] actual age upon marriage.

---

150. Entry for Massachusetts at http://topics.law.cornell.edu/wex/table_marriage#g.

151. Entry for Mississippi at http://topics.law.cornell.edu/wex/table_marriage#g.

152. Entry for California at http://topics.law.cornell.edu/wex/table_marriage#g.

In determining hadith authenticity, it is necessary to consider how many different narrators can relate a hadith back to the original source—be that source Prophet Muhammad[sa], Hadhrat Ayesha[ra], or a companion. The more narrators exist and the more in agreement they are with one another—the more authentic we may consider the hadith.

Perhaps knowing the incredibly weak narration alleging Hadhrat Ayesha's[ra] age at marriage as six, Wilders did not bother citing it. (Or perhaps he simply does not care to fact-check). Regardless, virtually every narration that relates Hadhrat Ayesha's[ra] marriage age as six is tied to Hisham ibn 'Urwah, who then reports on his father's authority. This is problematic for several reasons.

First, Hisham ibn 'Urwah is the only person to narrate this hadith. That only a single narration exists eliminates the opportunity for corroboration and validation. Next, Hisham related this hadith in his old age and after he migrated to Iraq—a time during which he admits he suffered severe memory loss. For example, *Tahzibut Tahzib*, a premier book on the credibility of hadith narrators, cites Yaqub ibn Shaibah to report, "Narratives reported by Hisham are reliable except those that are reported through the people of Iraq."[153] Likewise, "Malik ibn Anas objected on those narratives of Hisham which were reported through people of Iraq."[154] History records that after living in Medina for the first seventy-one years of his life, Hisham immigrated to Iraq in his old age and suffered severe memory loss.[155] More specifically, Yaqub ibn Shaibah relates, "He [i.e., Hisham] is highly reliable, his narratives are acceptable, except what he narrated after shifting to Iraq."[156]

The hadith that relates Hadhrat Ayesha's[ra] age as six at marriage was related by Hisham ibn 'Urwah after he immigrated to Iraq. Thus, this

---

153. Ibn Hajar Al-`Asqalaani, Tahzibut Tahzib, Dar Ihya al-turath al-Islami, vol. 11, 48–51.

154. Ibid.

155. Meezaan al-Ai`tidal, Vol. 4, pg. 301–302.

156. Tahzibut Tahzib, 50.

hadith is not only isolated in its claim but also unreliable due to Hisham's old age and admitted extensive memory loss. Wilders disregards these inconsistencies altogether.

On the contrary, several historical events and ahadith narrations demonstrate that Hadhrat Ayesha[ra] was likely fifteen or sixteen or as old as nineteen or twenty at the time of her consenting marriage to Prophet Muhammad[sa]. Wilders ignores each of these.

First, Hadhrat Ayesha[ra] was the daughter of Hadhrat Abu Bakr[ra]. Tabari reports, "All four of [Abu Bakr's[ra]] children were born of his two wives—the names of whom we have already mentioned—during the pre-Islamic period [i.e., pre-610 AD]."[157] Hadhrat Ayesha's[ra] marriage to Prophet Muhammad[sa] took place one year after Hijra (emigration to Medina), or around 624 AD. Therefore, even if Hadhrat Ayesha[ra] had been born as late as 609 AD, only a year before Prophet Muhammad[sa] claimed prophethood, she would have been roughly fourteen at the time of emigration to Medina in 623 and therefore no less than fifteen at the time of her marriage to Prophet Muhammad[sa]. This is a far cry from the age of six that Wilders asserts.

Likewise, most historians report that Hadhrat Asma[ra], Hadhrat Ayesha's[ra] elder sister, was ten years her senior.[158] The books *Tahzibut Tahzib* and *Al-Bidaayah wa an-Nihayah* both report that Hadhrat Asma[ra] died at the age of one hundred, in 73 AH (695 AD).[159] This means that Hadhrat Asma[ra] must have been no younger than twenty-seven at the time of emigration. Hadhrat Ayesha's[ra] marriage to Prophet Muhammad[sa] was in 1 AH, when Asma was twenty-eight. This means that at a

---

157. Al-Tabari, Tarikh al-umam wal-mamloo'k, vol. 4 (Beirut: Dar al-fikr, 1979), 50.

158. Imam Az-Zahabi, Siyar A`la'ma'l-nubala', vol. 2 (Beirut: Mu'assasatu'l-risala'h, 1992), 289.

159. Ibn-e-Kathir, Al-Bidaayah wa an-Nan-Nihaayah, vol. 8 (Al-jizah: Dar al-fikr al-`arabiy, 1933), 371–372.

minimum, Hadhrat Ayesha[ra] was eighteen upon her consenting marriage to Prophet Muhammad[sa].

The above examples are not exhaustive. Several other authentic ahadith and well-recorded events discredit Wilders's allegation that Prophet Muhammad[sa] married Hadhrat Ayesha[ra] when she was six. The examples I have presented, however, should more than suffice that Hadhrat Ayesha[ra] was not six, but instead, that she was a mature adult who married Prophet Muhammad[sa] of her own free will.

ALLEGATION 17

Muhammad^{sa} Caused Zainab^{ra} and Zaid^{ra} To Divorce

Wilders writes, "Soon afterward, when Muhammad fell in love with the wife of his adopted son, the latter offered to divorce her. Arab incest taboos, however, did not allow a man to marry the ex-wife of an adopted son. Hence, Allah ordered Muhammad to marry the woman so that, says the Koran, "it should become legitimate for true believers to wed the wives of their adopted sons if they divorced them. Allah's will must be done. No blame shall be attached to the Prophet for doing what is sanctioned for him by Allah.""[160]

REFERENCE: Qur'an 33:38–39.

RESPONSE: While Wilders cites the correct verse for the subject matter, his assertions that "Muhammad fell in love with the wife of his adopted son" and "the latter offered to divorce her" are arbitrary and without any historical support. Had Prophet Muhammad^{sa} engaged in any unbecoming behavior, no shortage of critics existed during his lifetime to point it out. Further, Hadhrat Zainab^{ra} was Prophet Muhammad's^{sa} cousin, and he had had ample opportunity to marry her before her marriage to Hadhrat Zaid^{ra} was even a nascent possibility. It is baseless to allege that his infatuation somehow spontaneously emerged only after her marriage to his adopted son.

---

160. Wilders, *Marked for Death*, 37.

While not a single critic of Prophet Muhammad's[sa] time attributed to him any wrongdoing, contemporary critics somehow find an opportunity to do so. To silence those critics, Christian scholar Reverend Boswell Smith writes:

> It should be remembered, however, that most of Muhammad's marriages may be explained, at least, as much by his pity for the forlorn condition of the persons concerned, as by other motives. They were almost all of them widows who were not remarkable for either their beauty or their wealth, but quite the reverse. May not this fact, and his undoubted faithfulness to Khadija till her dying day, and till he himself was fifty years of age, give us additional ground to hope that calumny or misconception has been at work in the story of Zainab.[161]

Again, perhaps if Wilders offered some authentic source to support his argument, I may have been obliged to provide a longer response. But as history records, critics during Prophet Muhammad's[sa] time and contemporary scholars both agree that Prophet Muhammad[sa] committed no wrong. Wilders's allegation here is, again, baseless.

---

161. Reverend Boswell Smith, Muhammad and Muhammadism (1946).

111

ALLEGATION 18

Muhammad[sa] Terrorized People to Accept Islam

In this allegation, Wilders cites a Qur'anic verse in an attempt to ascribe a violent character to Prophet Muhammad[sa]. Wilders writes, "Muhammad's scribe, who had to write down the prophet's revelations, renounced Islam and returned to Mecca. Others, however, were terrorized into submission. 'I shall cast terror into the hearts of the infidels. Strike off their heads, maim them in every limb!' declares the Koran."[162]

REFERENCE: Qur'an 8:13.

RESPONSE: Wilders correctly notes that one of Prophet Muhammad's[sa] scribes renounced Islam and returned to Mecca. But in noting this, Wilders contradicts himself in the very next sentence. Earlier in his book, Wilders claims that Islam teaches death for apostates. Now he casually cites an example where Prophet Muhammad's[sa] personal scribe renounced Islam. If Islam did in fact teach death for apostasy, here was a prime example for Prophet Muhammad[sa] to enforce this alleged teaching. But instead, as Wilders clearly writes, the scribe was allowed to leave Medina and travel all the way back to Mecca without hindrance or harm, let alone death.

Wilders then alleges that people were "terrorized into submission." While he does not provide even a single historical example to support his claim, he does cite the Qur'an 8:13. The verse in question states, "When

---

162. Wilders, *Marked for Death*, 37.

thy Lord revealed to the angels, saying, 'I am with you; so give firmness to those who believe. I will cast terror into the hearts of those who disbelieve. Smite, then, the upper parts of their necks, and smite off all fingertips.'"[163]

His lack of any training in Qur'anic hermeneutics notwithstanding, Wilders's refusal to study Islamic history further obstructs any chance that he might make a coherent statement about Islam. In this verse, God is relating the story of Badr—the battle that Muslims fought in self-defense against the invading Meccan army.

In the Battle of Badr, a woefully ill-trained, ill-equipped, and outmatched army of 313 Muslim men, women, and children defended their right to practice their faith peacefully against a well-trained and well-equipped army of a thousand Meccan soldiers. Badr took place near Medina. After Meccans had persecuted Muslims relentlessly in Mecca for thirteen years, they now had pursued Muslims a month's journey to Medina to murder them. In fact, many of the Muslims fought in self-defense with sticks and wooden swords—terrifying, isn't it? Despite the overwhelming odds, the scant Muslim army defeated the powerful Meccan army. In verse 8:13, God reminds the Muslims that their victory was as a result of His divine help with angels and not their own doing. Nothing in this verse indicates, suggests, or commands Muslims to strike terror into the hearts of those who do not submit to Islam. Rather, God declares in the Qur'an that He will cast terror into the hearts of the Meccans because of their desire to persecute and kill Muslims only for their faith.

Wilders's entire argument consists of a baseless allegation, a verse that he attempts to sensationalize as terrifying, and the sad hope that his readers assume a connection between the two. On the contrary, as Wilders is forced to admit, even Prophet Muhammad's[sa] personal scribe was allowed to leave Islam and Medina unharmed.

---

163. Qur'an 8:13.

ALLEGATION 19

Muhammad[sa] Launched Raids on Innocent Merchants

Once again ignoring history, Wilders next alleges, "From Medina, Muhammad began raiding the camel caravans of Arab traders travelling between Mecca and other Arab towns and oases. These plundering raids are called *ghazi* in Arabic, from which the word *razzia* is derived. Muhammad organized eighty-two *razzias*, twenty-six of which he personally led. "Fighting is obligatory for you, much as you dislike it," says the Koran."[164]

REFERENCE: Qur'an 2:117.

RESPONSE: As with the previous allegation, Wilders makes an unreferenced and meritless statement, cites a random verse from the Qur'an, and hopes the reader is naïve enough to assume a connection.

Still, I find it peculiar that Wilders confidently explains Arabic grammar and definitions, despite having absolutely no training in Arabic. It is also no surprise, likewise, that Wilders alleges caravan raids, again without so much as a single reference. He tries to jumble this allegation with the following verse: "Fighting is ordained for you, though it is repugnant to you; but it may be that you dislike a thing while it is good for you, and it may be that you like a thing while it is bad for you. Allah knows all things, and you know not."[165]

---

164. Wilders, *Marked for Death*, 37.

165. Qur'an 2:217 (Wilders also cites numerous other random verses in his footnote without offering any indication of how they connect to his opinion. Should the

114

What about this verse is troubling? The Qur'an reminds Muslims that even their thirteen years of nonviolent resistance in Mecca and peaceful emigration 240 miles away unfortunately had not changed the Meccans' massive hostilities against them. Therefore, they had to be ready to fight even though they did not wish to.

Of course the Muslims did not wish to fight. That is exactly why they bore persecution patiently for thirteen years and migrated to a different region altogether—to avoid fighting. The verse is a commentary on human nature. These Muslims had suffered for more than a decade in Mecca, left all their homes, properties, belongings, and ancestries to emigrate a month's journey, all for the sake of peace. Now war pursued them once more. It is completely reasonable to believe that some Muslims were tired of the persecution, suffering, and running. They simply wanted peace—but the Qur'an admonished them to remain firm, because God knew the consequences of their acquiescence to Meccan aggression. Commenting on this situation, Prophet Muhammad reassured the Muslims, "O ye Muslims! you should not desire to fight the enemy, and remain desirous of the peace and security of God. If however, contrary to your desire, you are compelled to fight an enemy then demonstrate steadfastness."[166]

This is a universal principle. Sovereign governments throughout history and even today enact mandatory drafts to ensure their nations remain secure against attack. By Wilders's logic, nations that obligate their citizens to fight, even in self-defense, are behaving unjustly.

Turning specifically to the issue of the alleged plundering raids, history records facts contrary to what Wilders fabricates:

---

reader require a response to those allegedly violent verses, we remind them that they can find a detailed analysis of each verse at www.alislam.org/quran.

166. Ṣaḥīḥul-Bukhārī, Kitābul-Jihādi Was-Siyar, Bābu Kānan-Nabiyyusa Idhā Lam Yuqātil Awwalan- Nahār, Ḥadīth Nos. 2631, 2966, and 4542.

Āṣim bin Kulaib relates from his father that an Anṣārī Companion narrates that, we set out on a Ghazwah with the Holy Prophet[sa]. On one occasion, the people were struck by severe hunger and became very much distressed (since they had no provisions with them). Upon this they caught a few goats from a flock, slaughtered them and began cooking them. Our pots were boiling with their meat when the Holy Prophet[sa] arrived. The Holy Prophet[sa] immediately upset our pots with his bow and angrily began grinding the pieces of meat beneath his feet and exclaimed, 'Plunder is no better than carrion.'[167]

This is the man that Wilders claims taught plunder? Let alone during times of prosperity, even in the face of severe hunger, Prophet Muhammad[sa] forbade plunder of any sort. In another famous hadith, Prophet Muhammad[sa] commanded the Muslims:

O ye Muslims! go forth in the name of Allāh and perform Jihād with the intention of protecting religion. But beware! do not embezzle the wealth of spoils and do not deceive a people. Do not mutilate the enemy dead, do not kill women and children,[168] nor religious recluses;[169] and do not kill the elderly. Create peace in the land, and treat the people with benevolence, for surely, Allāh loves the benevolent."[170]

---

167. Sunan Abī Dāwūd, Kitābul-Jihād, Bābu Fin-Nuhba Idhā Kāna Fit-Ta'āmi Qillatun, Ḥadīth No. 2705 and Sunan At-Tirmidhī, Kitabus-Siyar, Bābu Mā Jā'a Fī Karāhiyatin-Nuhbah, Ḥadīth No. 1600. (Emphasis added.)

168. Ṣaḥīḥul-Muslim, Kitābul-Jihādi Was-Siyar, Bābu Ta'mīril-Imāmil-Umarā' a 'Alal-Bu'ūth, Ḥadīth No. 4522.

169. Imām Abū Ja'far Aḥmad bin Muḥammad Aṭ-Ṭaḥāwī, *Sharḥu Ma'ānil-Āthār*, vol. 2, 126, Kitābus-Siyar, Bābush-Shaikhil-Kabīri Hal Yuqtalu Fī Dāril-Ḥarbi Am Lā, Ḥadīth No. 5067, Maktabah Raḥmāniyyah, Urdu Bazaar, Lahore.

170. Sunan Abī Dāwūd, Kitābul-Jihād, Bābu Fī Du'ā' il-Mushrikīn, Ḥadīth No. 2614.

Once again, Prophet Muhammad[sa], in word and deed, explains that the purpose of fighting is to protect religious freedom—not wealth, power, or terror. He specifically forbade Muslims from harming innocents, condemned violence, and implored benevolence.

So, then, what purpose did these raids serve, and why did Prophet Muhammad[sa] engage in them at all? Islamic history scholar Hadhrat Mirza Bashir[ra] Ahmad explains and demonstrates that the raids were not unjust, but a just form of defense that nations even today employ:

The fourth strategy employed by the Holy Prophet[sa] was that he began to intercept the trade caravans of the Quraish which travelled from Makkah to Syria passing by Madīnah enroute. The reason being that firstly, these caravans would spark a fire of enmity against the Muslims wherever they travelled. It is obvious that for a seed of enmity to be sown in the environs of Madīnah, was extremely dangerous for the Muslims. Secondly, these caravans would always be armed and everyone can appreciate that for such caravans to pass by so close to Madīnah was not empty of danger. Thirdly, the livelihood of the Quraish primarily depended on trade. Therefore, in these circumstances, the most definitive and effective means by which the Quraish could be subdued, their cruelties could be put to an end and they could be pressed to reconciliation, was by obstructing their trade route. As such, history testifies to the fact that among the factors which ultimately compelled the Quraish to incline towards reconciliation, the interception of these trade caravans played an extremely pivotal role. Hence, this was an extremely sagacious strategy, which yielded fruits of success at the appropriate time. *Fourthly, the revenue from these caravans of the Quraish was mostly spent in efforts to eliminate Islām. Rather, some caravans were even sent for the sole purpose that their entire profit may be utilized against the Muslims. In this case, every individual can understand that the interception of these caravans, was in its own right, an absolutely legitimate motive.*

Various prejudiced Christian historians...have raised the allegation that God-forbid, the Holy Prophet[sa] and his Companions would set out for the purpose of plundering the caravans of the Quraish. We would like to inquire of these people who are an embodiment of justice and equity, that do your nations, who you consider to be the epitomes of civility and nobility, not obstruct the trade routes of enemy nations? When they receive news that a trade vessel belonging to such and such enemy nation is passing by so and so place, do they not immediately dispatch a naval company in its pursuit so as to destroy it, or employ a strategy to subdue it and take possession of its wealth? Then for this reason can your leaders be labeled as robbers, pillagers and plunderers? Verily, if the Muslims intercepted the caravans of the Quraish, its purpose was not to take possession of the wealth of their caravans. Rather, military tactics demanded that the trade-route of the Quraish be obstructed, because there was no better means by which they could be brought to their senses and pushed to reconciliation. To assert that in the interception of these caravans, the Muslims were given teachings of pillage and plunder, is a grave injustice and far from equity.[171]

As usual, Wilders offers no references to support his claim. The multiple authentic references I have offered above, however, should clarify to any fair-minded reader that Prophet Muhammad[sa] did not engage in any injustice regarding war. On the contrary, he demonstrated extreme restraint and benevolence.

---

171. Mirza Bashir Ahmad, Seal of Prophets, 91–92.

ALLEGATION 20

Muhammad[sa] Violated the Chivalrous Arab War Code

By now I am left exasperated that Wilders works so hard to convince his readers, and perhaps himself, that pre-Islam Arabia functioned as a civilized society. He fails to provide even a single historical reference to substantiate his bold, unreferenced claim. Yet again he writes, "The pre-Islamic Arabs had a chivalrous war code. Muhammad, however, frequently violated it, allowing him to defeat his opponents who obeyed the rules and who simply could not imagine that their enemy would not do the same."[172] In Chapter 6 of his polemic, Wilders also asserts that Islam and Prophet Muhammad[sa] endorse civilian massacres. I address both allegations here.

REFERENCE: None.

RESPONSE: Wilders attempts to promulgate yet another fabrication without offering a single reference to support his claim. But, of course, this is because no such reference exists. Pre-Islamic Arabs had no rules of war—women, children, elderly, livestock, the dead, clergy, homes, and greenery were all fair game.

In fact, Wilders's favorite historian, Ibn-e-Ishaq, reports that after the Battle of Uhud, which the Muslims lost, "...the apostle went out seeking Hamza (his uncle) and found him at the bottom of the valley with his belly ripped up and his liver missing and his nose and ears cut

---

172. Wilders, *Marked for Death*, 38.

off."[173] Abu Sufyan, then a non-Muslim, said to Hadhrat Umar bin Khattab[ra], a Muslim, "There are some mutilated bodies among your dead. By God, it gives me no satisfaction and no anger. I neither prohibited nor ordered mutilation."[174]

Is this mutilation the Arab chivalry of which Wilders speaks?

The companions replied with anger and anguish upon hearing Abu Sufyan's statement that he did not forbid the Meccans from mutilating martyred Muslims. They were pained also upon seeing Prophet Muhammad's[sa] grief over his uncle's inhumane death. But Prophet Muhammad's[sa] response to the mutilations stands to this day as a model of unmatched leadership and compassion. Ibn-e-Ishaq reports:

> When the Muslims saw the apostle's grief and anger against those who had thus treated his uncle, they said, "By God, if God gives us victory over them in the future, we will mutilate them as no Arab has ever mutilated anyone." [Muhammad] replied, "If you endure patiently that is better. Endure thou patiently. Thy endurance is only in God. Grieve not for them, and be not in distress as to what they plot." So the apostle pardoned them and was patient and forbade mutilation. Humayd al-Tawil told me, "The Apostle never stopped in a place and left it without enjoining on us almsgiving and forbidding mutilation."[175]

Prophet Muhammad[sa] further declared, "Go forth in the name of Allah and in the cause of Allah. Fight whoever disbelieves (and rejects terms of peace). Go forth and *do not steal, do not commit treachery, do not muti-*

---

173. Guillaume, Life of Muhammad, 387.

174. Ibid., 386.

175. Ibid., 387–88.

late, and do not kill children."[176] At-Tirmidhi said, "The people of knowledge hate mutilation."[177]

Thus, through Prophet Muhammad's[sa] example, all these barbaric wartime practices that existed pre-Islam were now abolished. Prophet Muhammad's[sa] example is derived from the Qur'an itself, which compels Muslims to treat captives with dignity and compassion.[178] Hadhrat Abu Bakr[ra], first khalifa of Prophet Muhammad[sa], clearly related Prophet Muhammad's[sa] wisdom to the Muslim armies shortly after Prophet Muhammad's[sa] demise:

> O people! I charge you with ten rules; learn them well! Stop, O people, that I may give you ten rules for your guidance in the battlefield. Do not commit treachery or deviate from the right path. You must not mutilate dead bodies. Neither kill a child, nor a woman, nor an aged man. Bring no harm to the trees, nor burn them with fire, especially those which are fruitful. Slay not any of the enemy's flock, save for your food. You are likely to pass by people who have devoted their lives to monastic services; leave them alone.[179]

In another instance, Hadhrat Abu Bakr[ra] related an abbreviated form of this hadith: "Do not kill women or children or an aged, infirm person. Do not cut down fruit-bearing trees. Do not destroy an inhabited place."[180] These rules were necessary to enforce because the pre-Islam

---

176. Sahih Sunan At-Tirmidhi, Book of Compensation for Murder, #1408. (Emphasis added.)

177. Ibid.

178. Qur'an 76:8–10.

179. Al-Muwatta, vol. 21, #21.3.10 and Youssef H. Aboul-Enein and Sherifa Zuhur, Islamic Rulings on Warfare (Strategic Studies Institute, US Army War College; Darby, PA: Diane Publishing Co., 2004), 22

180. Al-Muwatta, vol. 21, #9, #10.

rules of warfare did not forbid such acts. Likewise, while the pre-Islam custom was to kill or enslave prisoners of war, Prophet Muhammad[sa] ordered them to be freed upon ransom—an astoundingly peaceful and progressive strategy.

Mutilation was common practice for pre-Islam Arabia. Thus, for Wilders to assert that Prophet Muhammad[sa] violated some alleged "chivalrous war code" is totally false. On the contrary, Prophet Muhammad[sa] advanced the rules of compassion and care for the enemy to a level that even today's most advanced societies have not reached.

Then, in his Chapter 6, Wilders cites Qur'an 48:29 to allege that Prophet Muhammad[sa] and the Qur'an endorse civilian massacres such as the one on Ambon City in 1999 and 2000.[181] I have already demonstrated that Islam forbids attacking civilians for any reason. The terrorists who murdered innocent civilians in Ambon City find no refuge or excuse in Islam. Wilders instead attempts to conflate the political and economic motivations of particular contemporary groups with Qur'anic exploitation. The full verse 48:29 cited reads, "He it is Who has sent His Messenger, with guidance and the Religion of truth, that He may make it prevail over all other religions. And sufficient is Allah as a Witness."[182] Apparently, Wilders believes this verse not only permits extremists, but also provokes moderates, to massacre non-Muslims.

The verse states that Prophet Muhammad[sa] was sent by God with a true religion so that it may take the place of the other religions. One might ask why—but not Wilders. Wilders is only concerned with the *how* of this prophecy.

The fact is that nothing in this verse, or any Qur'anic verse, implies or even suggests that bloodshed and mayhem are the "how" necessary for Islam to "prevail." Separate from those Qur'anic verses that deal with religiously persecuted Muslims and their rights to self-defense, the

---

181. Wilders, *Marked for Death*, 94.

182. Qur'an 48:29.

Qur'an repeats numerous verses that address spreading Islam through argumentation[183] and exhortation.[184] Various verses on the proper meaning of jihad—as discussed thoroughly in my Chapter 5—also support this position. The perpetrators of these attacks that Wilders cites violate Qur'anic injunctions about fighting to stop persecution[185] and not harming those who do not harm Muslims.[186]

The combined ignorance of Wilders and other extremists notwithstanding, no Qur'anic verse can be cited to support random acts of violence as necessary to bring about the triumph of Islam.

In sum, Prophet Muhammad[sa] did not violate some nonexistent, chivalrous Arab war code. Instead, he created a war code where there was none, a code that is unmatched in humanitarianism by even today's standards. Among other things, Prophet Muhammad's[sa] war code categorically forbids any attack on civilians for any reason. Wilders's concoction is nothing more than a figment of his own imagination.

---

183. Qur'an 29:27.

184. Qur'an 51:55–56.

185. Qur'an 2:194; 60:10.

186. Qur'an 60:9.

ALLEGATION 21

Muhammad^sa Actively Massacred the Quraishi Army at Badr

I briefly mentioned the Battle of Badr earlier and provide a more detailed analysis here due to Wilders's renewed allegation. Wilders writes, "In the Battle of Badr, in March 624, about 300 Muslims led by Muhammad defeated a Meccan escort three times their number and captured several important Quraishi leaders... Not content with mere robbery, Muhammad had the captured Quraishi leaders massacred because, according to the Koran, 'a prophet may not take captives until he has fought and triumphed in his land.' A Jewish poet from Medina was so indignant about this atrocity [the Battle of Badr] that he wrote a eulogy commemorating the slain leaders. Islam's prophet had the poet murdered for it."[187]

REFERENCE: None.

RESPONSE: I decline to respond to Wilders's allegation that Prophet Muhammad^sa had a Jewish poet killed after the Battle of Badr, as no reference is provided. In other words, I literally have no idea to what incident he refers. Suffice it to say, no such example exists in any authentic historical document. If Wilders provides some legitimate reference, or any reference at all, I will be happy to respond.

Regarding his allegations about the Battle of Badr, however, though Wilders makes no reference either—no surprise there—his description

---

187. Wilders, *Marked for Death*, 38.

of Badr is nothing less than outright deception. In short, this battle ensued after Muslims patiently suffered persecution and murder for nearly thirteen years in Mecca, then left their belongings and livelihoods and migrated peacefully to Medina, and then were pursued by Meccans who intended to kill them [the Muslims].

As a final resort, Muslims took up the sword—often wooden—to defend their right to religious freedom. As I've noted, at Badr, near Medina, some three hundred ill-trained and ill-equipped Muslims with two horses overcame a well-trained, well-equipped army of a thousand Meccan soldiers and one hundred horses. In total, fourteen Muslims and seventy Meccans were killed at Badr, and seventy Meccans were taken captive.

While seventy deaths in an army of a thousand is no small number, it is hardly a "massacre" (as Wilders paints it), considering that the Meccans were the instigating army. Likewise, Wilders's claim that the Muslims mistreated and even killed the Meccan POWs is patently false—history records the exact opposite. Here, I present the candid testimony of Sir William Muir:

> The Refugees had houses of their own, received the prisoners with kindness and consideration. "Blessings on the men of Medina!" said one of these in later days: "they made us ride, while they themselves walked afoot; they gave us wheaten bread to eat when there was little of it, contenting themselves with dates." It is not surprising, therefore, that some of the captives, yielding to these influences, declared themselves Believers, and to such their liberty was at once granted. The rest were kept for ransom. But it was long before Koreish could humble themselves to visit Medina for the purpose. The kindly treatment was thus prolonged, and left a favourable impression on the minds even of those who did not at once go over to Islam. Eventually the army of Badr was enriched by the large payments given. The captives were redeemed according to their several means, some paying a thousand, and others as

much as four thousand pieces. Such as had nothing to give were liberated without payment; but a service was required which shows how far Mecca was in advance of Medina in learning. To each were allotted ten boys, to be taught the art of writing; and the teaching was accepted as a ransom.[188]

Oh, the humanity! I challenge Wilders to produce another such noble example in world history. Far from the violent and false picture Wilders paints, even the captives could not help but testify that their captors treated them better than they treated themselves. At a time in Arabia when POWs were either put to death or enslaved, these men were allowed to purchase their freedom. Those who could not purchase their freedom "suffered" the responsibility of teaching ten children how to read. Education was their ransom. No example in history can even compare to this high standard Prophet Muhammad[sa] demanded of the Muslims.

Not content with fabricating history surrounding the POWs at the Battle of Badr, Wilders attempts to attribute his fabrication to the following Qur'anic verse: "It does not behoove a Prophet that he should have captives until he engages in regular fighting in the land. You desire the goods of the world, while Allah desires for you the Hereafter. And Allah is Mighty, Wise."[189]

Contrary to Wilders's bizarre interpretation that this verse requires Muslims to kill captives, this verse in fact condemns keeping captives at all *unless* it is during wartime. As mentioned earlier, the Qur'an compels Muslims to treat captives with dignity and compassion. "They fulfill their vow, and fear a day the evil of which is widespread. And they feed, for love of Him, the poor, the orphan, and the prisoner, Saying, 'We feed

---

188. Muir, Life of Mahomet, 233–34.

189. Qur'an 8:68.

you for Allah's pleasure only. We desire no reward nor thanks from you.'"[190]

Islam abolished the pre-Islamic custom to continuously imprison POWs after the end of a war. Islam forbids holding captives outside wartime and declares that such captives must be liberated immediately. Applying this teaching to contemporary times, any POW America may have captured during the Iraq War or Afghanistan War would categorically need to be released, as the wars are now over. Don't hold your breath for a book from Wilders condemning the detention of Guantanamo Bay inmates. Far from an unjust practice, this Islamic teaching to release POWs immediately is in danger of being called too liberal and free. This liberating teaching only becomes obscured behind Wilders's veil of ignorance.

---

190. Qur'an 76:8–10.

ALLEGATION 22

Muhammad^{sa} Ordered
a Woman Who Insulted Him Be Killed

I provided a detailed argument in Chapter 2 to demonstrate that Islam prescribes no worldly punishment for apostasy or blasphemy. I ask the reader to keep this in mind as I respond to Wilders's next allegation. Wilders writes, "When a woman spoke out against Muhammad for killing the [aforementioned] poet, the prophet beseeched his followers to murder her as well. 'Who will rid me of Marwan's daughter?' he asked. One of his followers obediently killed her in her house."[191]

REFERENCE: Alfred Guillaume, Life of Muhammad: A Translation of Ibn-e-Ishaq's Sirat Rasul Allah (Oxford University Press, 1955), 675–76.

RESPONSE: Once again Ibn-e-Ishaq's unreliability combined with Wilders's lack of scholarship integrity results in a sensationalized—and fabricated—event of epic proportions.

Ibn-e-Ishaq reports this event roughly a century after Prophet Muhammad's^{sa} demise. Prior to Ibn-e-Ishaq, both Ibn Sa'ad and Sunan Abu Dawud reported this incident. Neither mentions nor even implies that any companion (Umair bin Adi in this case) killed the poetess upon Prophet Muhammad's^{sa} directive. Neither mentions that Prophet Muhammad^{sa} gave such an order at all—yet somehow Ibn-e-Ishaq comes to this fantastic conclusion a century later, and Wilders calls it gospel.

---

191. Wilders, *Marked for Death*, 38.

Among those so-called historians whom Ibn-e-Ishaq cites to relate this incident, two names stand out as being of particular concern: Ikrama Maula Ibn-e-Abaad and Muhammad bin Al Hujaaj. Throughout history, Ikrama has been known for his falsehood in relating hadith. For example, advising his servant, a famous scholar, Sa'eed Bin Al Musayyab said, "Do not attribute untrue sayings to me, the way Ikrama attributes untrue sayings to Ibn-e-Abbas."[192] Likewise, Muhammad Ibn Al-Hajjaj is also not considered truthful in relating incidents of Islamic history. On the contrary, Imam Jozi cites Ibn-e-Adi to state, regarding the incident about Asma bint Marwan, that it is unclear if Muhammad ibn Al-Hujjaj fabricated this tradition.[193]

So far, we have three notable historians to consider. The earlier two, Ibn Sa'ad and Sunan Abu Dawud, are recognized as reliable and do not report the event the way Wilders alleges they do. The third, Ibn-e-Ishaq, whose integrity scholars repeatedly question, reports it based on a chain of narrators known for their falsehood. This alone should be enough factual data for any fair-minded researcher to determine which story to accept as authentic. But for the sake of argument, let us ignore facts and common sense and instead assume that Ibn-e-Ishaq has accurately recorded the event. I want the reader to see how ridiculous this story of alleged assassination actually is.

As Wilders acknowledges, this woman—Asma bint Marwan—belonged to the Bani Khitma Jewish tribe in Medina. According to Ibn-e-Kathir, this incident allegedly occurred after the Battle of Badr. Many strong Jewish tribes were established in Medina. As repeatedly mentioned, Prophet Muhammad[sa] signed the Charter of Medina with the Jews to form a peaceful alliance. The Banu Qainqa tribe breached the charter and was eventually exiled. The ironic question, however, is that if the incident of Asma bint Marwan were true, why would the Jews keep

---

192. Al Marefat Wal Tareekh LeAbi Yousuf Yaqoob Baab Ikrama Mola Ibn Abbas.

193. Al Halal Wal Mutanahiyya, vol. 1, 175.

quiet about it despite the fact that all three Jewish tribes were present at the time? This should have been all the proof they needed to demonstrate hostility from Muslims, a violation of peace, and thus an invalidation of the charter. Instead, every source—Jewish and non-Jewish—is completely silent regarding a Jewish reaction to the alleged unjust murder of Marwan's daughter. No protest or allegations exist to even allude that Prophet Muhammad[sa] violated the charter.

But perhaps the strongest argument that this story is fabricated is the set of events in the story itself. The companion who allegedly single-handedly murdered Asma, Umair bin Adi, was a blind man. According to Ibn Sa'ad, he reached Asma by groping around in an area of Medina unfamiliar to him—miraculously arriving at Asma's home. He entered it while she was home and awake. Her other five children were sleeping around her while she breastfed her infant.

In this condition, the blind man reached Asma and allegedly killed her by stabbing her chest with his sword—leaving even her infant child unharmed. He somehow did all this without making any noise to wake Asma's young adult children and while Asma lay there and watched him approach, sword in hand. Being awake and aware, Asma remained silent and did not once call for help because someone was there to kill her. Rather than try to protect her children or herself (or escape), Asma allegedly lay there and waited for a blind man to find his way through her house and fatally stab her precisely through the chest, leaving her children completely unharmed. One can only imagine how Umair knew it was Asma that he had stabbed and not some other person.

Yet Wilders believes this story and hopes his readers are naïve enough to believe it as well. The fact remains that Wilders cites Ibn-e-Ishaq, whom I have demonstrated is generally unreliable, and in this particular case is certainly so because of whom he cites in relating the story. Likewise, the fact that not even Jewish records offer any protest to this alleged unjust incident demonstrates the high likelihood that the event never occurred at all. Finally, the fantastic story of a blind man stumbling alone through an unfamiliar part of town, finding the right home, moving silently through that home, and killing a woman with exact precision—all without being detected—is both fantastic and fictitious. Had Wilders actually done his research instead of copying arguments from anti-Islamic websites, he might have at least left this one out.

ALLEGATION 23

Muhammad^{sa} Ordered and Approved of Torture

Wilders writes, "Muhammad also ordered people to be tortured, such as Kinana ar-Rabi, the man who had custody of the treasure of the Banu Nadir, a Jewish tribe from Yathrib. When ar-Rabi refused to reveal the location of the treasure despite a fire being lit over his chest, he was decapitated.[194] As the Koran says, "Lay hold of him and bind him. Burn him in the fire of Hell, then fasten him with a chain of seventy cubits long. For he did not believe in Allah, the Most High, nor did he care to feed the poor.""

I refute this allegation below.

REFERENCE: Alfred Guillaume, *Life of Muhammad: A Translation of Ibn-e-Ishaq's Sirat Rasul Allah* (Oxford University Press, 1955), 515; Sahih Jami' Bukhari, vol. 5, Book 59, #512; and Qur'an 69:31–36.

RESPONSE: Wilders, yet again, conflates treason against the state of Medina with something unrelated and hopes the reader is naïve enough to believe him. First of all, the Bukhari hadith he cites, 5:59:512,[195] does not mention Kinana ar-Rabi at all, so I am unsure why he cites it in the

---

194. Wilders, *Marked for Death*, 39.

195. Sahih Jami' Bukhari, vol. 5, Book 59, #512: Anasra relates, "The Prophet offered the Fajr Prayer near Khaibar when it was still dark and then said, 'Allahu-Akbar! Khaibar is destroyed, for whenever we approach a (hostile) nation (to fight), then evil will be the morning for those who have been warned.' Then the inhabitants of Khaibar came out running on the roads. The Prophet had their warriors killed, their offspring and women taken as captives. Safiya was amongst the captives, She first came in the share of Dahya Alkali but later on she belonged to the Prophet. The Prophet made her manumission as her 'Mahr.'"

first place. Likewise, the Qur'anic verses Wilders cites, 69:31–36,[196] have nothing to do with earthly punishments. The reader is encouraged to read the full Chapter at www.alislam.org/quran. A mere cursory read reveals that the entire Chapter is composed of metaphorical descriptions of the afterlife—and does not address some worldly punishment.

So, here we have a situation where Wilders cites authentic Islamic sources that, unfortunately for him, have nothing to do with his argument. Regardless, history records a much different story than what Wilders asserts.

Far from being tortured to death for hiding treasure, Kinana ar-Rabi was a war criminal, guilty of murder and treason. "Having left Medina and settled at Khaibar, the Banu Nadir started hatching a wide-spread conspiracy against Islam. Their leaders, Salam Ibn Abi-al Huqauaiq, Huyayy Ibn-e-Akhtab, *Kinana ar-Rabi* and others came to Mecca, met the Quraish and told them that Islam could be destroyed."[197] Wilders does not tell his readers the fact that even after agreeing to the Charter of Medina, Kinana ar-Rabi conspired to destroy Islam—thus making him guilty of treason.

Even leaving Kinana ar-Rabi's treason aside, history demonstrates that Wilders has fabricated the accusation that Prophet Muhammad[sa] tortured Kinana ar-Rabi. Islamic historian and scholar Allama Shibli Nu'Mani reports:

> The whole truth in the story is that Kinana was put to death. But it was not for his refusal to give a clue to the hidden treasure. He was put to death because he had killed Mahmud Ibn Maslama (also Muslima). Tabari had reported it in unambiguous words:

---

196. Qur'an 69: 31–36.
    http://www.alislam.org/quran/search2/showChapter.php?submitCh=Read+from+verse%3A&ch=69&verse=27.

197. Allama Shibli Nu'Mani, Sirat-Un-Nabi, vol. 2, 106. (Emphasis added.)

"Then the Holy Prophet[sa] gave Kinana to Muhammad Ibn Maslama (Muslima), and he put him to death in retaliation of the murder of his own brother, Mahmud Ibn Maslama (Muslima)."[198]

Recall my warning about Ibn-e-Ishaq's lack of veracity and authenticity when recording history. This is another example of the ramifications of combining Ibn-e-Ishaq's negligence with Wilders's lack of integrity. Allama Shibli Nu'Mani continues:

In the rest of the report, both Tabari and Ibn-e-Hisham have quoted it from Ibn-e-Ishaq, but *Ibn-e-Ishaq does not name any narrator*. Traditionalists, in books on Rijal, have explicitly stated that Ibn-e-Ishaq used to borrow from the Jews stories concerning the battle of the Prophet (peace and blessings of Allah be upon him). As Ibn-e-Ishaq does not mention the name of any narrator whatsoever in this case, there is every likelihood of the story having been passed on by the Jews.[199]

As mentioned, the Banu Nádir had conspired to revolt against the state of Medina, so they would reasonably have had motive to convey a fabricated incident. But whether the Jews passed on this story or not is secondary to the fact that no actual source exists regarding this incident. Ibn-e-Ishaq cites no one. The first "documented" recording of this incident is from Ibn-e-Ishaq himself more than a century after the "fact"— certainly not from the hadith Wilders cites. And in fact, history records that Kinana ar-Rabi could have relied on Prophet Muhammad's[sa] mercy but consciously chose otherwise:

---

198. Ibid., 173.
199. Ibid., 173–74.

As a matter of fact, Kinana Ibn Rabi Ibn al-Huquaiq had been granted his life on the condition that he would never break faith or make false statements. He had also given his word, according to one of the reports, that if he did anything to the contrary, he could be put to death. Kinana played false, and the immunity granted to him was withdrawn. He killed Mahmud Ibn Maslama (Muslima) and had, therefore to suffer for it, as we have already stated on the authority of Tabari.[200]

Thus, Prophet Muhammad[sa] did not torture Kinana Ibn ar-Rabi, nor did he order ar-Rabi's execution. In fact, Prophet Muhammad[sa] particularly forbade that fire be used to punish or kill anyone: "Punishment by fire does not behoove anyone except the Master of the Fire [i.e., God]."[201] Instead, Kinana Ibn ar-Rabi was guilty of treason and murder, and the family of the man whom he murdered held him accountable for that murder. And all this was only *after* ar-Rabi violated the single condition set to spare his life, a condition to which he had earlier willingly agreed.

Thus, to fabricate a story about torture without reference is disturbing enough. But to further ignore the plethora of historical fact that clarifies with absolute certainty that Kinana Ibn ar-Rabi committed murder and treason and received capital punishment accordingly is downright treachery. Welcome to Wilders-style censorship.

---

200. Ibid., 174.

201. Sunan Abu Dawud, Chap. Karahiya, Harqil Adu bin Naar.

ALLEGATION 24

Muhammad^{sa} Ordered the Murder of Eight Men for Apostasy

I have already demonstrated that Islam does not allow any worldly punishment, let alone death, for apostasy. But I am compelled to address this allegation here again. Wilders writes, "Tortured to death were also eight men from 'Ukil who had joined the Muslim state in Medina but had apostatized and run away. Muhammad had them apprehended, had their hands and feet cut off, and had them left to die in the desert. This was all in accordance with the Koran, which says that, "those that make war against Allah and His apostle and spread disorders in the land shall be put to death or crucified or have their hands and feet cut off on alternate sides.""[202]

REFERENCE: Wilders provides no historical reference to corroborate his allegation that Prophet Muhammad^{sa} tortured eight men from 'Ukil for their apostasy. Wilders cites Qur'an 5:34 as the guide for the alleged punishment for apostasy delivered to the eight men from 'Ukil.

RESPONSE: Wilders again provides no reference, likely knowing that if he cited the source, it would debunk his allegation. In fact, the eight men from 'Ukil were killed, but they were not killed for apostatizing. Rather, they were held accountable for committing a vicious murder, acts of terrorism, and treason.

---

202. Wilders, *Marked for Death*, 39.

I cite this event in full below. But first, I reiterate the heinousness that Islam attributes to murder. As already mentioned, murder and treason are the only two crimes for which the Qur'an allows the death penalty. Wilders correctly cites 5:34 as the commandment to put to death those who commit murder or treason. The verses immediately prior and subsequent to 5:34 are of paramount importance to this particular discussion, and for the reader's benefit I produce them below:

> On account of this, We prescribed for the children of Isra'el that whosoever killed a person—unless it be for killing a person or for creating disorder in the land—it shall be as if he had killed all mankind; and whoso gave life to one, it shall be as if he had given life to all mankind. And Our Messengers came to them with clear Signs, yet even after that, many of them commit excesses in the land.[203]

Here, the Qur'an equates the murder of one person to that of all mankind, demonstrating the high sanctity of life placed on every individual regardless of any differentiating factor. Likewise, the reward for saving one is that of having saved all mankind, demonstrating Islam's immense emphasis on protecting life. Having set this precedent, the Qur'an issues a warning to those who would dare "kill all mankind" in the subsequent verse 5:34:

> The reward of those who wage war against Allah and His Messenger and strive to create disorder in the land is only this; that they be slain or crucified or their hands and their feet be cut off on alternate sides, or they be expelled from the land. That shall be

---

203. Qur'an 5:33.

137

a disgrace for them in this world, and in the Hereafter they shall have a great punishment.[204]

As I mentioned in Chapter 1, Islam believes in neither absolute punishment nor absolute forgiveness, but in reform. Islamic punishments serve two purposes—to be reformative or to be a deterrent. When someone commits an act for which forgiveness will likely reform him or her, forgiveness is employed. Likewise, when someone commits a heinous crime for which reform is no longer possible—such as murder—or the likes of which leniency will fail to deter others from committing the same heinous act, Islam prescribes an exemplary punishment to deter future offenders. Such is the case here.

In 5:33, the Qur'an establishes the heinousness of murder, equating it to killing all mankind. Indeed, the pain an entire society suffers in response to the murder of even one individual ripples far beyond the murder victim. Thus, to ensure that murder remains as rare as possible, Islam prescribes an aggressive deterrence to would-be murderers.

The logic for this is simple. The burden on person A *not* to murder person B is extremely low. The harm caused to person B and all those who know person B, should person B be murdered, is extremely high. An extremely low burden not to murder combined with an extremely high level of pain, injustice, and suffering should the murder occur requires even higher consequence to would-be murderers. When applied justly, this strategy ultimately serves to mitigate the number of murders.

Keeping this in mind, the Qur'an still reverts to its dominant position on crime and punishment in the following verse: forgiveness. The Qur'an 5:35 declares, "Except those who repent before you have them in your power. So know that Allah is Most Forgiving, Merciful."[205] Thus, even those who commit the heinous act of murder may be forgiven if

---

204. Qur'an 5:34.

205. Qur'an 5:35.

they repent and submit to the government's authority—e.g., by stopping violence and turning themselves in. In other words, despite one's murder of "all mankind," Islam does not prohibit forgiveness altogether but allows flexibility for it should some possibility of reform exist. With this important background, I now turn to the event in question.

The Bukhari hadith relating the incident demonstrates that the eight men from 'Ukil were not executed due to apostatizing. Instead, they committed murder, theft, and treason, did not avail themselves of repentance, and were thus held accountable for their criminal actions. As even Wilders points out, they joined the "Muslim state." Their apostasy had nothing to do with the punishment they incurred. Hadhrat Anas bin Malik[ra] narrates:

A group of eight men from the tribe of 'Ukil came to the Prophet and then they found the climate of Medina unsuitable for them. So they said, "O Allah's Apostle! Provide us with some milk." Allah's Apostle said, "I recommend that you should join the herd of camels." So they went and drank the urine and the milk of the camels (as a medicine) till they became healthy and fat. Then they killed the shepherd and drove away the camels. And they became unbelievers after they were Muslims. When the Prophet was informed by a shouter for help, he sent some men in their pursuit. And before the sun rose high, they were brought. And he had their hands and feet cut off. Then he ordered for nails which were heated and passed over their eyes. And whey were left in the Harra (i.e. rocky land in Medina). They asked for water. And nobody provided them with water till they died (Abu Qilaba. a subnarrator said. "They committed murder and theft and fought against Allah and His Apostle and spread evil in the land.")[206]

---

206. Sahih Jami' Bukhari, vol. 4, Book 52, #261.

Compare Wilders's account of men who simply left Islam with this description of those who sought protection and help under the Medina state, were given whatever they asked, then murdered their caretaker, stole his property, spread violence in the land, and did not repent for their actions. At a time when the Medina state itself was subject to attack from all sides, punishments were necessary to ensure protection of the Muslim state as a whole and of Jewish and Muslim tribes alike.

Indeed, Prophet Muhammad[sa] loathed to harm anyone and inclined toward forgiveness as often as possible. He even forgave the man who caused his daughter to fall from a camel, have a miscarriage, and later also to die from injuries sustained in the fall. But this incident threatened the entire state. It would be unjust to risk the safety of the entire state of Medina by not delivering the preordained punishment for those who commit murder, terrorism, and treason. It is clear from a historical perspective that the fate of the men from 'Ukil was not based on their apostatizing, but on the protection of the state of Medina. These men committed violence, theft, murder, and treason, and were thus held accountable for their own actions.

This historical lesson should also serve to demonstrate that Islam does not endorse terrorism by anyone, nor does Islam permit the murder of innocent people. Those terrorists ascribing their acts to Islam are not acting as Muslims, rather they are acting as barbarians. In the aforementioned example, Prophet Muhammad[sa] ordered that these terrorists receive capital punishment due precisely to their acts of terrorism and murder of an innocent person. Extremist organizations today like the Taliban, Jamaat e Islaami, Boko Haram, and Al Qaeda should recognize this example and know that in the eyes of Prophet Muhammad[sa], they are nothing more than barbarians and terrorists.

ALLEGATION 25

Muhammad^{sa} Ordered the Execution of Seven Hundred Jews

This is one of the most common contemporary allegations levied against Prophet Muhammad^{sa}—that he ordered the execution of seven hundred Jews. It is also one of the most spurious. Wilders writes, "In order to stop this [Muhammad's] reign of terror, in March 627 a confederate army of Meccans, Jews, and other Arab tribes marched on Medina. The skirmish that followed, the so-called Battle of the Trench, was undecided. The anti-Muslim alliance then fell apart because of internal disagreements, ending the siege of Medina. Muhammad used the opportunity to exterminate his opponents in Yathrib. The Banu Qurayzah, one of the Oasis's largest Jewish tribes, was annihilated and all its men were decapitated on the order of Allah's prophet. Some 700 boys and men were butchered, with Muhammad himself actively participating in the massacre. The women and children were sold as slaves."[207]

REFERENCE: Alfred Guillaume, Life of Muhammad: A Translation of Ibn-e-Ishaq's Sirat Rasul Allah, (Oxford University Press, 1955), 461–64.

RESPONSE: What Wilders casually describes as a "skirmish" was the largest battle ever held on Arabian soil in Medina during Prophet Muhammad's life. The confederate army comprised no less than twelve thousand soldiers who launched an offensive assault on Medina to ex-

---

207. Wilders, *Marked for Death*, 39.

terminate Islam and murder all Muslims. The Muslims barricaded themselves in Medina along with their sworn allies, the Jews—per the Charter of Medina—and numbered roughly twelve hundred soldiers. Despite being outnumbered ten to one, the Muslims and Jews were victorious. However, though victorious, they came within moments of annihilation due to the Banu Qurayzah tribe's treason.

Wilders, along with virtually every anti-Islam Internet scholar, professes that Prophet Muhammad[sa] blindly executed the entire Banu Qurayzah tribe. Wilders goes a step further here and claims that Prophet Muhammad[sa] "actively participated in the massacre." I need not write another thesis for the reader of the dangers of relying on Ibn-e-Ishaq's testimony. Common sense, numerous scholars, and more authentic sources demonstrate that Ibn-e-Ishaq's testimony in regards to the Banu Qurayzah incident is false, as are Wilders's allegations. I proceed with a step-by-step analysis of this event.

In Chapter 2 I referred to the Charter of Medina's article 49, which states, "The parties to this Pact are bound to help each other in the event of an attack on Yathrib." The Banu Qurayzah tribe was an equal and willing party to this pact. Yet, despite the prior signed agreement, in the heat of battle the Banu Qurayzah sided with the enemy against the state of Medina. Fortunately, the remaining allied Medina army was able to withstand this treasonous act and win the battle against incredible odds.

The question remained, however: How to address the Banu Qurayzahs' treason? Adding to the dilemma was the fact that the Banu Qurayzah had committed this act once before, upon which Prophet Muhammad[sa] had merely exiled them. When they later asked his forgiveness, he granted it, which is why they had since reentered Medina. The nineteenth-century historian Stanley Lane-Poole accurately describes the events that followed the Battle of the Ditch:

> Of the sentences on the three clans, that of exile, passed upon two of them, was clement enough. They were a turbulent set, always setting the people of Medina by the ears; and finally, a brawl fol-

lowed by an insurrection resulted in the expulsion of one tribe; and insubordination, alliance with enemies and a suspicion of conspiracy against the Prophet's life, ended similarly for the second. Both tribes had violated the original treaty, and had endeavored in every way to bring Muhammad and his religion to ridicule and destruction. The only question is whether their punishment was not too light. Of the third clan a fearful example was made, *not by Muhammad*, but by an arbiter appointed by themselves. When Quraish and their allies were besieging Medina and had well-nigh stormed the defences, this Jewish tribe [the Banu Qurayzah] entered into negotiations with the enemy, which were only circumvented by the diplomacy of the Prophet. When the besiegers had retired, Muhammad naturally demanded an explanation of the Jews. They resisted in their dogged way and were themselves besieged and compelled to surrender at discretion. Muhammad, however, consented to the appointing of a chief of a tribe allied to the Jews as the judge who should pronounce sentence upon them. This chief gave sentence that the men, in numbers some 600, should be killed, and the women and children enslaved; and the sentence was carried out. It was a harsh, bloody sentence; but it must be remembered that the crime of these men was high treason against the State, during a time of siege; and one need not be surprised at the summary execution of a traitorous clan."[208]

Thus, contrary to Wilders's lie, Prophet Muhammad[sa] did *not* order any execution, nor did he participate in any. On the contrary, Prophet Muhammad[sa] graciously agreed to let the Banu Qurayzahs' own ally, Hadhrat Sa'd bin Mu'adh[ra] of Aus, deliver the verdict. Why blame Prophet

---

208. Stanley Lane-Poole, Studies in a Mosque (1883), 68. (Emphasis added.)

Muhammad[sa] for a decision he did not make and for a crime he did not commit?

Adding to the injustice in blaming Prophet Muhammad[sa] is the fact that Hadhrat Sa'd bin Mu'az[ra] did not deliver his decision based on the Qur'an. Rather, he delivered the judgment for the Banu Qurayzah based on the punishment for treason that *their* book, the Torah, prescribes:

> When thou comest nigh unto a city to fight against it, then proclaim peace unto it. And it shall be, if it make thee answer of peace, and open unto thee, then it shall be, that all the people that is found therein shall be tributaries unto thee, and they shall serve thee. And if it will make no peace with thee, but will make war against thee, then thou shalt besiege it: And when the Lord thy God hath delivered it into thine hands, *thou shalt smite every male thereof with the edge of the sword*: But the women, and the little ones, and the cattle, and all that is in the city, even all the spoil thereof, shalt thou take unto thyself; and thou shalt eat the spoil of thine enemies, which the Lord thy God hath given thee. Thus shalt thou do unto all the cities which the Lord thy God doth give thee for an inheritance, *thou shalt save alive nothing that breatheth: But thou shalt utterly destroy them*; namely, the Hittites, and the Amoiites, the Canaanites, and the Perizzites, the Hivites, and the Jebusites; as the Lord thy God hath commanded thee: That they teach you not to do after all their abominations, which they have done unto their gods; so should ye sin against the Lord your God.[209]

Thus, the Banu Qurayzah sealed their own fate with their own actions, according to their own arbiter and own book. Prophet Muhammad[sa] had nothing to do with it—other than agreeing to let an ally to the Banu

---

209. Deuteronomy 20:10–18.

Qurayzah arbitrate between them (an arbiter the Banu Qurayzah chose of their own free will) and to bind himself by that arbiter's decision.

Moreover, no Jewish tribes, Jewish historians, or Jewish scholars record this event. This is shocking because the Jewish people have recorded their history better than perhaps any other people. Yet, in regards to such an alleged massive execution, every Jewish historian, scholar, and tribe is silent. This fact (along with several other notable inconsistencies in Ibn-e-Ishaq's corrupted version not covered for the sake of brevity) suggests the likelihood that the event has been grossly exaggerated.

Dr. Barakat Ahmad, author of *Muhammad and the Jews*, argues, based on authentic sources from time periods well before Ibn-e-Ishaq, that it is highly probable that no execution took place at all. I gladly invite Wilders, or anyone for that matter, to respond to Dr. Ahmad's book.

As of now, however, it is clear that Prophet Muhammad[sa] committed no wrong against the Banu Qurayzah. History records that the Banu Qurayzah agreed to a constitution—the Charter of Medina—and that constitution explicitly required loyalty to the state of Medina, particularly in case of attack from an external army. After committing to Medina, the Banu Qurayzah violated that loyalty with a treasonous act *in the heat of battle*. The claimed execution that followed, if it happened, was the result of their choice to commit treason, per the judgment of a judge they demanded, according to the law elucidated in their own holy book. Prophet Muhammad[sa], far from being responsible for any of Wilders's allegations, interceded and even forgave those Jews who asked his forgiveness. To place even the slightest responsibility on anyone *but* the Banu Qurayzah is nothing less than ridiculous.

ALLEGATION 26

Muhammad[sa] Broke
a Truce to Mercilessly Conquer Mecca

Given all his fabrications so far, it should be no surprise that Wilders reinvents Prophet Muhammad's[sa] return to Mecca. Attempting to rewrite history, Wilders alleges, "In March 628, Muhammad signed a 10-year truce with the Meccans, giving him time to rebuild and strengthen his army. In January 630, sooner than expected, he was able to march on Mecca with 10,000 men. Outnumbered by a merciless enemy, Abu Sufyan, the 70-year-old leader of the largest Quraish clan and commander of the Meccan forces, surrendered the city to Muhammad without a fight."[210]

Wilders regurgitates this allegation in his Chapter 5—not surprisingly, also without reference.[211]

REFERENCE: None.

RESPONSE: Relating events vaguely, Wilders again presents a skewed and wholly incorrect version of history. That he does not cite any source simply defines his calling card as a propagandist. Here are the facts Wilders ignores. The Treaty of Hudaibiyah was a ten-year peace agreement—heavily in the Meccans' favor—signed in 628 between Prophet Muhammad[sa] and the Meccans. Prophet Muhammad[sa] represented the

---

210. Wilders, *Marked for Death*, 39.

211. Ibid., 88.

Muslims and the Medina State while Suhayl bin Amr represented the polytheists and the Meccan state.

In addition to ensuring a decade of peace, the Treaty unjustly held that "a young man, or one whose father is alive, if he goes to Muhammad without permission from his father or guardian, will be returned to his father or guardian. But if anyone goes to the Quraish [i.e. Meccans], he will not be returned."[212] Indeed just one of several lopsided provisions.

Prophet Muhammad[sa] had not yet signed the treaty when Abu Jandal, son of Suhayl bin Amr, presented himself to Prophet Muhammad[sa]. Abu Jandal had been beaten and was in shackles for accepting Islam. He begged Prophet Muhammad[sa] to give him amnesty and protection:[213]

> Suhayl bin Amr protested, "Muhammad, the agreement between us was concluded before this man [Suhayl bin Amr's own son] came to you." Muhammad replied, "You are right." As Abu Jandal shrieked for help, Muhammad replied, "O Abu Jandal, be patient and control yourself, for God will provide relief and a means of escape for you and those of you who are helpless. We have made peace with them and we and they have invoked God in our agreement and we cannot deal falsely with them."[214]

Though Prophet Muhammad[sa] had not signed the agreement yet, he acknowledged that he had given his word to the terms as written and held fast to his word. And history testifies that Prophet Muhammad[sa] was not merely attempting to gain some tactical advantage. Soon after the treaty was inked, Abu Jandal escaped Mecca and presented himself again to Prophet Muhammad[sa], once again seeking his protection. Yet

---

212. Sahih Jami' Muslim, Chap. 33, Book 19, #4404.

213. Guillaume, Life of Muhammad, 505.

214. Ibid.

Prophet Muhammad[sa] unhesitatingly sent him back to Mecca per the treaty's requirement.

Some critics object that Prophet Muhammad[sa] granted amnesty to women who escaped persecution in Mecca and sought protection in Medina, claiming that this violated the treaty. Those critics who would dare compel women to live under a regime of persecution should reevaluate their characters. But even considering the black letter of the law, the treaty explicitly stated that "any young man" must be returned. The subject "man," not "person," is employed, and no clause accounted for women. Therefore, Prophet Muhammad[sa] was completely within legal rights to offer amnesty to women who sought his protection in Medina from persecution in Mecca. It should be noted, additionally, that women did not flee Mecca without reason. These women willingly sought protection under Prophet Muhammad's[sa] leadership because they saw firsthand how Islam significantly elevated the rights and position of women to that of religious and social equality, especially as compared to their current lives.

But back to the crux of this discussion. Wilders next disingenuously attempts to blame Prophet Muhammad[sa] for violating the Treaty of Hudaibiyah. The treaty included a relatively common ally clause that extended the peace agreement to each party's respective alliances. Thus, should a Muslim ally attack a Meccan ally, it would be considered a breach of the treaty—and vice versa. Not two years after the treaty was signed, a Meccan ally, the Banu Bakr, attacked a Muslim ally, the Khuza'a, and killed several of its men.[215]

Upon learning that the Khuza'a had sent a delegation to Prophet Muhammad[sa] to report the breach, the Meccans sent Abu Sufyan as an emissary to convince Prophet Muhammad[sa] to renew the treaty.[216]

---

215. Mirza Bashiruddin Mahmood Ahmad, Life of Muhammad (Islam International Publications Ltd., 2005), 233–34.

216. Ibid., 234.

Prophet Muhammad^sa declined to renew it for obvious reasons—to agree to an unfair treaty is one thing, but to oblige oneself to another unfair treaty in the face of a breach that had cost human life is beyond injustice.

Wilders ignores these historical facts altogether and compounds his meritless argument with a peculiarly contradictory remark: "Outnumbered by a merciless army...Abu Sufyan surrendered the city to Muhammad without a fight." *Merciless* by definition means, well, without mercy. If Prophet Muhammad's^sa army truly had been merciless, then whether or not Abu Sufyan surrendered should have been irrelevant. An army without mercy by definition does not care about negotiating a peaceful accord. An army without mercy should have annihilated the Meccans without exception.

But even leaving his incoherent statement aside, Wilders misses the point. Throughout his book he describes Prophet Muhammad^sa as a man bent on destruction of the infidel and the forceful dominance of Islam. Yet, on the day that Prophet Muhammad^sa marches back to Mecca with ten thousand soldiers and has the city in the palm of his hand plus the opportunity to exact vengeance on any person for wrongs done to him over a span of twenty years—or for any reason—at that moment of truth as the de facto ruler, this alleged unjust warmonger offers...peace?

Even Washington Irving, by no means an Islamic apologist, is forced to admit:

> The sun was just rising as he entered the gates of his native city, with the glory of a conqueror, but the garb and humility of a pilgrim. He entered, repeating verses of the Koran, which he said had been revealed to him at Medina, and were prophetic of the

event. He triumphed in the spirit of a religious zealot, not a warrior.[217]

Stanley Lane-Poole likewise adds:

The day of Muhammad's greatest triumph over his enemies was also the day of his grandest victory over himself. He freely forgave the Quraish all the years of sorrow and cruel scorn to which they had inflicted him, and gave an amnesty to the whole population of Mecca.[218]

I repeat: "amnesty to the whole population of Mecca." This sounds like anything *but* a "merciless army." I challenge Wilders to find a single comparable example in world history. Find any comparable example where a man is beaten repeatedly, exiled from his native land, and pursued to be murdered; has had assassination attempts made on him on no less than five occasions, his family members mutilated and their corpses literally eaten, his companions dragged in the streets, the unfair peace treaty he signs savagely broken—and in response, on the occasion of his victory after two decades of persecution as the undisputed king of the land—he offers amnesty to all those who persecuted him. He demands no reparations, no apologies, and no enslavement—but instead offers outright forgiveness. No such example of compassion exists other than that of Prophet Muhammad's[sa], and I challenge any critic of Islam to prove otherwise.

In fact, Prophet Muhammad[sa] specifically asked his former persecutors, the Meccans:

---

217. Washington Irving, Mahomet and His Successors, vol. 1 (New York: G. P. Putnam's Sons, 1868), 253.

218. Stanley Lane-Poole, Selections from the Quran and Hadith (Lahore: Sind Sagar Academy, n.d.), 28.

What punishment should you have for the cruelties you committed against those whose only fault was that they invited you to the worship of one God?" The Meccans replied, "We expect you to treat us as Joseph treated his erring brothers." Prophet Muhammad[sa] smiled and replied, "No blame shall lie upon you today. You are free to go.[219]

As the de facto ruler of Arabia, Prophet Muhammad[sa] and his allegedly "merciless" army forgave all their tormentors and set them free. Yet, Wilders censors this entire series of events and fabricates a story to the contrary. Such is the height of his deception.

Having established that Prophet Muhammad[sa] did not break the treaty and that he demonstrated unmatched compassion upon returning to Mecca, I am compelled to add Abu Sufyan's testimony regarding Prophet Muhammad[sa]. This is simply because Wilders repeatedly cites Abu Sufyan as a trustworthy and reliable individual—a fair-enough representation. After all, by Wilders's own admission, Abu Sufyan was the chief of the largest Meccan tribe and leader of their forces. Thus, any fair-minded reader would agree that Abu Sufyan's testimony—as leader of the allegedly persecuted Meccans and ostensibly the leading opposition to Prophet Muhammad[sa]—carries significant weight.

Throughout his prophethood, Prophet Muhammad[sa] sent letters to numerous kings and emperors of his time, inviting them to accept Islam. Per chance, Abu Sufyan was in Ghaza, near Jerusalem, where Heracles Caesar received Prophet Muhammad's[sa] letter. This incident occurred after the Treaty of Hudaibiyah was signed, but before the Meccans violated it. Caesar held a grand court and invited Abu Sufyan to approach. When he did, Caesar questioned him about the Prophet:[220]

---

219 Ibn-e-Hisham, Tuwaful Rusool Bil Bait wa Dukhoolihi Al Haram wa Ibn-e-Kathir, Ibn-e-Sa'ad wa Zarqani wal sayeratul Hilbiya Victory of Mecca.

220. Sahih Jami' Bukhari, vol. 4, Book 52, #191.

Caesar: To what sort of family does the Claimant to Prophethood belong?

Abu Sufyan: A noble one.

Caesar: Did someone else in his family claim Prophethood?

Abu Sufyan: No.

Caesar: Did someone from his family happen to be a King?

Abu Sufyan: No.

Caesar: Are the people who have accepted this religion poor or influential?

Abu Sufyan: They are poor people.

Caesar: Are his followers growing in number or decreasing?

Abu Sufyan: They are growing.

Caesar: Have you ever experienced untruthfulness from him?

Abu Sufyan: No.

Caesar: Does he ever break a promise or agreement?

Abu Sufyan: Thus far he has never done it. But it is seen if he adheres to the new peace pact which has just been concluded.

Caesar: Have you ever fought a battle against him?

Abu Sufyan: Yes.

Caesar: What was the result of the battle?

Abu Sufyan: Sometimes we were victorious and sometimes he was successful.

Caesar: What does he teach?

Abu Sufyan: He says, "Worship One God—Allah. Associate none else with Allah. Say prayers. Take to piety. Speak the truth. Treat relatives with kindness.

Caesar: Did anyone else make such a claim before him in his people?

Abu Sufyan: No.

Later Abu Sufyan exclaimed, "By God! Throughout the conversation, except the statement [regarding the new pact], I did not get any chance to say anything against Muhammad." The discussion continued and Heracles Caesar then explained why he asked those particular questions.

Caesar: When I asked you about the lineage of the claimant of the prophethood, you stated that he belongs to a very noble family. Messengers always belong to noble families. I asked you if there has been a king in his forefathers? You responded no. From this I concluded that had there been a king in his forefathers, he might be desirous of regaining the kingdom of his forefathers. I asked you about his followers, whether they are rich and powerful? You replied they are weak and poor. In the beginning, always the poor and weak accept the Messengers. I asked you, Did you ever blame him for telling a lie before he claimed to be a prophet? You said "No." I was convinced that the one who does not tell a lie to the people, how can he tell a lie about God? Then I asked you, Did anyone of his followers apostatize after accepting Islam due to disliking Islam? You said, "No." This is the case with a true faith. When

153

someone accepts a faith with clarity of mind, it is very difficult for him to turn away from that faith. I asked you, whether they are increasing or decreasing in number? You said, they are increasing in number and also in steadfastness. This is always the case with true faiths. I asked you, did you ever fight a battle with him? You said, we have fought several battles. Sometimes they had the upper hand in the battle and other times we had the upper hand. Sometimes we were successful while the other times they were successful. This is the case with the Messengers of God. In the beginning, they went through many trials but ultimately they were triumphant. I asked you, did he ever break an agreement or deal treacherously? You said, "No." Such is the high status of the Prophets. They never break an agreement. Then I asked, has anyone among your people claimed to be a prophet before him? You said, "No." From this, I concluded that since there had not been a prophet in his people; he is not imitating anyone.

Abu Sufyan said that then Caesar asked him, "What did [Muhammad] command you to do?"

The answer was, "He commanded us to observe prayer, pay Zakaat, strengthen the ties of kinship, tell the truth, be pious and chaste." Hearing this, Caesar said,

If everything you have told is true, then definitely he is a prophet. I was expecting the coming of a prophet. However, I did not know that the prophet would be commissioned from among your people. Had the circumstances permitted me, I certainly would have gone to see this prophet. Had I visited him, I would have washed his feet. The kingdom of this prophet will reach the land where I stand.

Caesar then asked for Prophet Muhammad's^sa letter and read it before his court.

The Meccan named Abu Sufyan, whom Wilders correctly cites as the leader and general of the allegedly oppressed and persecuted Meccans, could not help but admit that Prophet Muhammad^sa was truthful, just, honest, and noble. Caesar could not help but admit that Prophet Muhammad^sa was indeed God's true prophet, dignified and honorable. This is the true story of Prophet Muhammad's^sa life and victory at Mecca—not the unreferenced fabrication Wilders asserts.

Prophet Muhammad^sa broke no treaty. And—let alone with justice—he acted with unprecedented compassion upon returning to Mecca. This is what even his enemies readily admitted to then, and this is what every educated and fair-minded person—Muslim or non-Muslim—admits to today.

ALLEGATION 27

Muhammad[sa] Promised
Women in Heaven for Martyrs

Wilders writes that "...Muhammad [vowed] that Muslims who die while waging Jihad, Islam's holy war, go straight to heaven and have sex with beautiful women for eternity."[221] Wilders repeats these allegations in his Chapter 7.[222]

REFERENCE: Qur'an 44:55; 52:21; 55:73; 56:23.

RESPONSE: In classic Wilders form, he makes an outlandish statement, cites a few verses of the Qur'an, hopes his readers naively make a connection between the two, and calls it research. The full text of the verses Wilders cites are as follows:

> Thus will it be. And We shall consort them with fair maidens, having wide, beautiful eyes.[223]

> "Reclining on couches arranged in rows." And We shall consort them with fair maidens having wide, beautiful eyes.[224]

---

221. Wilders, *Marked for Death*, 42.

222. Ibid., 125.

223. Qur'an 44:55.

224. Qur'an 52:21.

These verses make no mention of jihad, holy war, or any type of fighting as the precondition to attain paradise. Later I refute Wilders's incorrect explanation of jihad. For now, suffice it to say that Wilders conveniently and unjustly imposes his own interpretations.

Next, both Prophet Muhammad[sa] and the Qur'an reject this concept of heavenly reward via "sex with beautiful women for eternity." Prophet Muhammad[sa] clarified that such an interpretation could not be applicable to the aforementioned verses:

> Allah the Exalted and Glorious, said: "I have prepared for My pious servants which no eye has ever seen, and no ear has ever heard, and no human heart has ever perceived but it is testified by the Book of Allah." He then recited: "No soul knows what comfort has been concealed from them, as a reward for what they did" (32:18).[225]

Therefore, to limit divine reward to something as hedonistic as "eternal sex" is not only contrary to Islam, but an insult to God's infinite bounty for those who earn paradise. The rewards of paradise are far beyond what any human can conceive or perceive in this life, so I ask Wilders to spare us his meritless interpretations.

But another issue exists. The verse Wilders cites is another classic demonstration of Wilders's ignorance of Qur'anic hermeneutics or the Arabic language.

In Arabic, as in many Semitic languages, nouns are either masculine or feminine. Appropriately enough, a masculine noun is used when referring to a male. In referring to a female, an additional "*ta marbuta*" is

---

225. Sahih Jami' Muslim, Book 40, #6780–83.

added to the end of the masculine noun to make it feminine.[226] For example, the Qur'an states:

> And thou, O soul at peace! Return to thy Lord well pleased with Him and He well pleased with thee. So enter thou among My chosen servants, And enter thou My Garden.[227]

These four short Qur'anic verses describe the soul in paradise, referring both to females (89:28–29), and males (89:30–31). According to Islamic theology, unlike the human being, the soul is neither male nor female. This background builds the platform to properly understand the verses Wilders incorrectly claims promise sexual gratification.

The Arabic noun translated to "fair maidens" is derived from the three Arabic letters: *ha*, *vow*, and *ra*, yielding the word *hour* [hoor]. The Arabic *hour* is applicable to both men and women. It is applicable to both also in its plural form, *ahwar*. This title bestowed upon an individual indicates the character of having beautiful eyes—a reward for the righteous souls themselves. It also indicates an intense whiteness to the eye. Both descriptions refer to spiritual qualities having nothing to do with any sort of hedonistic physical gratification.

Moreover, *hour* has no gender. But Islam teaches that no soul can reach its full potential until it has a spouse. Thus, this verse demonstrates that one reward of paradise is that the soul of each person—whether male or female—will be given a companion with which to celebrate paradise.

To be sure, these are metaphorical explanations that will yet more effectively be understood in the afterlife. In the meantime, suffice it to say that Wilders's allegation that the reward of martyrdom is hedonistic

---

226. An Arabic dictionary is available at
http://www.languageguide.org/arabic/grammar/.

227. Qur'an 89:28–31.

pleasure is a belief that finds no support in Islam in any capacity. This is clear from a sincere study of the Qur'anic Arabic—something Wilders has unfortunately not attempted.

ALLEGATION 28

Islam is Anti-Semitic

Islam's alleged anti-Semitism is one of the few topics I address in two places, mainly because Wilders repeats this allegation numerous times and in different capacities. In this Chapter Wilders writes, "Islam [has a] zeal for dehumanizing and slaughtering Jews. 'We changed [the Jews] into detested apes,' says the Koran. 'We said to them: "You shall be changed into detested apes,"' 'transforming them into apes and swine.'"[228] Wilders made the same allegation earlier in his book and makes it again in his Chapters 5[229] and 7.[230]

REFERENCE: Qur'an 7:167, 2:666, 5:61.

RESPONSE: I have already referenced Dr. Philip Jenkins to refute Wilders's previous assertion that the Qur'an is somehow anti-Semitic. To recap: Dr. Jenkins performs a thorough analysis of the Qur'an's alleged anti-Semitic verses and concludes:

> In order to make such texts look vicious, anti-Islamic critics systematically exaggerate the Jewish element in the passage...[231] The Qur'an offers nothing vaguely as explicit as the New Testament passages in which Jesus himself, who is for Christians the incarnation of the Divine, speaks so furiously against "the Jews." It is the

---

228. Wilders, *Marked for Death*, 43.

229. Ibid., 84.

230. Ibid., 115.

231. Jenkins, *Laying Down the Sword*, 89.

Jesus of the New Testament who calls his enemies the children not of Abraham but of the Devil, the Father of Lies. That same Jesus denounces the Jews of his day, warning that "this generation will be held responsible for the blood of all the prophets that has been shed since the beginning of the world." He was not condemning all Jews in any racial sense, but was rather attacking rival factions and leaders in his day. And that is the model we find in the Qur'an.[232] In reality, the Qur'an has nothing that need be taken as a condemnation of Jews, or of any ethnic group.[233]

But lest I am accused of avoiding the three verses Wilders cites, I provide a cogent analysis of one of them (7:167). My analysis is equally applicable to all three of his cited verses because the principle that refutes him is the same in all. That is, the Qur'an does not "have a zeal for dehumanizing and slaughtering Jews" but a zeal for justice and mercy.[234] The Qur'an consistently demonstrates its condemnation of unjust behavior while lauding just behavior—regardless of the person or people committing the act. To help illustrate this point, I include below the verse prior to 7:167 to provide the proper context:

And when [the Jews] forgot all that with which they had been admonished, We saved those who forbade evil, and We seized the transgressors with a severe punishment because they were rebellious. And when they insolently rebelled against that which they had been forbidden, We said to them, "Be ye apes, despised!"[235]

---

232. Ibid., 91.

233. Ibid., 94. (Emphasis added.)

234. We again remind the reader to visit www.alislam.org/quran for a detailed explanation of any Qur'anic verse in question.

235. Qur'an 7:166–67.

In this verse, the Qur'an refers to an incident in Jewish history when the Jews violated God's covenant with Prophet Moses[as] and profaned the Sabbath. As a consequence of their violation of God's commandment, God applied the principles of justice and "seized the transgressors" because "they were rebellious." Note that God does not seize Jews "because they were Jewish" but seizes only those Jews who transgressed because they were rebellious. God specifies in the Qur'an, "We saved those [Jews] who forbade evil," i.e., those Jews who behaved righteously. Yet we hear nothing from Wilders about the Qur'an's praise of righteous Jews.

The fact is that no scripture prior to the Qur'an so much as acknowledges salvation as a possibility for adherents to other faiths. The Qur'an explicitly and repeatedly declares that the Jews will be amongst the parties of paradise: "Surely, the Believers, and the Jews, and the Christians and the Sabians—whichever party from among these truly believes in God and the Last Day and does good deeds—shall have their reward with their Lord, and no fear shall come upon them, nor shall they grieve."[236]

The Qur'an repeatedly praises noble characteristics while condemning injustice—irrespective of the person or people performing the act. For example, addressing all humankind—Muslim and non-Muslim—the Qur'an declares, "Surely, We have created man in the best make; Then, if he works iniquity, We reject him as the lowest of the low; Except those who believe and do good works; so for them is an unending reward."[237]

---

236. Qur'an 2:63. The Qur'an then reemphasizes the same principle that Jews, Christians, and Sabians will also be rewarded with paradise in 5:70. "Surely, those who have believed, and the Jews, and the Sabians, and the Christians—whoso believes in Allah and the Last Day and does good deeds, on them shall come no fear, nor shall they grieve."

237. Qur'an 95:5–7.

Here, condemnation is of those who "commit iniquity," just as in the verse Wilders referenced where condemnation came to those who rebelled. But this verse I cite regarding all of humanity is far more harsh due to the phrase "lowest of the low," translated from *as falaa saafileen*. *As falaa saafileen* refers to a condition of such moral bankruptcy that even the filthiest animal—including an ape or swine—is above it. God condemns a person who commits iniquity to that humiliated and degraded low level—excepting those, Muslim and non-Muslim alike, who "believe and do good works." The Qur'ans reference to apes alludes to animalistic behavior—it should not be understood to mean that God literally transformed man into ape. Such bizarre concepts are indeed espoused by ignorant extremists and have no place in intellectual and common sense dialogue.

Finally, for those who still insist that this Qur'anic verse endorses anti-Semitism, compare it with the biblical condemnation of Jews who violate the Sabbath: "For six days, work is to be done, but the seventh day is a Sabbath of rest, holy to the LORD. Whoever does any work on the Sabbath day *must be put to death*."[238] So, according to Wilders, a book that teaches capital punishment for every Jew who violates the Sabbath is just fine, but another that differentiates between just and unjust behavior among Jews evidently automatically condemns all Jews.

It is also necessary to refute Wilders's regurgitated assertions of Islam's alleged anti-Semitism from Chapters 5 and 7 of his book. Wilders claims that Islam actually conditions Muslims to work toward Judaism's destruction.[239] Not surprisingly, Wilders does not quote the Qur'an or another authority on Islam to prove another one of his sweeping statements. Contrary to Wilders's meritless allegations, the Qur'an dedicates a whole Chapter (17) to the *Bani Isra'el*—the Children of Israel—and

---

238. Exodus 31:15.

239. Wilders, *Marked for Death*, 84.

considers the Israelites to be a nation bestowed with special divine fa-vor.[240]

The Qur'an details the life of Prophet Moses[as] by name more so than any other prophet's. His name is cited over 150 times, and he is referred to as *kaleemullah*— "one who spoke with God directly." Of the twenty-six prophets mentioned by name in the Holy Qur'an, more than twenty are Israelite prophets. A Muslim's faith is incomplete without believing in the truth of all prophets of God and all books of divine origin, includ-ing the Torah and the Psalms of David. The Holy Qur'an also declares that no single religion can monopolize salvation.[241] No other ancient religious scripture can compare to the Qur'an in terms of respecting oth-er faiths.

Islam does not censure Jews *because* they are Jews. The Qur'an spe-cifically states that Jews will be amongst the parties of paradise[242] and that Muslims can marry from among the People of the Book.[243] The Qur'an does censure certain Jews, however, who have strayed from the teachings of the Torah; the Torah and Gospels, too, censure such Jews. This Qur'anic censure serves not only to urge those particular Jews to rectify their behavior, but also as an example for Muslims.[244]

As explained in my Chapter 2, Prophet Muhammad's[sa] treatment of Jews in Medina—vis-à-vis the Charter of Medina—demonstrates the benevolence of Muslims toward Jews. Indeed, the Jews of Medina demonstrated their love for Prophet Muhammad[sa] by their actions. Saf-waan bin Assal relates, "some people among the Jews kissed the hands and feet of the Prophet[sa]."[245] It is impossible to consider that a man could

240. Qur'an 2:48, 123; 45:17.

241. Qur'an 2:63, 112–114; 3:114–116; 5:67, 70; 7:160; 22:69.

242. Qur'an 2:63; 3:114–116; 5:70.

243. Qur'an 5:6.

244. Qur'an 5:45.

245. Sunan Ibn Majah, vol 5, Chapter 16, 34. (Hadith No. 3705)

garner such love from his citizens with force or violence. On the contrary, this was a reflection of the immense compassion and justice with which Muhammad[sa] ruled. And this compassion and justice embodied Muslim leadership long after Muhammad's[sa] demise. Had Islam endorsed the destruction of Jews, why did Jews flourish in parts of North Africa, Jerusalem, Persia, and Spain under Muslim rule?[246]

Moreover, if blaming the Jews for wrongdoing is anti-Semitic, then the New Testament, which Wilders repeatedly defends, is just as (or more) anti-Semitic.[247] If inciting fear of the dangers Jews posed to Christ is anti-Semitic, then the New Testament is anti-Semitic.[248] If naming Jews dogs, swine, or snakes is anti-Semitic, then the New Testament is anti-Semitic.[249] If saying that the Jews' father is the devil is anti-Semitic, then the New Testament is anti-Semitic.[250] Prominent Christian theologians, based on their study of the Bible, also endorsed anti-Semitism:

Justin Martyr: [Circumcision's] purpose [...] was that you and only you might suffer the afflictions that are now justly yours; that only your land be desolated, and your cities ruined by fire, that the fruits of your land be eaten by strangers before your very eyes; that not one of you be permitted to enter your city of Jerusalem.[251]

---

246. See http://www.thejc.com/comment-and-debate/comment/68082/so-what-did-muslims-do-jews.

247. Matthew 23:13–38; 27:25; Mark 11:18; Luke 20:19; Acts 2:22–23, 36; 3:12–15; 4:10; 6:8–8:3; 7:51–53; 8:30; 9:23–25; 17:6–8; II Corinthians 11:23–26; Galatians 4:29, 5:11.

248. John 7:1–9, 12–13; 20:19.

249. Matthew 7:6; 12:34; 23:31, 33.

250. John 8:44.

251. Justin Martyr, *Dialogue with Trypho*, trans. Thomas B. Falls, 27.

John Chrysostom: Again the Jews, the most miserable and wretched of all men... But today the Jews, who are more dangerous than any wolves, are bent on surrounding my sheep; so I must spar with them and fight with them so that no sheep of mine may fall victim to those wolves... Isaiah called the Jews dogs and Jeremiah called them mare-mad horses. This was not because they suddenly changed natures with those beasts but because they were pursuing the lustful habits of those animals.[252]

Saint Augustine: How hateful to me are the enemies of your Scripture! How I wish that you would slay [the Jews] with your two-edged sword, so that there should be none to oppose your word! Gladly would I have them die to themselves and live to you![253]

Saint Thomas Aquinas: As the laws say, the Jews by reason of their fault are sentenced to perpetual servitude and thus the lords of the lands in which they dwell may take things from them as though they were their own.[254]

Martin Luther: What then shall we Christians do with this damned, rejected race of Jews? ...their synagogues should be set on fire...their homes should likewise be broken down and destroyed...rabbis must be forbidden under threat of death to teach

---

252. John Chrysostom, "Homily 4," in Eight Homilies Against the Jews [Adversus Judeaus], vol. 98. Patrologia Greaca.

253. Saint Augustine, The Confessions of Saint Augustine, trans. Edward Bouverie Pusey, vol. 12.

254. Saint Thomas Aquinas, Letter on the Treatment of the Jews.

any more... [let us] be free of this insufferable devilish burden—the Jews.255

John Calvin: [Jews'] rotten and unbending stiff-neckedness deserves that they be oppressed unendingly and without measure or end and that they die in their misery without the pity of anyone.[256]

Pope Clement VIII: All the world suffers from the usury of the Jews, their monopolies and deceit. They have brought many unfortunate people into a state of poverty, especially the farmers, working class people and the very poor. Then, as now, Jews have to be reminded intermittently that they were enjoying rights in any country since they left Palestine and the Arabian desert, and subsequently their ethical and moral doctrines as well as their deeds rightly deserve to be exposed to criticism in whatever country they happen to live.[257]

Prominent "Westerners," as Wilders would call them, held views many consider anti-Semitic: Diderot, Voltaire, Henry Ford, T. S. Eliot, Peter Stuyvesant, G. K. Chesterton, H. G. Wells, Henry Adams, H. L. Mencken, Immanuel Kant, Richard Wagner, Thomas Edison, Aleksander Pushkin, Pierre Renoir, Charles Lindbergh, Charles de Gaulle, Edgar Degas, Shakespeare, Roald Dahl, Geoffrey Chaucer, Charles Dickens, William Blake, John Dryden, the Fireside Poets, Fyodor Dos-

---

255. Martin Luther, On The Jews and Their Lies: Luther's Works, trans. Martin H. Bertram, vol. 47 (Philadelphia: Fortress Press, 1971).

256. [John Calvin, "Excerpt from Ad Quaelstiones et Objecta Juaei Cuiusdam Responsio," in] (The foregoing may not match with the following source info?) Gerhard Falk, The Jew in Christian Theology (Jefferson, NC and London:, McFarland and Company, Inc., 2013).

257. See http://www.biblebelievers.org.au/repute.htm. Accessed March 6, 2014.

toyevsky, Ernest Hemingway, Arnold Toynbee, Frederic Chopin, and more. Prominent "Western" literature such as *The Merchant of Venice*, "The Prioress's Tale" from Chaucer's *Canterbury Tales*, *Oliver Twist*, and *The Jew of Malta* also endorses anti-Semitism. Concepts such as su-persessionism and "the wandering Jew" also owe their births and prolif-eration to traditional Christian theology.

In practical terms, thousands upon thousands of Jews were murdered during the Crusades, the Spanish Inquisition, and at various times in Europe and Russia. The word *ghetto* owes its origin to the slums of Ven-ice where Jews lived. Father Charles Coughlin, who commanded a week-ly radio audience of more than thirty million Americans in the 1930s, openly supported anti-Semitism and the likes of Adolf Hitler and Beni-to Mussolini. Coughlin also blamed Jews for the Great Depression, the Russian Revolution, and Marxism.

More recently, the Anti-Defamation League, in its 2012 report on anti-Semitism in ten European countries (including the Netherlands), concluded, "As with previous surveys, data from this latest 2012 Euro-pean tracking poll indicates that significant percentages of European re-spondents continue to believe in some of the most pernicious anti-Semitic stereotypes."[258] A 2011 ADL poll found that about 15 percent of Americans—forty-five million people—"fall into the most anti-Semitic co-hort."[259]

Wilders ignores all the facts, data, and history imaginable and instead somehow argues that Islam is anti-Semitic. This allegation is dangerous because it creates fear of Islam and of Muslims when no such basis for that fear exists. Those few and far between extremists ascribing to Islam,

258. See http://www.adl.org/Anti_semitism/adl_anti-semitism_presentation_february_2012.pdf. Accessed August 12, 2012.

259. See http://www.adl.org/anti_semitism_domestic/ADL-2011-Anti-Semitism_Presentation.pdf. Accessed August 12, 2012).

who engage in anti-Jewish propaganda, do so contrary to Prophet Muhammad's[sa] clear, compassionate, and tolerant example.

Wilders may claim that he wants peace and harmony, but deceptive tactics like this allegation prove quite to the contrary. The bottom line is that Islam recognizes Jews as equal human beings, a fact that Prophet Muhammad[sa] demonstrated in the Charter of Medina. Wilders's allegations are, once again, without merit.

ALLEGATION 29

Islam Rejects the Golden Rule and Forbids Befriending Non-Muslims

Not content with fabricating an allegation of anti-Semitism against Islam, Wilders next claims that Islam rejects the Golden Rule and that Islam forbids Muslims to befriend Christians and Jews. He writes, "...there is no Golden Rule in Islam. In fact, the Koran states explicitly that non-Muslims are to be treated much worse than Muslims. "Believers, take neither Jews nor Christians for your friends," it says. It further commands, "When the sacred months are over slay the idolaters wherever you find them. Arrest them, besiege them, and lie in ambush everywhere for them.""[260] Wilders cites known anti-Islam personality Nonie Darwish in his Chapter 4 to rekindle this allegation.[261]

REFERENCE: Qur'an 5:52, 3:29, 9:5.

RESPONSE: Hadhrat Anas[ra] relates that Prophet Muhammad[sa] said, "None of you has faith until he loves for his brother what he loves for himself."[262] Some critics assert that "brother" in this hadith refers only to fellow Muslims, but nothing supports this presupposition. In fact, Islam not only champions the Golden Rule, it goes beyond the Golden Rule in teaching to respond to others with an even greater act. Prophet Muhammad[sa] said, "'Help your brother, whether he is an oppressor or he is

---

260. Wilders, *Marked for Death*, 44.

261. Ibid., 68.

262. Sahih Jami' Bukhari, vol. 1, Book 2, #15.

oppressed.' The Prophet was asked: 'It is right to help him if he is op-pressed, but how should we help him if he is an oppressor?' He replied: 'By preventing him from oppressing others.'"[263] Thus, it is not just the duty of Muslims to treat others as they would want to be treated, but also to have compassion for the oppressed and help them win their free-dom from oppression without them even having to ask.

Wilders adds that Darwish—a self-proclaimed religious scholar—"points out another characteristic of authentic religions that Islam lacks: it does not teach the golden rule—that we should treat others as we would have them treat us. Instead, Islam institutionalizes inequality, sanctioning discrimination against certain groups of people such as women and non-Muslims."

In fact, Islam's teaching is superior to the Golden Rule. Islam teaches that Muslims must treat others well no matter how others treat them: "Verily, Allah enjoins justice, and the doing of good to others; and giving like kindred."[264] Unlike the Old Testament's teaching of equal retribu-tion, the Qur'an urges Muslims to forgive:

And the recompense of an injury is an injury the like thereof; but whoso forgives and *his act* brings about reformation, his reward is with Allah. Surely, He loves not the wrongdoers.[265]

The Qur'an teaches that Muslims must deal justly with everyone, even those who may hate them:

O ye who believe! be steadfast in the cause of Allah, bearing wit-ness in equity; and let not a people's enmity incite you to act oth-erwise than with justice. Be always just, that is nearer to

---

263. Sahih Jami' Bukhari, vol. 3, #624.

264. Qur'an 16:91.

265. Qur'an 42:41.

righteousness. And fear Allah. Surely, Allah is aware of what you do.[266]

The Golden Rule teaches us to do unto others as we would have them do unto us. In the aforementioned verse, the Qur'an commands Muslims to *always* treat others with justice, even if they act with animosity and injustice toward them. In other words, the Qur'an commands Muslims to treat others as they would like to be treated, *even if* the Muslim must suffer through negative treatment.

The aforementioned example of amnesty that Prophet Muhammad[sa] offered to his Meccan persecutors upon the victory of Mecca excellently personifies this teaching. In fact, Prophet Muhammad[sa] added that "a Muslim who kills a covenanting disbeliever, would not even be able to perceive the breeze of paradise."[267] The Qur'an likewise teaches that a Muslim who kills a covenanting disbeliever even unintentionally or by mistake must, in addition to fully paying the blood money to the heirs of the deceased, also free a slave. (Incidentally this was also a means to systematically purge slavery from society, a matter I discuss at length in Chapter 6). Such is the level of respect afforded to those with whom Muslims have pacts.

True to Wilders's modus operandi, however, he next cites partial Qur'anic verses to argue that Islam forbids a Muslim to befriend Christians and Jews. This is another wholly false allegation. The Qur'an only forbids Muslims from befriending those individuals who attack or wage war against Muslims, while it emphatically encourages ties of kinship and alliance otherwise:

---

266. Qur'an 5:9.

267. Ṣaḥīḥul-Bukhārī, Kitābul-Jizyati Wal-Muwāda'ati, Bābu Ithmi Man Qatala Mu'āhidan Bi-Ghairi Jurmin, Ḥadīth No. 3166.

Allah forbids you not, respecting those who have not fought against you on account of your religion, and who have not driven you forth from your homes, that you be kind to them and act equitably towards them; surely Allah loves those who are equitable. Allah only forbids you, respecting those who have fought against you on account of your religion, and have driven you out of your homes, and have helped others in driving you out, that you make friends of them, and whosoever makes friends of them—it is these that are the transgressors.[268]

Wilders censors this teaching from his readers; it appears nowhere in his book. The Qur'an clearly says that Muslims are *not* forbidden from befriending those who have not fought them, instead commanding Muslims to "be kind to them and act equitably towards them." Contrary to Wilders's allegation, no religious qualifications are required before a people can be befriended. This demonstrates that the verses regarding "arresting and seizing" the idolaters apply only to those individuals who have persecuted Muslims on account of their faith, driven them out of their homes, and have incited others to persecute Muslims—just as the plain text of the aforementioned verse clarifies. In such instances, God has permitted Muslims to fight in self-defense.

But exactly *when* does Islam permit a Muslim to take up arms in self-defense? The Qur'an explains, "Permission to fight is given to those against whom war is made, because they have been wronged—and Allah indeed has power to help them."[269] Thus, preemptive war finds no justification in Islam. Permission—not a commandment—is only granted once another party imposes war upon a nonviolent party. Having established this principle, the Qur'an adds:

---

268. Qur'an 60:9–10.
269. Qur'an 22:40.

Those who have been driven out from their homes unjustly only because they said, "Our Lord is God"—And if God did not repel some men by means of others, there would surely have been pulled down cloisters and churches and synagogues and mosques, wherein the name of God is oft commemorated. And God will surely help one who helps Him. God is indeed Powerful, Mighty.[270]

This verse—the like of which does not exist in any other religious scripture and did not exist in any secular constitution for centuries after—commands Muslims to champion universal religious freedom for all faiths. Unlike any other ancient scripture, the Qur'an specifically protects those who attend "cloisters, churches, and synagogues." Moreover, Muslims must prefer protection of other faiths even to their own, as demonstrated by the Qur'an mentioning mosques last. Muslims are thus permitted to fight in self-defense when they are attacked and to protect universal religious freedom for people of all faiths.

This verse recognizes and preempts what happens when a tyrant oppresses one faith and no one speaks up: the oppression spreads. Thus, fourteen hundred years prior to Martin Niemoller's famous words,[271] the Qur'an made it incumbent upon Muslims to fight for universal religious freedom. The Qur'an in fact teaches compassion beyond the Golden Rule. It encourages interfaith friendship and is the only divine scripture to mandate its adherents—Muslims—to fight on behalf of any person of any faith to ensure universal religious freedom. The restriction on befriending Christians and Jews is only on those who have proactively reli-

---

270. Qur'an 22:41.

271. "First they came for the communists, and I didn't speak out because I wasn't a communist. Then they came for the trade unionists, and I didn't speak out because I wasn't a trade unionist. Then they came for the Jews, and I didn't speak out because I wasn't a Jew. Then they came for me and there was no one left to speak out for me."

giously persecuted Muslims. Otherwise Muslims are commanded to behave compassionately and equitably to *all* people.

ALLEGATION 30

Muslims Who Fight Jews Today Do So per Muhammad's[sa] Orders

I have already dismantled Wilders's allegation that Islam is anti-Semitic. Yet he finds multiple means to continue asserting it. Here, he alleges that modern-day Muslims who commit violence toward Jews are merely acting in accordance to Prophet Muhammad's[sa] directives. He writes, "[The previous allegation that the Qur'an is anti-Semitic] is consistent with Muhammad's infamous order to his followers, so often repeated throughout the Islamic world today, 'You will fight with the Jews till some of them will hide behind stones. The stones will betray them saying "O Abdullah [slave of Allah]! There is a Jew behind me; so kill him.'"[272]

REFERENCE: Sahih Jami' Bukhari, vol. 4, Book 52, #177; Sahih Jami' Muslim, Book 41, #6985.

RESPONSE: Recognizing that Islam is not anti-Semitic, I address this hadith with the same word, but with caution: Wilders's sensationalism should not obstruct the reader from viewing this hadith with a sober mind. An objective analysis demonstrates that nothing about this hadith is anti-Semitic; neither is the statement itself unlike how past prophets have admonished certain factions of their respective societies. First I present the full hadith. Hadhrat Abu Huraira[ra] reported that Prophet Muhammad[sa] said:

---

272. Wilders, *Marked for Death*, 44.

The last hour would not come unless the Muslims will fight against the Jews and the Muslims would kill them until the Jews would hide themselves behind a stone or a tree and a stone or a tree would say: "Muslim, or the servant of Allah, there is a Jew behind me; come and kill him; but the tree Gharqad would not say, for it is the tree of the Jews."[273]

First, this hadith does not speak against the Jews as a whole but against unjust Jews. The same argument previously explaining the allegedly anti-Semitic Qur'anic verses is also applicable here. Prophet Muhammad's[sa] reputation for justice ensured that he praised noble qualities and condemned injustice, no matter in whom the qualities were found. For example, this allegedly anti-Semitic hadith notwithstanding, Prophet Muhammad[sa] reserved his harshest language to describe none other than his own people—the Muslims—and the Muslim clerics of the anticipated latter days. Hadhrat Ali[ra], fourth khalifa of Prophet Muhammad[sa], narrates that Prophet Muhammad[sa] said:

A time will come in the near future when there will be nothing left of Islam except its name. And there will be nothing left of the Holy Qur'an except its words [the Qur'an would not be understood/followed]. The mosques of that age will apparently be full of people, but will be empty of righteousness. Their *ulema* [religious clerics] will be *the worst creatures under the heavens*. Discord will rise from them and will come right back to them [the ulema will be the source of all evils].[274]

---

273. Sahih Jami' Muslim, Book 41, #6985.

274. Al-Baihaqi as quoted in al-Mishkat Kitab ul-Ilm, chap. 3, 38; Kanzul 'Ummal, chap. 6, 43. (Emphasis added.)

Though Prophet Muhammad[sa] calls the Muslim clerics the "the worst creatures under the heavens," it is naïve to assume that this hadith condemns every Muslim cleric alive. And the same principle applies to Jews. Prophet Muhammad's[sa] statement regarding the Jews addresses those Jews deserving of censure. It cannot mean he is censuring Jews simply because they are Jews—if so, then he is equally censuring all Muslims for being Muslim. Both views are equally nonsensical. Furthermore, as mentioned earlier, Jesus Christ[as] equates the Jews of his time to the children of Satan—yet Wilders is silent on this declaration. Why?

Next, in this allegedly anti-Semitic hadith in question, the verb *qata-la* (قَتَلَ) does not only mean "kill." Indeed, any standard Arabic lexicon dictionary notes that the word has numerous meanings: to kill, boycott, be hostile, eliminate carnal desires, lessen or weaken, curse, acquire full knowledge (thus killing doubt), quarrel, wage war, commend or approve, to humble another.

When interpreting hadith, we either understand it completely literally or completely metaphorically. We cannot pick and choose what part is literal and what part is metaphorical, as that leaves the hadith to an entirely subjective and unreliable standard. In this hadith, nothing demands, much less suggests, literally translating *qatl* as "to kill." But if we must literally translate it as that, then we must also literally seek out talking stones and trees. Thus, Muslims would only be able to actually kill Jews once they found talking stones and trees. Even a small child would laugh at the idea of a talking stone or talking tree—yet Wilders somehow takes the passage as literal. In other words, if the "stones and trees" that talk are metaphorical, what right does one have to insist that the "killing" is literal?

The bottom line is that both Islam and Prophet Muhammad[sa] have consistently spoken up for justice while condemning injustice—regardless of the person or people committing the act. As the Qur'an clarifies, "O ye who believe! Be strict in observing justice, and be witnesses for Allah, even though it be against yourselves or against parents and kindred. Whether he be rich or poor, Allah is more regardful of them both than you are."[275] The Jews that Prophet Muhammad[sa] critiques in this hadith receive censure because they are worthy of censure, not because they are Jews.

---

275. Qur'an 4:136.

Conclusion

Even more so than in his Chapters 1 and 2, Wilders avails himself of every opportunity in his Chapter 3 to misdirect and deceive his readers about Prophet Muhammad^{sa}. Wilders's refusal to cite the vast majority of his allegations makes his propaganda all the more bizarre. I implore the reader that any ignorant hate-monger can make wild and sensational allegations, but it takes a true seeker after truth to present an objective, authentic, and independently verifiable argument. Wilders does none of this.

I deliberately did not address an earlier remark Wilders makes that Adolf Hitler allegedly admired Islam, but I have chosen to address it here. First, how Islam could be to blame for Hitler's view of it is a mind-boggling mystery. But if such a relationship amounts to some sort of guilt, then I remind the reader that convicted Norway "Christian" terrorist Anders Breivik actively and vociferously praises Wilders. Breivik calls Wilders a hero, repeatedly demanding that Europe pay him homage.

Moreover, while Wilders finds the time and audacity to quote Hitler to attempt to malign Islam, he ignores that Hitler claimed his actions in the name of Christianity. For example, Wilders does not even acknowledge that Hitler claimed that his Christian faith motivated his horrific extermination of the Jews, Gypsies, and numerous other minorities. Hitler wrote in *Mein Kampf*, "Hence today I believe that I am acting in accordance with the will of the Almighty Creator: by defending myself against the Jew, I am fighting for the work of the Lord."[276] Hitler likewise stated in a speech in Passau on October 27, 1928:

> We are a people of different faiths, but we are one. Which faith conquers the other is not the question; rather, the question is whether Christianity stands or falls...We tolerate no one in our ranks who attacks the ideas of Christianity...in fact our movement is Christian. We are filled with a desire for Catholics and Protestants to discover one another in the deep distress of our own people.[277]

While I would object if Wilders attempted to blame Christianity for Hitler's atrocities, I reference Hitler's self-stated motivation for only one reason—to demonstrate how warped Wilders's worldview actually is. While Hitler declared in no uncertain terms that he was a Christian and that he acted as a Christian, according to Wilders his actions were somehow Islam's fault. Finally, and shockingly, Wilders's closing Chapter 3 comments to demonize Muslims frighteningly mimic Hitler's comments to demonize Jews. Hitler wrote:

---

276. Adolf Hitler, *Mein Kampf*, 60,
http://www.jewishvirtuallibrary.org/jsource/Holocaust/kampf.html.

277. Richard Steiggman-Gall, The Holy Reich: Nazi Conceptions of Christianity, 1919–1945(Cambridge University Press, 2004), 61–62. Citing BAZ NS 26/55 (27 October 1928: Passau).

If, with the help of his Marxist creed, the Jew is victorious over the other peoples of the world, his crown will be the funeral wreath of humanity and this planet will, as it did thousands of years ago, move through the ether devoid of men. Eternal Nature inexorably avenges the infringement of her commands. The ignorance of the broad masses about the inner nature of the Jew, the lack of instinct and narrow-mindedness of our upper classes, make the people an easy victim for this Jewish campaign of lies.[278]

By comparison, Wilders writes:

While President Obama is apparently unaware that Islam is a cult of hatred, that fact has been widely known for many centuries in both the West and the East. Defenders of Western civilization should not sugarcoat Islam... Otherwise, we risk repeating the mistake made by the tolerant inhabitants of Yathrib and Mecca before their cultures were wiped away by the aggressive ideology they had once welcomed within their walls.[279]

Both Hitler and Wilders make sweeping allegations and broad threats about entire, worldwide communities of people, warning with similar bigotry and ignorance that if either is given power, it will destroy all

---

278. Adolf Hitler, Mein Kampf, 60.

279. Wilders, *Marked for Death*, 45.

others. Hitler wanted to destroy and exile Jews; Wilders quotes President Adams's recommendation to use force to dispel Muslims. Hitler censored anything related to Judaism; Wilders wants to ban the Qur'an altogether. To an unbiased observer, Wilders's desire to eradicate Muslims and Islam is no different from Hitler's desire to eradicate Jews and Judaism. Contrary to Wilders's hallucinations about Islam and Prophet Muhammad[sa], Sir William Muir writes:

> The courteous treatment which the deputations of these various clans experienced from the Prophet, his ready attention to their grievances, the wisdom with which he composed their disputes, and the politic assignments of territory by which he rewarded early declaration in favour of Islam, made his name to be popular, and his fame as a great and generous Prince to spread throughout the peninsula."[280]

This Chapter was Wilders's first substantive attempt to make a case against Islam. While he fails miserably, the good news for readers is that more than half of Wilders's arguments within EXTREMIST's scope have already been addressed. In his Chapter 4, Wilders aggressively attacks the role and rights of women in Islam. Let us proceed now to that discussion.

---

280. Muir, *Life of Mahomet*, 399.

Chapter 4

Wilders Invents a New Religion

"I wanted to know the best of the life of one who holds today an undisputed sway over the hearts of millions of mankind... I became more than ever convinced that it was not the sword that won a place for Islam in those days in the scheme of life. It was the rigid simplicity, the utter self-effacement of the Prophet the scrupulous regard for pledges, his intense devotion to his friends and followers, his intrepidity, his fearlessness, his absolute trust in God and in his own mission."

— MAHATMA GHANDI

In just twenty-five pages, Wilders manages to hurl nearly thirty allegations against Islam. Among other objections, he alleges that Islam approves of wife beating and honor killing. He alleges Islam is not a religion at all, but a backward, fatalistic, militant political ideology opposed to freedom, modernity, innovation, theology, philosophy, rationalism, and democracy. He further alleges that Islam seeks to establish a caliph-governed, theocratic world.

He claims that Allah is unknowable—which, if anything, reflects his own atheism or agnosticism. Such an allegation can be levied against any faith. He asserts that nonbelievers are doomed in Islam; that zakaat is used for holy war in Kashmir, Palestine, and other places. He mischaracterizes martyrdom and fasting and accuses Prophet Muhammad[sa] of making inappropriate exceptions in the latter. Wilders raises many of these allegations again in his Chapter 10.[281] In short, Wilders invents a new, never-before-heard-of religion and tries to label it Islam. Not surprisingly, he fails, and I respond to each of these allegations here.

---

281. Wilders, *Marked for Death*, 48–50.

ALLEGATION 31

Islam Teaches "Honor Killings"

This is the first in a series of allegations Wilders makes in his attempt to argue that Islam is misogynist. Specifically, Wilders alleges that Prophet Muhammad[sa] turned Arabia into a misogynist society, giving women a low status in Islam.[282] Wilders laments that "honor killings are a pervasive problem throughout the Islamic world," and implicates Islam as the cause, stating, "If women behave 'lewdly,' their families sometimes kill them in order to save the family's honor. 'Confine them in their houses till death overtakes them,' says the Koran."[283]

REFERENCE: Qur'an 4:16.

RESPONSE: Honor killings have no place in Islam and no relation to the verse Wilders cites to claim some connection exists. The extremists who engage in such acts are criminals in every sense of the word. The Qur'an instructs: "There should be no compulsion in religion"[284] and "Admonish, therefore, for thou are but an admonisher; thou hast no authority to compel them."[285] It is unquestionably un-Islamic for any Muslim to compel another person to abide by Islamic teachings.

The verse Wilders cites reads: "And such of your women as are guilty of any flagrant impropriety—call to witness four of you against them;

---

282. Ibid., 163.

283. Ibid., 51.

284. Qur'an 2:257.

285. Qur'an 88:21–22.

and if they bear witness, then confine them to the houses until death overtakes them or Allah opens for them some other way."[286]

Wilders cites only the portion of the verse he finds convenient. The verse actually lays down three conditions, all of which Wilders ignores: first, a woman must in fact be guilty of such impropriety (which should be flagrant and damaging to the moral fabric of society); second, not one but four separate, reliable witnesses must testify to this—lest the woman suffer any injustice; and finally, confinement to her home is administered only until such a time as "Allah opens for [her] some other way," meaning repentance, reform, marriage, and so on.[287]

Lewd conduct is not just un-Islamic, it is also illegal in America.[288] Wilders, without reference, lies when claiming, "If a woman, however modest, awakens the lust of a Muslim man, then she, not he, is to blame." The Qur'an first commands men to "restrain their looks," to avoid arousing their own lust,[289] and only then does it tell women to do the same.[290] Prophet Muhammad[sa] further instructed, "Be chaste and your women will be chaste."[291] Thus, men are responsible and will be held accountable for their actions. Men have the greater burden and obligation to maintain chastity—not women. Nothing in Islam substantiates Wilders's allegation.

---

286. Qur'an 4:16.

287. Hadhrat Mirza Bashiruddin Mahmud Ahmad, *Al-Tafsir as-Saghir, The Holy Qur'an 1-Volume Commentary* (Tilford: Islam International Publications, Ltd., 2002), 190.

288. See e.g., Cal. Pen. Code § 288 (criminalizing lewd conduct with fine, imprisonment, or both). Virtually, if not every, state has a detailed penal code criminalizing lewd behavior. This makes it all the more puzzling that Wilders would object to the Qur'an's condemnation of lewd behavior fourteen hundred years ago, since modern societies are in unanimous agreement that such laws are necessary to protect their moral fabrics.

289. Qur'an 24:31.

290. Qur'an 24:32.

291. Al-Tabaraani, al-Mu'jam al-Awsat, Book 6, #241.

Furthermore, the Qur'an repeatedly states that true believing men are those who safeguard their private parts from everyone except their wives.[292] Finally, Wilders also fails to convey that the Qur'an prescribes male fornicators and adulterers be punished the same for such acts.[293]

Indeed, at Islam's advent, it was common practice in Arabia for men to bury their infant daughters alive to spare shame to the family. The Qur'an categorically rejected this horrific and barbaric act, ending it once and for all. Muslims who engage in any form of "honor killing" today do so in spite of Islam, never because of Islam. In short, nothing in Islam justifies or accepts any form of honor killing.

But a deeper issue exists and herein also lays Wilders's double standard. He attempts to present violence against women as a "Muslim only" issue. He ignores the human rights atrocities and rising gang rape cases against women in Hindu majority India. He ignores that every nine seconds a woman is assaulted in Christian majority America. In America, for example, 3 women are killed daily by their husbands or boyfriends. The vast majority of these women are Christian women murdered by their Christian male counterparts. This amounts to a thousand women a year killed in acts of domestic violence in Christian majority America—shall we ignorantly call this "Christian honor killing"?

Wilders is hypocritically silent on this. As a Muslim I reject this extremist style thinking because it is not only illogical, it does nothing to remedy the situation for those women suffering under domestic violence. I present the examples of India and America not to detract from the serious issue of domestic violence among some Muslim majority nations, but to once again provide something Wilders won't—a true picture of reality. Violence against women is not just a "Muslim only" issue. It is a serious worldwide epidemic independent of color, caste, or creed. Men as a whole must take ownership over this disease and root out this

---

292. Qur'an 23:2–7.
293. Qur'an 24:3.

barbaric behavior from among themselves. It is not only ignorant, but also offensive to put blame on any faith—as Wilders and religious extremists do with Islam only. In blaming a religion, Wilders and other extremists become enablers. Rather than blindly blaming religion, Wilders should recognize this as an opportunity to provide education to abused women on how to remove themselves from violent situations, education to youth on why it is unacceptable to harm women—ever, and advance criminal justice reform to hold abusive men more accountable and prevent repeat offenses.

Violence against women will stop when men take the lead and make it stop—not when we ban Islam as Wilders ignorantly recommends.

ALLEGATION 32

Prayer is Annulled If a Woman Passes in Front of a Man

Wilders cites the horrific deaths of fifteen Saudi schoolgirls—killed in a fire because Saudi police refused to let them exit the burning building without wearing burqas—to allege that such behavior is ingrained in Islamic teaching. He writes, "The tragic fate of the fifteen Saudi school-girls is indicative of the low status of women in Islam, a 'religion' that deems prayers to be nullified if a dog, a donkey, or a woman pass in front of praying men."[294] Wilders cites a Bukhari hadith to allege that a man's prayer is annulled if a woman passes in front of him.

REFERENCE: Sahih Jami' Bukhari, vol. 1, Book 9, #490.

RESPONSE: Islam categorically condemns the Saudi police's actions. Earlier in this book, I discussed the immense value Islam places on even a single life—equating its murder to having murdered all mankind. There-fore, absolutely nothing justifies the barbaric action to prevent school-children from escaping a burning building. The individuals who prevented those innocent children from escaping a blazing fire are guilty of murder—nothing less.

That condemnation clear, I transition to Wilders's allegation that a person's prayer is nullified should a woman—whom he alleges has the status of a dog—cross in front of him. While I am pleased that Wilders cites an actual Islamic source, I am shocked at his inability to understand

---

294. Wilders, *Marked for Death*, 47–48.

a simple hadith. In fact, the hadith, offered below, shows the exact *opposite* of what Wilders alleges:

> Hadhrat Ayesha[ra] states, "The things which annul the prayers were mentioned before me. They said, 'Prayer is annulled by a dog, a donkey and a woman (if they pass in front of the praying people).' I said, 'You have made us (i.e., women) dogs. I saw the Prophet praying while I used to lie in my bed between him and the Qibla. Whenever I was in need of something, I would slip away. for I disliked to face him.'"[295]

In this hadith, Hadhrat Ayesha[ra] explains that "they" (some group of people) mentioned before her what they understood to nullify prayer if it passed in front of them while they pray—dogs, donkeys, and women. In response, Hadhrat Ayesha rebuked them, saying, "You have made us (i.e., women) dogs." On the contrary, "[she] used to lie between [Prophet Muhammad[sa]] and the Qibla" whenever Prophet Muhammad[sa] prayed; i.e., she would lie on the ground in front of Prophet Muhammad[sa] when he prayed, and he never once objected.

In another hadith, Hadhrat Ayesha[ra] relates, "I used to sleep in front of Allah's Apostle[sa] with my legs opposite his qibla (facing him); and whenever he prostrated, he pushed my feet and I withdrew them and whenever he stood, I stretched them."[296] Not a single Islamic resource—the Qur'an, sunna, or hadith—substantiates Wilders's baseless accusation. Wilders made his assertion without fully reading the hadith and hopes his readers do the same.

---

295. Sahih Jami' Bukhari, vol. 1, Book 9, #490.

296. Sahih Jami' Bukhari, vol. 1, Book 9, #492.

ALLEGATION 33

In Islam, a Woman's Testimony is Worth Half That of a Man's

Wilders argues that because the Qur'an prescribes either two men as witnesses or one man and two women, "in Islam, a woman has half the worth of a man."[297]

REFERENCE: Qur'an 2:283.

RESPONSE: This verse Wilders cites is the single longest in the Qur'an and provides guidelines regarding finance.[298] (For the sake of brevity, I have made the entire verse available in the footnotes instead of in the

297. Wilders, *Marked for Death*, 50.

298. The full text of the Qur'an 2:283 reads, "O ye who believe! when you borrow one from another for a fixed period, then write it down. And let a scribe write it in your presence faithfully; and no scribe should refuse to write, because Allah has taught him, so let him write and let him who incurs the liability dictate; and he should fear Allah, his Lord, and not diminish anything therefrom. But if the person incurring the liability be of low understanding or be weak or be unable himself to dictate, then let someone who can watch his interest dictate with justice. And call two witnesses from among your men; and if two men be not available, then a man and two women, of such as you like as witnesses, so that if either of two women should err in memory, then one may remind the other. And the witnesses should not refuse when they are called. And do not feel weary of writing it down, whether it be small or large, along with its appointed time of payment. This is more equitable in the sight of Allah and makes testimony surer and is more likely to keep you away from doubts; therefore omit not to write except that it be ready merchandise which you give or take from hand to hand, in which case it shall be no sin for you that you write it not. And have witnesses when you sell one to another; and let no harm be done to the scribe or the witness. And if you do that, then certainly it shall be disobedience on your part. And fear Allah. And Allah grants you knowledge and Allah knows all things well."

main text.) Wilders, however, casts aside the verse's clear context and scope. Although two women are called to bear witness—i.e., pay attention to and affirm the transaction when it takes place (and in financial dealings only) in place of a second man, the testimony of one woman suffices. The only reason a second woman is called is "so that if either of two women should err in memory, then one may remind the other."[299] Moreover, while Wilders attempts to convey that two women are *always* called for in all testimonies, the Qur'an demonstrates that a second woman is called only in financial matters—nowhere else. But before delving into the need to call a second woman, it is necessary to understand the full context of the verse in question.

First, the Qur'an directs that financial transactions be written down to protect both parties. Second, the Qur'an protects the borrower from exploitation by giving him or her the right to dictate the terms. Third, the Qur'an shows consideration for those borrowers of "low understanding" or who are "weak" or "unable [...] to dictate," by stipulating a representative in their best interests. Fourth, not one but multiple people are called to bear witness for the borrower's and lender's protection. Finally—and getting to the crux of this discussion—in terms of calling witnesses, the Qur'an says:

> And call two witnesses from among your men; and if two men be not available, then a man and two women, of such as you like as witnesses, *so that if* either of two women should err in memory, then one may remind the other. And the witnesses should not refuse when they are called.[300]

Thus, the Qur'an does not command both women to testify but instead elucidates an "if/then" clause. The more accurate question, then,

---

299. Mirza Tahir Ahmad, Khalifatul Masih IV, "Ask Islam." November 17, 1983, accessed August 15, 2012. http://www2.alislam.org/askislam/inp3/MEI_19841117_08.inp3.

300. Qur'an 2:283. (Emphasis added.)

should be that if one woman's testimony shall suffice, why does the Qur'an even bother calling two women in the first place?

The Qur'an itself answers this question: the purpose of calling two women is so that "if either of the two should err in memory, then one may remind the other."[301] This, like the previous four stipulations in the verse, is also for the protection of the borrower (and lender), and reflects a historical and present-day reality that Wilders ignores (or is wholly ignorant of). In seventh-century Arabia, illiteracy abounded, and women were not accustomed to financial and business dealings—largely because the pre-Islamic misogynist society did not allow women to partake substantively in financial affairs. Women like Hadhrat Khadija[ra] who ran profitable trade businesses were exceptions.

But even today, seven hundred million women worldwide (one in every five) are illiterate.[302] Women are marginalized in societies across the globe, unable to participate fully in the economy. In 2012, American women earned only $.79 for every $1 an American man earned.[303] Thus, Islam granted women unprecedented legal rights in participating in financial dealings, and this verse demonstrates that process.

This verse affords a female witness the *option* of conferring with another person. If, however, the first female witness testifies of her own accord, she has every right to do so. Nothing in the Qur'an or ahadith stipulates that her testimony alone is not enough or that she is obliged to confer with the second female witness. Thus, if during some financial matter—which I remind the reader is the only place this teaching ap-

---

301. Qur'an 2:283.

302. UNESCO Institute for Statistics, *Adult and Youth Literacy*, September 2011, accessed August 15, 2012. http:// www.uis.unesco.org/FactSheets/Documents/FS16-2011-Literacy-EN.pdf.

303 PolitiFact.com, "Tim Kaine says Virginia women earn 79 cents to every $1 made by men," June 6, 2012, accessed August 15, 2012. http://www.politifact.com/virginia/statements/2012/jun/15/tim-kaine/tim-kaine-says-virginia-women-earn-79-cents-every-/.

plies—one man and one woman testify, then the testimony of both is equal. Its weight is determined not on gender but on accuracy and truthfulness, just as if two men testified or two women testified.

For women, this teaching developed access to, and successful participation in, political and economic life. It is peculiar that as of 2014, the three largest Muslim countries in the world—Indonesia, Bangladesh and Pakistan—have all had female heads of state, unlike the Netherlands or America.[304] Over time, Muslim women have been able to gain stronger understandings of financial matters—something of which pre-Islam misogynistic societies had deprived them.

In short, contrary to Wilders's claim, nothing in Islam requires or even suggests "two female witnesses for one male witness." Those Muslim majority nations that impose this unjust requirement commit a grave crime against women specifically and society at large. I implore them to repeal this discriminatory practice and instead adhere to the honest and just example that the Qur'an implores.

---

304. Megawati Sukarnoputri, president of Indonesia from 2001–2004; Khaleda Zia, prime minister of Bangladesh from 1991–1996 and 2001–2006; Hasina Wazed, prime minister of Bangladesh from 1996–2001 and 2009–present; Benazir Bhutto, prime minister of Pakistan from 1988–1990 and 1993–1996.

ALLEGATION 34

Islam Requires a Female Rape Victim to Produce Four Witnesses

Wilders rightly laments that, "some Islamic states consider female rape victims to be adulterers liable to be stoned to death."[305] However, he explains this by misrepresenting a verse of the Qur'an: "This stems from the Koran's injunction that a female rape victim has to present four male witnesses to support her claim that she has been raped."[306] In reality, nothing in Islamic jurisprudence supports Wilders's (or the so-called Muslim government's) belief.

REFERENCE: Qur'an 24:14.

RESPONSE: Before even delving into this response, let me make one thing clear at the onset. In Islam, rape is a crime and one of the most horrific crimes imaginable. Thus, those who commit rape are criminals and Islam demands the state or governing authority hold them criminally liable. Moreover, rape is never the fault of anyone but the rapist. That clarified, let's move on to repudiate Wilders's baseless allegation.

The verse in question actually reads: "Why did not those, *who gave currency to this charge*, bring four witnesses to *prove* it? Since they have not brought the *required* witnesses, they are indeed liars in the sight of Allah."[307] As the reader will soon see, this verse has nothing to do with

305. Wilders, *Marked for Death*, 49.

306. bid., 59.

307. Qur'an 24:14.

rape—which is a criminal act. Instead, this verses addresses adultery—which is not a criminal act—and the Islamic teaching to *not* expose people's private lives.

First, Islam is a religion of modesty. Sexual behavior is considered a private matter, not for public display. Accordingly, this verse calling for four witnesses *protects* women and upholds Islamic ideals of modesty and chastity. Of note, Islamic modesty derives its core principles from the example set forth by the woman that the Qur'an recognizes as the greatest woman of all time—Mary[ra] Mother of Jesus[as]. Islam teaches that God chose Mary[ra] to be the mother of the Messiah due to her unmatched piety, righteousness, and chastity. When Mary[ra] conceived Jesus[sa], she was unjustly accused of unchaste behavior though no person had a shred of evidence to prove such an accusation. Accordingly, the Qur'an forbids that any woman should face accusations of unchaste behavior without a minimum of four witnesses. But this is just one part of the equation.

Next, as mentioned this verse does not address rape; it addresses those who accuse women of unchaste behavior. If, for example, someone accuses a woman of adultery, then he or she must produce four truthful witnesses to corroborate the accusation. Failing that, meaning if the accuser only produces one, two, or three witnesses, then the minimum threshold of proof is unfulfilled, and the accuser is deemed a liar. The Qur'an prescribes harsh punishments for those who make such false allegations against women.

It is worth noting that the same rules apply when someone accuses a man of adultery—i.e. four witnesses must substantiate the claim. Wilders ignores this altogether. Thus, I am focusing on accusations against women because it more directly addresses Wilders's allegation.

But why four witnesses? For context, consider that for crimes of murder or rape, Islam teaches that even one witness or the rape victim's testimony alone can suffice. Why then, would Islam suddenly require four witnesses for accusations of adultery? It is crucial to understand the overall Islamic philosophy behind requiring an astounding four witnesses. The fact is that Islam does not allow just anyone impose him or herself into another person's private life. While Islam considers adultery a sin, it does not permit individuals from invading another person's privacy rights and exposing their private behavior. Indeed, the reader should recall the earlier discussion on Islam's immense emphasis on privacy rights.

On the other hand, however, if a woman (or man) becomes so open about their sexual promiscuity that they display it openly, Islam sets a limit because now that once private behavior has a public impact. That limit is described as "Why did not those, who gave currency to this charge, bring four witnesses to prove it?" That is, if someone's private behavior is exposed due to his or her own display (as evidenced by four truthful witnesses), rather than through anyone invading that person's privacy, only then does it become a public matter liable to public response. On the contrary, whatever a person's private behavior, though Islam may frown upon it, it is a private matter between that person and God, and therefore must be kept private.

But Islam's requirement of proving adultery with four witnesses has another important application. In the West, a common insult to demean and demonize women is "slut-shaming." This derogatory term describes an attempt to make a woman feel guilty about her private life or personal choices. The Islamic practice of requiring four truthful witnesses to levy an accusation of unchaste behavior not only prevents this demonization from occurring, it also better ensures that the only time a woman's private life is exposed is when she chooses to do so of her own accord. Otherwise, Islam categorically forbids any person from invading or commenting on a woman's private life. No other scripture affords women this level of protection. Indeed, nothing in the Qur'an or ahadith validate Wilders's highly offensive allegation that a woman must provide four witnesses to prove she was raped. Extremists ascribing to Islam who hold this belief commit a grave injustice against women.

It is the height of absurdity to suggest that a rape *victim* should face punishment. On the contrary, numerous ahadith related to rape prove that the woman is not to be punished under any circumstance. Abdul

Jabbar ibn Wa'il ibn Hujr reported on the authority of his father that a woman was raped in the time of Prophet Muhammad[sa]. Prophet Muhammad punished the rapist but prescribed no punishment for the victim.[308] In another hadith, Alqamah ibn Wa'il Kindi reports that Prophet Muhammad[sa] punished a rapist but not the victim.[309] I challenge Wilders to cite any hadith in which Prophet Muhammad[sa] punished the victim, or a Qur'anic verse that prescribes such injustice.

Wilders also makes a side allegation that "Mohammad so hated his daughters that even after their deaths he called them 'filth and whores' and ranted that someone should defecate 'on their graves.'"[310] This shameless lie reflects only Wilders's ignoble imagination, nothing more. True to his calling, Wilders makes this outlandish claim without citing any Islamic source. No Qur'an, no hadith, no Islamic historian. Instead, Wilders cites a *Wall Street Journal* news article, which itself provides no references.

Contrary to Wilders's pathetic claim, Prophet Muhammad[sa] loved his daughters immensely and implored the same of his companions. When one of his daughters died, he directed Muslim women to wash her body thoroughly to give her a clean, dignified, and proper burial.[311] Whenever his daughter, Hadhrat Fatima, entered the room, he would stand in her honor, offer her his seat, and then sit next to her.[312] He gave

---

308. Imam Muhammad ibn 'Isa Tirmidhi, "Chapter 22, #1458" in *Jami' Tirmidhi* vol. 1, (Karachi: Darul Ishaat Urdu Bazar, 2007), 620.

309. Ibid., #1459, 621.

310. Wilders, *Marked for Death*, 51–52.

311. Sahih Jami' Bukhari 2.347, narrated Um 'Atiyya: "When we washed the deceased daughter of the Prophet, he said to us, while we were washing her, 'Start the bath from the right side and from the parts which are washed in ablution.'" Sahih Jami' Bukhari 2.348, narrated Um 'Atiyya: "The daughter of the Prophet expired, and he said to us, 'Wash her three or five times, or more if you see it necessary, and when you finish, notify me.' So, (when we finished) we informed him and he unfastened his waist-sheet and told us to shroud her in it."

312 Sahih Jami' Bukhari Hadith 8.301, narrated by Aisha, Mother of the Believers.

her the most honorable rank as "chief of the believing women in Paradise," demonstrating both his love for her and that women would certainly attain paradise.[313] He gave the glad tidings of paradise to his companions who raised their daughters virtuously and with honor.[314] This is the man Wilders claims loathed his daughters? Wilders's claim is nothing more than a lie.

In short, it is worth repeating that Wilders sadly judges Islam by the actions of a small group of Muslims who have twisted the religion to suit their own ends. Yes, there exist misguided and barbaric clerics who believe that a woman who is raped must produce four witnesses. As mentioned earlier, Prophet Muhammad[sa] preemptively dissociated himself from such clerics and called them the "worst creatures on Earth." I condemn their false interpretations and condemn their barbaric actions, and appeal to them and their followers to resort to reason. It is unfortunate that Wilders continues to look to these worst creatures in promoting his false narrative.

---

313 Ibid.

314 Sahih Jami' Muslim 2631.

ALLEGATION 35

Islam Teaches Misogynistic Inheritance Laws

Wilders takes issue with sons inheriting twice as much as daughters in Islam and repeats this complaint again in Chapter 10 of his book.[315] He cites a British Islamic family law ruling [Sharia court]: "The Shariah court gave the sons twice as much as the daughters, in accordance with the Koranic pronouncement that a woman is only worth half a man."[316]

REFERENCE: Qur'an 4:12.

RESPONSE: Wilders is correct that the Qur'an prescribes, in general, that a male inherits twice what a female inherits. His unwarranted personal commentary that this is unjust, or that the Qur'an pronounces that a woman is only worth half a man, however, is incorrect.

When we study Prophet Muhammad's[sa] example, we find a remarkable and unique financial philosophy heavily in favor of women. For example, Islam does not impose any financial obligation on women—none whatsoever. The Qur'an primarily charges men—not women—with being the breadwinners for their families.[317] Muslim men are financially accountable for and liable to their wives, children, and parents. Likewise, while women have a right to their husbands' incomes, husbands have no right to their wives' incomes. Anything a husband earns, he must spend on his family to provide for its members. Anything a wife earns, she has full right to spend on whatever and whomsoever she pleases—or not

---

315. Wilders, *Marked for Death*, 169.
316. Ibid.
317. Qur'an 4:35.

spend it at all. Of course, a wife has the right to choose to spend on her husband and her family, but her husband has no right to oblige or compel her to do so. Should a wife earn more than her husband, he has no right to demand she pay any family expenses. Upon marriage, a man must give his wife a handsome dowry as a gift, for her sole use and at her discretion, while she has no financial obligation to him. Therefore, because men have the greater financial burden, they receive a correspondingly higher inheritance.

A simple exercise demonstrates that this is practical and still heavily in favor of women. Let us assume that a family comprises parents, a son, and daughter. They have $1500 in the bank. When the parents die, the son receives $1000 in inheritance and the daughter receives $500. Islam obliges the son to spend his $1000 on his family. His actual share of the $1000 is likely a few hundred, if anything at all, because he is obligated to distribute it among his wife and children. Comparatively, of the $500 the daughter receives, she keeps every penny. She only shares with her family what she chooses to share. Even if the two children are not yet married, ultimately the son will be Islamically obliged to spend his finances, income, and inheritance on his future family, while the daughter will not.

Moreover, consider that people inherit perhaps a few times in their lives, while they earn throughout their lives. Thus, even if one were to argue that a man's double inheritance is somehow unjust, the reality is that by the same logic, it is unjust that men must share their wealth with their families throughout every paycheck of their entire lives, while women may keep every penny they ever earn. It sounds nonsensical to suggest it is unjust for men to share their wealth with their families, but I present the point only to demonstrate that even this fundamental obligation is something men must take primary (and, if needed, exclusive) responsibility for. Meanwhile, Islam holds women free from this burden altogether.

Thus, nothing here indicates that the daughter is "worth half" of the son. Rather, this is a practical law that ensures a male receives a correspondingly higher amount to share with his wife and children due to his significantly higher financial obligation, while a female receives a substantive amount exclusively for herself.

Finally, while expectedly Wilders does not delve into it, it is crucial to note that Islam gave women rights of inheritance fourteen hundred years ago. This is a right that women pre-Islam were not afforded. Likewise, it is a right that women in the West only recently received through civil law—not religion.

ALLEGATION 36

Islam Confers Superior Divorce Rights on Men Than on Women

Wilders openly lies when alleging, "A man can also divorce his wife at will, even if she is blameless, while a woman has no equivalent power toward her husband."[318] Nothing in Islam substantiates this claim. In fact, the Qur'an specifically rejects this myth.

REFERENCE: None.

RESPONSE: I find it increasingly difficult to believe that Wilders has read the Qur'an at all, let alone the "many many times" he professes. Had Wilders made it past its chapter 2, he would have read, "And they (the women) have rights similar to those (of men) over them in equity."[319] Wilders's unsubstantiated allegation holds no water and finds no validation in the Qur'an or in the hadith, and in fact is specifically repudiated.

When a Muslim man and woman are married or divorced, the woman is afforded a *wali* (a protector). Critics baselessly assert that because the woman must inform her wali of her desire to divorce, she is under a form of oppression. On the contrary, the wali's function is to ensure a woman's rights are not being usurped and that an unjust man is held accountable for his actions. A woman is not required to inform her wali of her intent to divorce; only the court—just as a woman today must

---

318. Wilders, *Marked for Death*, 50.

319. Qur'an 2:229.

inform the court of her intent to divorce. In fact, the concept of wali is ingrained in contemporary society vis-à-vis lawyers. A lawyer represents his or her client to ensure the client's rights are protected against the un-just actions of an opposing party. Islam, recognizing that women have been historically oppressed and disenfranchised, assigns women—not men—an advocate, and does so without any need for consideration, i.e. payment. Far from oppression, this is in fact an advanced teaching that the rest of the world did not embrace until centuries later.

That in mind, when a woman chooses to divorce, she may exercise that equal right through her wali. This does several things. First, should a woman choose divorce because she is in an unhappy marriage, her wali removes her from the situation. That is, her wali deals with her husband directly; she does not, which affords her peace of mind. And, if the hus-band were abusive, it would not be wise for her to confront him with a divorce, as it might well result in more violence. Thus, her wali's in-volvement affords her physical protection. Furthermore, the wali en-sures—whether in marriage or divorce—that a woman has not been coerced or is making a coerced decision, the same way a lawyer would for a client today. Additionally, the wali ensures a woman is making an in-formed decision, again, just as a lawyer would for a client today.

Finally, as the wali is often a woman's father, brother, or uncle, she is assured appropriate accommodations should she need it, should she re-move herself from the marital home until the divorce is finalized and marital assets can be appropriately divided. Thus, a wali protects a wom-an's rights even more so than a lawyer, because a wali provides for more of her rights and needs beside simply the financial ones.

Several ahadith also demonstrate that women have the equivalent power as men to divorce and can do so even if their husbands are blame-less.

Jamilah bint Saul[ra], for example, complained to Prophet Muham-mad[sa] that although she found no fault in her husband's character (Thabit bin Qais[ra]), she simply could not endure to live with him. Thereupon, Prophet Muhammad[sa] granted her a divorce.[320] Of note, Prophet Muhammad[sa] required no approval from Thabit bin Qais[ra] before granting the divorce.

Likewise, Hadhrat Ayesha[ra] reports, "Allah's Apostle gave us the option (to remain with him or to be divorced) and we selected Allah and His Apostle."[321] So when Prophet Muhammad[sa] demonstrated that his wives had unilateral rights to divorce even him, on what grounds can Wilders dare assert otherwise?

One point remains. Wilders defends the Bible as a progressive book compared to the Qur'an, despite being an atheist or agnostic. In the same BBC *Hardtalk* interview I mentioned in the introduction, Wilders stated:

> There are so many differences between on one side Christianity, Judaism, and the other side [Islam]. It is complete nonsense to [allege that you can justify violence and discrimination from the Bible]. The Old Testament has been followed by a more moderate New Testament. There has not been any new Koran so far.[322]

Wilders forgets that in Europe and the United States, it was not the Bible that gave women the right to divorce, but secular and civil law. For example, women in the United Kingdom gained the right to divorce only in 1857—and even then only if their husbands were cruel to them. British women did not gain unilateral divorce rights until 1891—a full thirteen hundred years after Islam granted such rights to women. But cruelty from their husbands did not spare American women. In a heartbreaking 1862 North Carolina case, a woman petitioned the court to

---

320. *Sahih Jami' Bukhari*, vol. 7, Book 63, #199.

321. *Sahih Jami' Bukhari*, vol. 7, Book 63, #188.

322. Wilders, interview by Stephen Sackur, BBC *Hardtalk*.

grant her a divorce after her husband mercilessly horsewhipped her. The North Carolina Supreme Court's chief justice denied her, stating, "The law gives the husband power to use such a degree of force necessary to make the wife behave and know her place."[323] French women could not legally divorce until 1885.[324] Women in Latin America—a largely Christian region of the world—could not divorce until the late nineteen or early twentieth centuries—depending on the country.

Moreover, as far as Wilders's claim that the New Testament is more moderate than the Old Testament and likewise more moderate than the Qur'an, I cite Mark 10:12: "And if she divorces her husband and marries another man, she commits adultery." As such, to avoid the risk of adultery, certain Christian denominations to this day have banned divorce altogether. Wilders is silent on these matters but instead gives them the blanket approvals "progressive" and "tolerant"—more progressive and tolerant, apparently, than the Qur'an, which granted women equal divorce rights fourteen hundred years ago.

Islam was the first, and arguably the only ancient religion to afford women equal divorce rights. Indeed, the West has only recently "caught up" to Islam in this regard. Wilders's insistence otherwise is in shameless denial of undeniable evidence and all civilized persons should divorce him or herself from such propaganda.

---

323. Heidi Hemming and Julie Hemming Savage, *Women Making America* (Clotho Press, 2009),76–78.

324. Richard J. Evans, *The Feminists: Women's Emancipation Movements in Europe, America and Australasia, 1840–1920.*

ALLEGATION 37

Islam Allows a Man to Beat His Wife

Wilders writes, "In light of the inferior position Islam assigns to women, it should be no surprise that the Koran approves of wife beating."[325] To the reader I say, it should be no surprise that Wilders has made yet another baseless allegation.

REFERENCE: Qur'an 4:35.

RESPONSE: Earlier I demonstrated that Islam views men and women as equal human beings with equitable responsibilities and rights. Now, I further state clearly and directly that Islam does not endorse, approve, or permit a man to beat his wife. In fact, Islam specifically rejects this behavior. To elaborate, I begin by presenting the full verse in question, which reads:

> Men are guardians over women because Allah has made some of them excel others, and because they (men) spend of their wealth. So virtuous women *are those who* are obedient, and guard the secrets *of their husbands* with Allah's protection. And *as for* those on whose part you fear disobedience, admonish them and leave them alone in their beds, and chastise them. Then if they obey you, seek not a way against them. Surely, Allah is High, Great.[326]

---

325. Wilders, *Marked for Death*, 50. (Emphasis added.)

326. Qur'an 4:35

Before defining the exact meaning of the term *wadribu-hunna* ["and chastise them"], it is logically important and necessary to understand the context of the verse. The nuclear family is a fundamental feature of Islam in which men and women are encouraged to embrace their respective equal-but-different roles, with women as wives and mothers and men as husbands and fathers.

Like all human relationships, the husband-wife relationship is complex and at times given to disagreement. This verse in question, and the one following, prescribes a means of addressing that disagreement with conflict resolution—not violence. Against the backdrop of divorce, which is the most hated act permitted in Islam,[327] verses 35 and 36 prescribe sequential steps that should be taken to achieve reconciliation between husband and wife. Nothing in the verse is a general permission allowable in every circumstance. Rather, it is conditional—much like the state of mortal hunger, which must be present for a believer to have recourse to the consumption of pork. In such situations, pork can be eaten as an alternative to starvation until other food can be found, after which the eating of pork is once again forbidden.[328] Likewise, the actions described in verses 35 and 36 are permissible only when a serious disagreement exists and grave disobedience is feared.

So what are these conditions? The wife must have first engaged in some form of disobedience. Arabic lexicon provides that what is translated as "disobedience" means that the wife has either deserted her husband unjustly or attempted to destroy the family altogether. In other words, "fearing disobedience" does not mean a husband is given carte blanche rights should he disagree with his wife. Nothing in Islam supports this perspective—which I readily admit some extremists believe. Rather, it applies to specific behavior well beyond difference of opinion.

---

327. "The most hated permissible act before Allah is divorce." *Sunan Abu Dawud*, #1863.

328. Qur'an 2:174.

Once that prerequisite is fulfilled, 4:35 prescribes admonition as the first step toward reconciliation. If a husband simply admonishes his wife of his disapproval and she concedes her previous behavior, no more steps are necessary.

If admonition should fail, however, the Qur'an prescribes the second step—separating beds. Typically, this period is understood to not exceed three months. If either side is behaving unreasonably, this period affords time for reflection and reconciliation.

If, however, neither admonition nor separating of beds is successful and the wife continues to engage in inappropriate behavior—as described above—step three is permitted. That is, chastisement—the meaning of which is explained below. If chastisement fails, the next verse prescribes arbitration. The period of chastisement is fleeting, as evidenced by the grammatical construct of the *fi'l amr* (imperative), and it is to take place between separation of beds and arbitration.[329] Failing arbitration, the Qur'an allows for divorce—revocable, then irrevocable. With this background, let us proceed to understand the exact meaning of "chastise."

The root *da-ra-ba* is one of the richest words in the Arabic language. Its proper definition must be understood within the context of its use in a sentence. The average entry for an Arabic word in *Lane's Lexicon*, for example, covers a half page. The entry for *da-ra-ba* covers six full pages and includes hundreds of meanings.[330] Wilders, like many anti-Islam critics and like extremists purportedly subscribing to Islam, choose the most egregious for their own purposes.

In Islam, "chastising," if understood as physical, can amount to no more than a soft push or weightless tap—the kind used to get the atten-

---

329. When multiple verbs are separated by "and" (*wa*), it is an accepted convention that they should take place in sequence.

330. Edward W. Lane and Stanley Lane-Poole, *An Arabic-English Lexicon*, vol. 5 (New York: Cosmo Classics, 2011), 1777–83.

tion of a person but never to cause injury. This is derived through a simple study of ahadith.

First, Prophet Muhammad[sa] never hit his wives. Hadhrat Ayesha[ra] narrates, "Allah's Messenger never hit anything with his hand ever, except when fighting in the path of Allah. Nor did he ever hit a servant or a woman."[331] He did, however, hit his companions—a push or gentle tap on the body—to get their attention: "The Messenger of Allah, may Allah bless him, hit the chest of Umar bin Khattab with his hand three times when he embraced Islam and he said, 'O Allah remove the malice from his heart and replace it with faith.'"[332] Hence, even the actual hitting was out of love and friendship—as close friends of a variety of cultures do to this day—not anger or malice.

Then we have the following hadith: "[Jarir] made this complaint to [Prophet Muhammad[sa]]: 'I cannot sit upon the horse with firmness,' whereupon [Prophet Muhammad[sa]] struck his chest with his hand and prayed: 'O Allah, make him steadfast and rightly guided.'"[333]

As for those who proceed to get their wives' attention in this manner, Prophet Muhammad[sa] said three things: it should be done so lightly as not to leave a mark;[334] it should cause no injury to the wife; and that those who do chastise their wives are not the best of men.[335]

Prophet Muhammad[sa], whose example the Qur'an commands Muslims to follow,[336] advised against any hitting of women. "Feed them from your food, and dress them from (the same class and quality of) your

---

331. Ibn Majah.

332. *Sahih Jami' Muslim,* Book 4, #1787.

333. *Sahih Jami' Muslim,* Book 31, #6051.

334. Long Commentary of the Holy Qur'an under 4:35, from *Jami' at-Tirmidhi, Kitab ar-Rida.* See www.alislam.org/quran.

335. Long Commentary of the Holy Qur'an under 4:35, from *Tafsir Ibn-e-Kathir,* iii.

336. Qur'an 3:33, 3:133; 4:60; 5:93; 8:21, 8:47.

clothes, and *do not chastise* them, nor ascribe them to ugliness."[337] The Arabic for "chastise" in this hadith, *tadribu-hunna*, is from the same root as that in the Qur'anic verse under discussion: *da-ra-ba*. Likewise, in another place Mu'awiyah al-Qushayri reports, "I went to the Messenger of Allah (saaw) and asked him: What do you say about our wives? He replied: Give them food that you have for yourself, and clothe them by which you clothe yourself, *and do not beat them*, and do not revile them."[338] Thus, in clear and direct terms, Prophet Muhammad[sa] forbade Muslims to beat women.

Furthermore, had the verse 4:35 intended to mean physical harm, the word *hatumhoo* was available. *Hatumhoo* indicates to strike with the intent to cause pain or injury. On the contrary, the Qur'an does not use *hatumhoo* but instead *da-ra-ba*. This particular word choice further demonstrates an action that does *not* cause any form of physical injury. Thus, the facts demonstrate that Prophet Muhammad[sa] forbade ever beating or harming women, never beat or harmed women himself, and taught that Islam does not allow such a thing. To continue to insist that Islam endorses beating women is to deliberately remain oblivious to Prophet Muhammad's[sa] example and basic Arabic grammar.

Finally, we cannot forget that husbands also have obligations to their wives, and wives have rights over their husbands. Thus, as for a woman who fears the disobedience of her husband, Islam affords her an even easier route—to demand her husband reform his behavior or consequently divorce him. As thoroughly explained in the previous section, Islam afforded women divorce rights fourteen hundred years ago— rights that Western nations have only recently granted women through civil law improvements. Wilders unfortunately ignores the deep wisdom behind 4:35 and incorrectly assumes it permits men to beat women. On the contrary, this verse forces all men to communicate their complaints

---

337. *Sunan Abu Dawud*, vol. 2, #2144 (Lebanon: Dar al-Kutub al-Ilmiyyah, 2008), 230.

338. *Sunan Abu Dawud* 11:2139.

effectively, stop and reflect for several months to cool down, and channel their anger in a manner that causes no harm to women. Thus, this verse taken as a whole focuses on anger management, reformation, and reconciliation—a fact Prophet Muhammad[sa] himself demonstrated.

ALLEGATION 38

Islam Opposes
Scientific Advancement and Free Inquiry

Wilders next alleges that Islam is anti-modern and anti-innovation; it is anti-theology, anti-philosophy, anti-rationalism, and against the spirit of free inquiry.[339]

REFERENCE: Daniel Pipes.[340] Urbain Vermulen.

RESPONSE: Wilders—whose Arabic expertise is nonexistent—conflates *bid'ah* with *ibtida'* when alleging, based on his "original research," that "Islam is extremely wary of *bida [sic]*, or innovation."

Stemming from the same root, *ba-da-'a*, the former (*bid'ah*) is a term of Islamic jurisprudence that denotes corruption of religion through the creation of false beliefs and harmful practices. Examples include prostrating before or praying to anyone besides Allah (e.g., the tombs of saintly Muslims); consecrating sham "temporary marriages" (*mut'ah*) to fulfill physical pleasure; and carrying out acts of terrorism in the name of Islam. These harmful innovations have no place in Islam, and it is to these acts that *bid'ah* refers.

In contrast, *ibtida'*, or innovation stemming from reflection, research, and development designed to progress society, is highly encouraged in Islam.

---

339. Wilders, *Marked for Death*, 54, 70.

340. For a rebuttal of Daniel Pipes, see "In Defense of Islam: Confronting the Critics" in *The Muslim Sunrise* (Summer 2012). http://www.muslimsunrise.com.

The fact is that the Qur'an itself repeatedly calls upon Muslims to ponder and reflect on hundreds of different occasions: "*This is* a Book which We have revealed to thee, full of blessings, that they may reflect over its verses, and that those gifted with understanding may take heed."[341]

In another chapter we read: "This is a sufficient admonition for mankind *that they may benefit by it,* and that they may be warned thereby, and that they may know that He is the only One God, and that those possessed of understanding may ponder."[342]

Again, God explains inward reflection as one purpose of the Qur'an: "Allah sets forth similitudes for men that they may reflect."[343] Likewise, Muslims are encouraged to constantly recite chapter 20:115 of the Qur'an, which clearly declares, "Oh my Lord, increase me in my knowledge."

Remarkably, secular innovation throughout Islamic history has come as a *result* of adherence to the Islamic faith, not departure from it. Wilders himself grudgingly admits as much when conceding, "Islam also made a contribution to mathematics...because it is useful for astronomy and for determining the Qibla, the direction toward the Ka'aba shrine in Mecca, which Muslims must face when they pray."[344]

But Islam's contribution to mathematics is but the tip of the iceberg. Dr. Abdus Salam, a theoretical physicist and devout Muslim, won the Nobel Prize in Physics in 1979. Known for his work on the electroweak theory as well as the magnetic photon, vector meson, supersymmetry, and the grand unified theory, he was without doubt one of the brightest minds of the twentieth century. His landmark work paved the way for the recent Higgs boson discovery. Dr. Salam credited his success to the

341. Qur'an 38:30.
342. Qur'an 14:53.
343. Qur'an 14:26.
344. Wilders, *Marked for Death,* 57.

Holy Qur'an. "The Holy Qur'an enjoins us," he wrote, "to reflect on the verities of Allah's created laws of nature; however, that our generation has been privileged to glimpse a part of His design is a bounty and a grace for which I render thanks with a humble heart."[345]

In another article, Dr. Abdus Salam wrote:

> According to Dr. Mohammed Aijazul Khatib of Damascus University, nothing could emphasize the importance of sciences more than the remark that "in contrast to 250 verses which are legislative, some 750 verses of the Holy Quran—almost one-eighth of it—exhort the believers to study Nature—to reflect, to make the best use of reason and to make the scientific enterprise an integral part of the community's life." The Holy Prophet of Islam—peace be upon him—said that it was the "bounden duty of every Muslim—man and woman—to acquire knowledge."[346]

Although Wilders asserts that "thinkers like Ibn-e-Sina and Ibn-e-Rushd are exceptions," the truth is that they are simply among the most recognized Islamic thinkers in the West. Throughout history, from Ibn Sina and Ibn Rushd to Abdus Salam, devout Muslims have unlocked doors to humanity's progress through research and study, invention, and innovation, inspired by Islamic teachings. Muhammad al-Khwarizmi's (circa 780–850 AD) contributions to mathematics, astronomy, and geography are legendary—even if Wilders only credits him with being the namesake for the word algorithm.

Throughout Islamic history, and most remarkably in the universally recognized Golden Age of Islam, Muslims have made significant contri-

---

345 See www.nobelprize.org/nobel_prizes/physics/laureates/1979/salam-bio.html. Accessed June 6, 2012.

346 Abdus Salam, A. Kidwai and C. H. Lai, *Ideals and Realities: Selected Essays of Abdus Salam*, 3rd ed. (London: World Scientific Publishing Co., 1989), 343–44.

butions to mathematics, sciences, and the arts. Abbas ibn Firnas (810–887) was an Andalusian inventor and scientist who created magnification lenses for vision and undertook early attempts at controlled flight a thousand years before the Wright Brothers. Omar Khayyam (1048–1131) was a Persian mathematician and poet who developed still-standing quadratic equations. And Dr. Salam is not the only twentieth-century Muslim thinker of note. Dr. Cheikh Anta Diop (1923–1986), for example, was a historian, anthropologist, and physicist, considered one of the greatest African historians of the twentieth century. (The interested reader may learn more at www.1001Inventions.com.)

Islam criticizes those philosophies with an atheistic or blasphemous bent that argue that there is no God (or an imperfect one). But why should this be any surprise? After all, Islam came to establish and argue the reality of God, not His absence. Reason, however, is an important part of Islamic thought. The practice of *ijtihad*, or decision-making in Islamic law based upon its primary sources, has helped to keep Islam relevant for fourteen hundred years and will keep it so far into the future.

Regarding theology, no religion in the world—including Christianity, despite its six-hundred-year head start—has a more developed theological study than Islam. Its sciences, including *'ilm ul-Qur'an* (Qur'anic science), *'ilm ul-Hadith* (hadith science), and *usul ul-fiqh* (methodologies of jurisprudence), have helped guide Muslims to preserve and promote their religion since its inception.

Finally, I present a few important ahadith to demonstrate the immense emphasis that Prophet Muhammad[sa] placed on attaining knowledge and education. He declared, "Seeking Knowledge is obligatory upon every Muslim male and Muslim female."[347] Likewise, teaching knowledge to the next generation is a crucial part of Islam. "Whoever is asked about a knowledge that he knows about and then hides it and keeps it away, he will be bridled on the Day of Judgment with a bridle of

---

347. Related by Ibn 'Adiyy, Al-Bayhaqi & Al-Tabarani.

fire."[348] He added, "The cure for ignorance is to question."[349] Finally, Prophet Muhammad[sa] placed immense emphasis on Muslims to expand their horizons and worldviews: "Seek knowledge even [if you must travel to] China."[350]

In short, the allegations Wilders asserts here are not only contrary to the clear direction provided in the Qur'an and ahadith, but also contrary to established world history. I encourage the reader to research Islam and science to truly understand the vast contribution Muslim scientists have made to the world and humanity at large.

---

348. Related by Ahmad, Abu Dawud, and Al-Tirmidhi.

349. Reported by Ahmad, Abu Dawud, and Ibn Maajah. (Hasan).

350. Related by Anas by al-Bayhaqi in Shu`ab al-Imaan and al-Madkhal, Ibn `Abd al-Barr in Jami` Bayaan al-`Ilm, and al-Khatib.

ALLEGATION 39

The Qur'an Has 6,360 Verses

Wilders writes that the ordering of the Qur'an consists of 6,360 verses and is based on length from longest to shortest.[351] He is wrong on both accounts.

REFERENCE: None.

RESPONSE: Critics have alleged that humans arranged the Qur'an as opposed to God Himself. This is incorrect. The Qur'an actually consists of 6,348 verses and is arranged by divine guidance and subject matter, not mere length.[352] The first chapter is only seven verses while the second is 287. Each successive chapter is related to the preceding in terms of subject matter. Accordingly, chapter 1 includes the prayer, "Guide us on the right path."[353] Chapter 2 then furnishes an answer of what the right path is, saying, "This is a perfect Book; there is no doubt in it; *it is* a guidance for the righteous."[354]

The conjugated verb *ihdina*, or "guide us," in the first chapter corresponds exactly to the word *huda*, or "guidance," in the second—both stemming from the same root: *ha-da*.[355] With regard to numbering,

---

351. Wilders, *Marked for Death*, 58.

352. For a detailed explanation, refer to, Mirza Bashir-ud-Din Mahmud Ahmad, *The Introduction to the Study of the Holy Qur'an* (Guildford: Islam International Publications Ltd., 1996), 368–71.

353. Qur'an 1:6.

354. Qur'an 2:3.

355. Hans Wehr, *A Dictionary of Modern Written Arabic*, 4th ed. (Urbana: Spoken Language Services, 1994), 1199

some Muslims follow the practice of counting the verse "In the Name of Allah, the Gracious, the Merciful" in every chapter in which it appears, which leads to a total of 6,348. Other Muslims exclude it in the numbering for all but the first chapter for a count of 6,236.

By any count, by claiming that the Qur'an has 6,360 verses, it appears Mr. Wilders has added a few of his own. What sort of Qur'anic study did Wilders perform that he cannot even count its verses properly?

ALLEGATION 40

Allah Is Unknowable and
Requires Unquestioned Submission

Wilders next claims that Islam's purpose is the total surrender of oneself
and others to the unknowable Allah, whom we must serve through total
obedience to the teachings of Muhammad[sa].[356]

REFERENCE: None.

RESPONSE: With the exception of the ridiculous notion that Allah is
unknowable (addressed shortly)—and perhaps replacing "surrender"
with "submission"—this might conceivably pass as a correct statement.
Indeed, all religions instruct believers to adhere completely to the will of
God Almighty. Pure, sinless prophets bring this message, and their example is to be followed closely. It appears that Wilders takes issue with
the basic concept of religion itself—again, not a surprise, considering his
agnosticism or atheism. In reality, Wilders's allegation is applicable
against all people of all faiths, not just against Muslims and Islam.

Accordingly, I would be remiss if I did not mention Wilders's hypocrisy here. As an atheist or agnostic with no appreciation for Christianity,
Wilders's views contradict Jesus Christ's[as] beautiful teachings. Yet in his
book—marketed to the conservative Christian community in America—he presents himself as a friend of Christians.

On the contrary, 75 percent of the twelve hundred Christian leaders
polled in the *Netherlands Dagblad*, a Christian-perspective daily news-

356. Wilders, *Marked for Death*, 60.

paper, say that Christians cannot vote for Wilders's political party.[357] One minister explained succinctly, "Wilders and the PVV's views contradict Christianity."

Indeed, Christians should be wary of joining forces with a hypocritical opportunist only for his anti-Islamic stance. It is no wonder that the vast majority of Christian leaders in his own country would not even cast a vote for him.

Regarding the allegation that "Allah is unknowable," the Qur'anic verse Wilders cites reads: "*He is* the Maker of the heavens and the earth. He has made for you pairs of your own selves, and of the cattle *also He has made* pairs. He multiplies you therein. There is nothing whatever like unto Him; and He is the All-Hearing, the All-Seeing."[358]

How this means Allah is unknowable is beyond me. The verse explains that Allah is unique in that He is the sole Creator of the Universe, and only He hears and sees all. This verse does not mean a Muslim cannot know Allah. Indeed, a primary reason why many Americans who convert to Islam do so is the clearer knowledge they gain of God through the Holy Qur'an and ahadith.

In Dawn's Early Light: Short Stories by American Converts to Islam,[359] Miguel David Caliz, a former Catholic Christian, writes:

I was always curious about Islam, but never got the chance to learn about it. Then I met an [Muslim] Imam named Rashid Ahmad. After three lessons, that is, about three Fridays, I knew I

---

357. "Christians can't vote for Wilders, say vicars," *Dutch News*, February 25, 2010, accessed June 3, 2012.
http://www.dutchnews.nl/news/archives/2010/02/christians_cant_vote_for_wilde.php.

358. Qur'an 42:12.

359. Majlis Khuddamul Ahmadiyya USA, *By the Dawn's Early Light: Short Stories by American Converts to Islam* (2008). http://www.alislam.org/library/books/Short-Stories-American-Converts-to-Islam.pdf.

was in the right place. They believed in what I believed: One God Who is the Creator of heaven and earth, Who also created the angels and everything in the universe, and has no partners, Who sent prophets for the benefit of the mankind, Who is Gracious, Merciful, and Just, among many other attributes.[360]

The Qur'an and ahadith contain more than a hundred attributes of Allah, which help us to know the One God. Through prayer, Muslims establish a direct relationship with Allah. Accordingly, the God of Islam promises: "And when My servants ask thee about Me, say: 'I am near. I answer the prayer of the supplicant when he prays to Me. So they should hearken to Me and believe in Me, that they may follow the right way.'"[361]

Knowledge does not fall on us through osmosis; rather, we must pursue it. Whether that knowledge is medicine, physics, law, hermeneutics, or spirituality—we must pursue it before we can attain it. We ask the reader to again reflect that Prophet Muhammad[sa] declared, "The cure for ignorance is to question."[362]

Wilders does not object to Islam's description of God so much as he objects to the idea of God in general. But—at the risk of sounding like a broken record—I already knew he would.

In any case, if a person does not have a direct, living relationship with God, if they do not experience true dreams, if their prayers are not regularly answered, and they do not see miracles and fulfillments of prophecies, they owe it to themselves to test this promise of Allah: He shall answer your prayer if you pray to Him—this is what Islam and indeed all religious teach. But the burden is on humankind to pursue the goal of knowing God. Indeed, Wilders's claim that the God of Islam is unknowable is a claim the Qur'an and ahadith thoroughly refute. It is only a re-

---

360. Ibid., 169–70.

361. Qur'an 2:187.

362. Reported by Ahmad, Abu Dawud, and Ibn Maajah. (Hasan).

flection of his own personal ignorance of God and in fact an attack on all religions in general.

ALLEGATION 41

Islam Teaches That God No Longer Reveals Himself

Wilders writes "Koran claims to be God's final revelation to man."[363]

REFERENCE: Qur'an 33:41.

RESPONSE: While the Qur'an states that Islam will be the final divine-ly revealed religion,[364] this is a far cry from alleging that revelation has ended altogether. Islam is a living religion, and God Almighty continues to communicate with His chosen ones on Earth now as He had done in times past. *Auliya* (saints), *mujaddidin* (reformers) and holy people in the *ummah* have received revelation and have experienced true dreams and visions for fourteen hundred years.[365]

Hadhrat Mirza Ghulam Ahmad[as] of Qadian, the promised Messiah, directly answers Wilders's allegation:

---

363. Wilders, *Marked for Death*, 60.

364. Qur'an 5:4.

365. Numerous Muslim saints—most of whom are well-regarded by mainstream Mus-lims—have recorded their revelations and visions in their writings throughout the fourteen-hundred-year history of Islam. It merits mention that mainstream Muslims believe that God shall raise the Imam Mahdi and Jesus[as], son of Mary, as two sepa-rate individuals in the latter days (ignoring the Holy Prophet's[sa] hadith, "La mahdi il-la 'Isa," i.e., "There is no Mahdi but Isa"), yet they paradoxically believe revelation ended with Prophet Muhammad[sa], so that these two men of God, prophets, shall go about the earth without receiving revelation from God—a completely indefensible position under the concept and history of Islamic prophethood (*nubuwwah*, which actually means receiving news from God; a *nabi*, or prophet, is one who conveys such news).

Some ignorant clerics go so far in their denial that they assert that the door of revelation is altogether closed and that it is not open to a Muslim to enable him to perfect his faith through this bounty and then to act righteously under the urge of his faith. ... The truth is that those who think like this are themselves foolish and stupid.[366]

Explaining the continuity of revelation, the Promised Messiah[as] writes:

Obviously, if man cannot escape error through his own knowledge and if God (Who is Gracious and Merciful and is free from every mistake and knows the truth of every matter) does not help His servants through His true revelation, how could we humble creatures emerge out of the darknesses of ignorance and error, and how could we be delivered from the calamities of doubt and suspicion? I, therefore, affirm with full conviction that the wisdom and mercy and sustaining love of God Almighty demand that from time to time, when He deems it right, He should create men who should be recipients of revelation for the purpose of ascertaining true doctrines and establishing correct morals, and who should have bestowed upon them the capacity of impressing their teachings upon others so that mankind, who have been created for true guidance, should not be deprived of their needed good fortune.[367]

Moreover, Wilders reference to 33:41 has nothing to do with the Qur'an declaring itself the final revelation to mankind. This verse states, "Muhammad is not the father of any of your men, but he is the Messenger of Allah, and the Seal of the Prophets." This is a beautiful Qur'anic

---

366. Barahin-e-Ahmadiyya, Ruhani Khaza'in, vol. 21, 310–11.

367 Purani Tehrirain, Ruhani Khaza'in, vol. 2, 20–21.

verse that recognizes Prophet Muhammad[sa] as the Seal, or validation of all prophets who ever lived. However, even if "Seal" meant last, it still would not substantiate Wilders's claim that revelation from God has eternally ceased.

Thus, countless Mujaddadeen, saints, and scholars throughout Islamic history have laid claim to revelation. But again, I appreciate that no amount of evidence will convince Wilders otherwise—not just because he is anti-Islam, but also and more specifically because he is anti-God. He may sympathize with Christianity and Judaism, but he believes such faiths are hollow fairy tales all the same. Wilders is only doing what he would do to any faith—attacking its concept of God. It should come as no surprise that Wilders disguises attacks on God as attacks on Islam.

ALLEGATION 42

Islam Requires the Muslim Ummah to Act Like An Army

Wilders, again without reference, writes, "Islam commands the Umma to act like an army."[368]

REFERENCE: None.

RESPONSE: As in numerous other instances, Wilders here insinuates that Islam promotes militancy. The Qur'an is a perfect book, regulating human behavior in every aspect, including warfare. To take issue with the Holy Qur'an for bringing morality to war—absent in other religious scriptures, and something the West only finally addressed more than twelve hundred years after the advent of Islam,[369] is absurd.

Wherever the Qur'an permits fighting, it does so only for defensive purposes—a just teaching that I've thoroughly elucidated upon earlier. Before fighting is allowed, one should resort to patience, prayer, and even emigration. But if fighting is the only option, God commands:

> And fight in the cause of Allah against those who fight against you, but do not transgress. Surely, Allah loves not the transgressors.[370]

---

368. Geert Wilders, *Marked for Death*, 61.

369. The Hague Conventions of 1899 and 1907, coupled with the Geneva Conventions, constituted the first attempts to regulate warfare from a moral perspective in secular international law.

370. Qur'an 2:191.

And if they incline towards peace, incline thou also towards it, and put thy trust in Allah.[371]

Granted, some extremists ascribing to Islam promote militancy and violent extremism, but they do so for national, political, or other purposes. They have no basis for doing so in Islam. But this is irrelevant; as Wilders repeatedly admits, he has no problem with Muslims. His issue is with Islam and its evidently violent ideology.Earlier in this book, I explained the advanced rules of war that Prophet Muhammad[sa] enacted: forbidding mutilation, forbidding civilian attacks, etc. I also demonstrated that the Qur'an commands Muslims to fight on behalf of other faiths to champion universal religious freedom. Finally, I have clarified numerous times that Islam does not allow preemptive attacks, and that, as explained in the above verses, it implores Muslims to be ever inclined toward peace.

Wilders, in ignoring these points, is no different from the minority of extremists ascribing to Islam about whom he complains. Both such extremists and Wilders promote a false narrative, and are guilty of twisting verses to suit to their own evil ends and interpretations.

---

371. Qur'an 8:62.

ALLEGATION 43

Islam Teaches That All Non-Muslims Are "Doomed"

Wilders writes, "Muhammad said, "Every child is born with a true faith of Islam but his parents convert him to Judaism, Christianity or Magainism [Zoroastrianism]. Hence, if some of us today are not Muslims, this is either through our own fault or through the apostasy of our parents. Islam teaches that the unbeliever is doomed; he is always *kafir* ("guilty"), whether by his own or his forefathers' fault."[372]

REFERENCE: Bukhari 2:23:441.

RESPONSE: Wilders's vague accusations make the task of responding all the more cumbersome. To do so properly, I must first review the hadith he cites and then determine what Wilders means by "doomed."

Unsurprisingly, Wilders only cites part of the hadith he references. I present it in full below:

> Hazrat Abu Huraira[sa] narrates: Allah's Apostle said, "Every child is born with a true faith of Islam but his parents convert him to Judaism, Christianity or Magainism, as an animal delivers a perfect baby animal. Do you find it mutilated?" Then Abu Huraira recited the holy verses: "The pure Allah's Islamic nature with which He has created human beings. No change let there be in

---

372. Wilders, *Marked for Death*, 61.

the religion of Allah. That is the straight religion but most of men know, not."[373]

In this hadith, Prophet Muhammad clarified Islam's teaching that man is born to worship one God by nature. This is a concept that Wilders admits to knowing when he writes, "Islam is a universal religion that stands for the unity of God and the oneness of mankind."[374] The jump Wilders makes from this understanding of Islam's concept of human nature to distinguishing a set of "doomed unbelievers" is laughable.

Though it is unlikely that even Wilders knows, for the sake of discussion I shall assume that "doomed" and "always *kafir* (guilty)" mean that an unbeliever is worthy of eternal divine punishment in this world and/or in the next.

Before addressing each of these criticisms, I must properly define the word *kafir*, which Wilders mistranslates as "guilty" for some preposterous reason (a Freudian slip, perhaps). From the root *ka-fa-ra*, the word *kafir* means to conceal, be ungrateful, deny, or disbelieve. In the context of Islam, it means "one who disbelieves in Allah," and is thus translated in *Lane's Lexicon* as "disbeliever," "unbeliever," "infidel," etc.[375] Nowhere does the word *guilty* appear in *Lane's Lexicon* (which is based on the famous classical Arabic dictionary *Tajul-'Urus*) or even modern dictionaries like Hans Wehr's *Dictionary of Modern Written Arabic*. So, Wilders's unreferenced argument is also factually incorrect.

The word *kafir* properly defined, I turn next to the question of punishment for *kafireen* (plural of *kafir*). Proceeding to both these criticisms, we read in the Holy Qur'an, "I will inflict My punishment on whom I will; but My mercy encompasses all things."[376]

---

373. Sahih Jami' Bukhari, vol. 2, Book 23, #441.

374. Wilders, *Marked for Death*, 61.

375. Lane and Lane-Poole, *Arabic-English Lexicon*, vol. 7, 2622.

376. Qur'an 7:157.

Islam is the only ancient religion that does *not* monopolize salvation exclusively to its adherents. Islam, instead, teaches that non-Muslims can and shall attain paradise. Based on the above-quoted verse and similar verses, it is not for humans to say how God will judge those who pass away. No guarantee or promise exists that every Muslim will go directly to paradise after death or that every non-Muslim is somehow automatically hell bound.

Islam teaches that whoever you are—be it a Muslim, Christian, Jew, or even atheist—you must first be cleansed of sin before entering paradise. This cleansing may be of incorrect beliefs—which are held both by non-Muslims and misguided Muslims—or for sinful actions (applicable to everyone). Hell is the reformatory abode for this purification after death—for Muslims and non-Muslims equally. As such, we read in the Holy Qur'an, "But as for him whose scales are light [upon judgment], Hell will be his *nursing* mother. And what should thee know what [hell as a mother] is? *It is* a burning Fire."[377]

The Qur'an makes no distinction between a believer and a disbeliever in this verse. In fact, the Qur'an and ahadith confirm that some Muslims (hypocrites, for example) shall go to hell.[378] Yes, Islam teaches that hell is a painful experience:

> As for those who will prove unfortunate, they shall be in the Fire, wherein there shall be for them sighing and sobbing, abiding therein so long as the heavens and the earth endure, excepting what thy Lord may will. Surely thy Lord does bring about what He pleases.[379]

---

377. Qur'an 101:9–12.

378. Qur'an 4:141.

379. Qur'an 11:107–108.

The verse is clear, "excepting what thy Lord may will," which corroborates with the earlier referenced verse, "[God's] mercy encompasses all things." Moreover, once again the Qur'an does not distinguish between Muslims and non-Muslims. However, Prophet Muhammad[sa] explained that hell is temporary in nature: "A time will come when no one will be left in Hell; winds will blow and the windows and doors of Hell will make a rattling noise on account of the blowing winds."[380]

Contrast this with the New Testament, for example, which teaches the concept of an "everlasting fire" for those who are hell bound.[381] Again, I cite this New Testament teaching only because Wilders repeatedly calls it "progressive" as compared to the Qur'an. Contrary to Wilders's allegations, Islam does not "doom" the unbeliever to hell, exclusively or eternally, but ultimately offers glad tidings of paradise to all of humanity.

---

380. Tafsir-ul Maalam-ut Tanzil, under Qur'an 11:107.

381. Matthew 25:41 says, "Then he will say to those on his left, 'Depart from me, you who are cursed, into the eternal fire prepared for the devil and his angels.'"

ALLEGATION 44

Zakaat Finances Holy War in Kashmir and Palestine

Wilders maligns the purpose of zakaat, writing, "The third pillar [of Islam] is *zakat*, the giving of alms, which is given either on behalf of poor Muslims or 'in the cause of Allah' for purposes such as building mosques. Some of these religiously mandated donations are used to finance Jihad, or 'holy war.'"[382]

REFERENCE: Yusuf al-Qaradawi, head of the European Council for Fatwa and Research and founder of the Islam Online website.

RESPONSE: Al-Qaradawi and Wilders share two things in common: they both hold extreme views[383] and they were both banned from entering the United Kingdom for espousing these extremist views—the for-

---

382. Wilders, *Marked for Death*, 61.

383. Although al-Qaradawi enjoys widespread popularity, while calling for discussions and mutual cooperation with the West, the controversial cleric has issued a fatwa permitting the killing of all Americans in Iraq, including civilians; he has also called for a fresh holocaust to kill off the Jews; and he supports the death penalty for apostasy and blasphemy—endorsing, for example, Ayatollah Ruhollah Khomeini's fatwa calling for Salman Rushdie's assassination after the publication of his book, *The Satanic Verses*. Al-Qaradawi is a hypocritical opportunist who tells his varying audiences what they wish to hear. Interestingly, thousands of Muslim clerics have denounced al-Qaradawi for his views. From August to September 2004, deep in the struggle to bring stability to a post-Saddam Iraq, al-Qaradawi was busy circulating his above-noted anti-American fatwa. For this, the former dean of the Sharia faculty at Qatar University blasted al-Qaradawi for "fanning the fire" in Iraq by aiding armed militias and hindering the local security forces and by encouraging a jihad "that has no goal other than slaughter." He also dismissed al-Qaradawi's later attempts to backpedal from the fatwa.

mer from the United States as well.[384] It is fitting that Wilders continues to resort to his own ilk when levying allegations against Islam. But, such references must be dismissed, as we are discussing the teachings of *Islam* (not those of notorious clerics). And this is precisely the problem with critics like Wilders: they cherry-pick extreme misinterpretations of Islam by a minority of extremists ascribing to Islam as Muslim leaders and prop them up as the actual teachings of Islam.

Though much more damning information on al-Qaradawi is included in the footnotes, one example should suffice to prove his extremism: in 2004, he issued a fatwa permitting the killing of all Americans in Iraq, including civilians.[385]

The Qur'an, in contrast, forbids transgression of any kind,[386] including terrorism, and couples zakaat with enjoining good and forbidding evil.[387] Likewise, I have already provided numerous ahadith in which Prophet Muhammad[sa] forbade killing civilians for any reason. The notion that charitable alms should be spent on violence and terrorism, therefore, even if couched as "jihad" by misguided clerics like al-Qaradawi, is laughable. And all this notwithstanding, Wilders again incorrectly defines jihad as "holy war" when it actually means "to struggle." For the reader's edification, in Arabic, "holy war" is actually *"al-harb al*

---

384. Al-Qaradawi has been banned from entering the United Kingdom since 2008 (and the United States since 1999) for espousing extremist views (see previous and following notes for a few examples); Wilders was banned in 2010, albeit temporarily, for inciting hatred through his widely discredited short film, *Fitna*.

385. Aside from this 2004 fatwa permitting the killing of all Americans inside Iraq, including civilians, al-Qaradawi has also permitted the killing of Jewish fetuses on the logic that they might grow up and join the Isra'eli army. Then, on July 3, 2004, he issued a fatwa (published in *al-Ahram al-Arabi*) permitting the killing of … Muslim intellectuals, claiming that Islam justifies the killing of such apostates. See "Arab Liberals: Prosecute Clerics Who Promote Murder," *Middle East Quarterly* (Winter 2005), 84–86 (http://www.meforum.org/700/arab-liberals-prosecute-clerics-who-promote-murder, accessed June 3, 2012).

386. Qur'an 2:191.

387. Qur'an 9:71; 22:42.

muqaddasah." The reader will note that *al-harb al muqaddasah* in fact is rather different from *jihad.* Moreover, *al-harb al muqaddasah* never once appears in the Qur'an.

Adding to the irony here is the fact that it was not some Muslim organization but the United States that supported, trained, armed, funded, and helped indoctrinate the Taliban with extremist literature to "wage Jihad" against Communist Russia.[388] Even educational material for young Afghan children that taught radicalism and violence was printed "in the early 1980s under a U.S. Agency for International Development (AID) grant to the University of Nebraska-Omaha and its Center for Afghanistan Studies."[389] Dr. Susmit Kumar, who has written extensively on this history, remarks:

> The Reagan Doctrine had a narrow vision of defeating Soviets by providing overt and covert aids, and it did not care for the long lasting effects. It did not hesitate to term the war against the Soviets in Afghanistan as a religious war, but they did not realize its long term effects in the Middle East or in other Islamic countries.[390]

This is not to shield extremists and so-called Islamic governments from blame—they are just as guilty. But Wilders's censorship of information on Western involvement with the Taliban combined with his deliberate attempt to instead blame Islam is simply pathetic.

---

388. Joe Stephens and David B. Ottaway, "From U.S., the ABC's of Jihad; Violent Soviet-Era Textbooks Complicate Afghan Education Efforts," *The Washington Post*, March 23, 2002.

389. Craig Davis, "'A' is for Allah, 'J' is for Jihad," *World Policy Journal*, March 22, 2002; and Susmit Kumar, "Afghanistan in Agony and the Rise of Frankenstein—A Failed Reagan Policy," accessed December 1, 2013. http://www.susmitkumar.net/index.php?option=com_content&view=article&id=64&Itemid=82.

390. Kumar, "Afghanistan in Agony."

Indeed, Wilders's earlier claim that he has no problem with Muslims but instead only with Islam is an outright lie. Wilders repeatedly blames Islam and all Muslims for the actions of the minority extremists who ascribe to Islam. Rather than citing any Islamic source to support his claim, he cites his own opinion as evidence that such extremist actions are justified in Islam. This is also one reason why so few allegations from the second half of his book are addressed. That is, the vast majority of his book's second half involves Wilders's complaints about extremists acting under the guise of Islam. Wilders would be better served if he simply admitted what everyone already knows—he hates both Islam and Muslims. For now, once again, his allegation against the purpose of zakaat is entirely unfounded.

ALLEGATION 45

Muhammad^sa Violated His Own Rules of Fasting

Wilders alleges that Islamic fasting is "not a total fast, but an obligation to abstain from food, drink and sex from dawn to dusk." Likewise, he alleges that Prophet Muhammad made selective exemptions to the prohibition on sex for himself and others.[391] As usual, this claim is baseless.

REFERENCE: Hadith Sunan Abu Dawud, Kitab-us Saum.

RESPONSE: Wilders fails to explain the meaning of "a total fast," so I am unsure to exactly what he refers. The Islamic fast calls for more than mere proscription from food, drink, and sex during the day.

First, spiritual development is the primary purpose of the Islamic fast. The Qur'an declares, "O ye who believe! Fasting is prescribed for you, as it was prescribed for those before you, so that you may become righteous."[392]

Believers achieve this spiritual development by giving up physical pleasure and all manner of sin for the sake of God. Abu Hurairah^ra relates that Prophet Muhammad^sa said, "Whoever does not give up forged speech and evil actions, Allah is not in need of his leaving his food and drink (i.e., Allah will not accept his fasting)."[393]

Further, those fasting are encouraged to intensify their prayers, their study of the Qur'an, and their distribution of charity. It is related that during Ramadan, Prophet Muhammad's^sa "own concern for and care of

---

391. Wilders, *Marked for Death*, 62.

392. Qur'an 2:184.

393. Sahih Jami' Bukhari, vol. 3, Book. 31, #127.

the poor, the needy, the sick and the orphan was intensified manifold, and that his charity knew no limit."[394]

With this understanding of fasting in mind, I address Wilders's allegation. Wilders states that "some groups are exempted from the requirement, such as old men, whom Muhammad allowed to have sex during Ramadan," citing a narration from *Sunan Abu Dawud* as support. Wilders's assertion is false. The hadith reads:

A man asked the Messenger of Allah[sa] about approaching his wife while he was fasting (i.e., to kiss her, fondle her...without having sexual relation with her), and the Messenger of Allah[sa] gave him concession. Another man came and asked him (about the same), and he forbade him. Behold! Such as was given concession was an old man, and the other who was forbidden was a young man.[395]

The translator himself explicates the meaning of *al-mubasharah*, or "approaching his wife," in parentheses because in other contexts, the term can mean sexual intercourse. However, it is obvious that sexual intercourse is prohibited during a fast, and such exceptions were never granted to anyone. It was unclear, however, whether one could engage in lesser forms of intimacy (also a meaning of *al-mubasharah*). As the young man in question may have been carried away by his lustful passions during lesser intimacy, he was not allowed this concession. Elder men were allowed, including Prophet Muhammad[sa], who was already forty at the advent of Islam, and older still when married to Hadhrat Ayesha[ra].

---

394. Muhammad Zafrulla Khan, "Fasting: The Fourth Pillar of Islam," *The Review of Religions* (March 1994).

395. Sunan Abu Dawud, (Lebanon: Dar al-Kutub al-Ilmiyyah, 2008), 56. Wilders cites the hadith as Abu Dawud 13:2381, whereas the edition of Abu Dawud we cite records the same hadith as 14:2387.

Hadhrat Ayesha[ra] also reports (in the other hadith that Wilders cites) that the two were intimate during the fast without engaging in sexual intercourse. This is an important distinction that Wilders ignores—perhaps because it undermines his point altogether. Thus, we need look no further than the hadith Wilders himself cites to recognize that his argument is baseless. Islam offers no exemption or permission to anyone, and did not give an exemption to Prophet Muhammad[sa], to engage in sexual intercourse while fasting.

ALLEGATION 46

Islam Teaches Fatalism, Not Individual Freedom

Wilders alleges, "Since Islam lacks a commitment to individual freedom, it is unsurprising that the ideology downplays the notion that man is responsible for his own fate. To the contrary, Islam teaches Muslims to be fatalistic, because Allah has predestined everyone's future."[396]

REFERENCE: Qur'an 57:22, 9:52, 54:50, 3:146, 14:5. Ibn-e-Warraq.

RESPONSE: On the contrary, Muslims are wholly accountable for their own actions. First, individual freedom is enshrined throughout the Qur'an and has been discussed a number of times, including at the outset of this chapter.

Likewise, *qadr*, meaning "divine decree," is one of the six articles of the Islamic faith[397] and far deeper than Wilders can envisage. For brevity's sake I will stick to a simple rebuttal of Wilders's allegation.

Islam teaches that God's decree (*taqdir*) controls the eventual outcome of actions in the universe (though prayer has an important role in Allah's shaping one's destiny). At the same time, humanity has the ability to make decisions that run counter to God's guidance. The Qur'an states, "And if thy Lord had *enforced* His will, surely, all who are on the earth would have believed together. Wilt thou, then, force men to become believers?"[398] This verse could not be clearer that humans have free

---

396. Wilders, *Marked for Death*, 63.

397. The remaining articles of faith are belief in Allah, Angels, Books, Prophets, and the Day of Judgment.

398. Qur'an 10:100.

will and free choice to act as they please. Likewise, this verse also importantly declares that in matters of belief, whatever a person believes, neither shall God enforce His own will to the contrary nor may humans enforce their own wills to the contrary. Each person has true freedom.

Furthermore, the Qur'an states, "Do you suppose that you will enter Heaven while Allah has not yet distinguished those of you that strive in the way of Allah and has not yet distinguished the steadfast?"[399]

Taken together, these verses explain that we have free will to make our own decisions and that God will judge each of us based upon those actions that play a role in determining if we go to paradise. Furthermore, despite Wilders's assertion to the contrary, Islam holds Muslims responsible for their individual actions. The Qur'an states, "Beware of the Day when every soul shall find itself confronted with all the good it has done and all the evil it has done."[400] Likewise, "And fear the day when no soul shall serve as a substitute for another soul at all, nor shall any ransom be accepted from it, nor any intercession avail it, nor shall they be helped."[401]

Fatalism has many forms, and Wilders defines it in the pages of his book much like *murji'ah* or defeatism: the acceptance of defeat without struggle. Both this form of fatalism (*murji'ah*) and its opposite extreme, i.e., the rejection of destiny altogether (known as *qadriyyah*), are un-Islamic. Accordingly, Prophet Muhammad[sa] said, "Two groups of my ummah have no share in Islam: the *Murji'ah* and the *Qadriyyah*."[402] Islam prescribes a middle ground, teaching that there is a destiny, but one that believers have a role in shaping through actions like prayers and good deeds.

---

399. Qur'an 3:143.

400. Qur'an 3:31.

401. Qur'an 2:124.

402. Imam Muhammad ibn 'Isa Tirmidhi, Jami' Tirmidhi, vol. 1, Abwab-ul Qadr, Ch. 13, No. 2156, (Karachi: Darul Ishaat Urdu Bazar, 2007), 879.

The verses that Wilders cites in support of his allegation that Islam teaches fatalism are actually designed to either bring contentment to one's heart (i.e., fear not; good shall come eventually), or further emphasize freedom of religion (as noted above).

Indeed, if Islam had been fatalistic, Prophet Muhammad[sa] would not have led a ragtag group of 313 Muslims against an army more than three times that size; rather, they would have accepted their "fate" and their slaughter. Wilders's allegations once again demonstrate nothing more than his ignorance of Islamic theology and jurisprudence.

ALLEGATION 47

Only Martyrdom While Making Others Suffer Assures Paradise

Wilders writes, "According to Islam there is only one assurance that a Muslim will go straight to paradise: martyrdom. However, the concept of Islamic martyrdom is fundamentally different from Christian martyrdom, which refers to suffering unto death for the sake of faith. In contrast, the Koran says that Allah promises his garden to those who "fight for His cause, slay, and be slain." Such is the true pledge which He has made them in the Torah, the Gospel and the Koran. Islamic martyrs are not those who suffer and die for the truth, but those who are killed while making others suffer and die."[403]

REFERENCE: Qur'an 9:111. Passing reference to an irrelevant passage in Salman Rushdie's *The Satanic Verses* (213).

RESPONSE: I again find it remarkable that an agnostic or atheist so adamantly defends Christianity—a faith that according to many Christian scholars promises Wilders eternal damnation for rejecting the blood of Christ.

Wilders's allegation against Islam is twofold: first, Muslim martyrs are only "those who are killed while making others suffer and die," and not "those who suffer and die for truth;" second, only martyrdom carries the promise of paradise in Islam. Both of these allegations are meritless.

---

403. Wilders, *Marked for Death*, 64.

Although the Islamic concept of martyrdom, or *shahadah*, is profoundly deep, I confine this discussion to a prima facie reading. Those *killed* on account of their faith are indeed considered martyrs in Islam. But Islam nowhere requires—let alone permits—a Muslim to impose willful suffering on others to attain martyrdom. It should be no surprise that Wilders makes his allegation without a reference.

Furthermore, Prophet Muhammad[sa] taught that there are many kinds of martyrs, including those who die from any of the following: the plague, cholera, drowning, and a falling wall.[404] And there are other kinds yet.

For example, I can offer a personal example—one quite near and dear to me. on December 23, 2006, armed gunmen killed an American Ahmadi Muslim in Chicago named Muhaimin Karim. Muhaimin, an attribute of God that means "protector," heard his employees yelling for help outside his barbershop and ran out to defend them and his store. In saving the lives of his employees, both Christian, he sacrificed his own—dying of multiple gunshot wounds.[405] His Holiness the Khalifa of Islam, Hadhrat Mirza Masroor Ahmad[aba], declared Muhaimin a martyr and led his funeral prayer in absentia. This corresponds to the hadith of Prophet Muhammad[sa], "He who is killed in defense of his property is a martyr."[406] Here, a Muslim literally gave his life so that his Christian friends might live—and they did. But according to Wilders, this is not enough for him to be declared a martyr.

As for martyrs killed in warfare, Islam permits fighting only after several nonviolent means of escaping religious persecution have been exhausted. I have thoroughly discussed this matter throughout this book.

---

404. Imam Nawawi, "Hadith #1358," in *Gardens of the Righteous* (translation of *Riyad us-Salihin*), (Tilford: Islam International Publications, Ltd., 1996), 228.

405. Annie Sweeney, "Suspect Arrested in 2006 Slaying," *Chicago Tribune*, June 17, 2010, accessed June 6, 2012. http://articles.chicagotribune.com/2010-06-17/news/ct-met-barber-cold-case-20100617_1_abdul-karim-slaying-barbershop.

406. Nawawi, "Hadith #1360," *Gardens of the Righteous*, 228.

Accordingly, in its chapter 3, the Qur'an states: "You are from one another. Those, therefore, who have emigrated, and have been driven out from their homes, and have been persecuted in My cause, and have fought and been killed, I will surely remove from them their evils and will cause them to enter Gardens."[407]

Turning to Wilders's reference of Qur'an 9:111, the full verse reads:

Surely, Allah has purchased of the believers their persons and their property in return for the Garden they shall have; they fight in the cause of Allah, and they slay and are slain—a promise that He has made incumbent on Himself in the Torah, and the Gospel, and the Qur'an.[408]

Wilders alleges, "In contrast to Christianity, the Koran says that Allah promises his garden to those who 'fight for His cause, slay, and be slain'"[409] and that, "according to Islam, there is *only one assurance* that a Muslim will go straight to paradise: martyrdom."[410]

Wilders is guilty of muddling the issue, as the verse promises the Garden to "the believers"—not to the martyrs—in return for the purchase of "their persons and their property," signifying a person's time and effort and financial sacrifice in the cause of Allah. When God says, "they fight in the cause of Allah, and they slay and are slain," Allah is describing just a few of the many qualities of the believers (*mu'minin*)—not of martyrs (*shuhada'* or *shahidin*).

And, contrary to Wilders's claim, no such teaching in Islam exists that "only assures martyrs [a] straight path to paradise." Thus, again it is no coincidence that Wilders does not cite a reference to support his

---

407. Qur'an 3:196.

408. Qur'an 9:111.

409. Wilders, *Marked for Death*, 64.

410. Ibid., 64. (Emphasis added.)

claim, because no such reference exists. Indeed, throughout the Qur'an, Allah attributes many other traits to the believers, promising them paradise. In chapter 23, we read:

> Surely success does come to the believers, who are humble in their Prayers, and who shun all that which is vain, and who are active in paying the Zakaat, and who guard their chastity—except from their wives of what their right hand possess, for then they are not to be blamed; but those who seek *anything* beyond that are the transgressors—and who are watchful of trusts and their covenants, and who are strict in the observance of their Prayers. *These are the heirs who will inherit Paradise.* They will abide therein."[411]

Here, Allah promises paradise to "the believers." In the six qualities mentioned, fighting or martyrdom is not even remotely suggested.

In chapter 70, Allah promises paradise to *al-musallin*, or "those who pray." He describes *al-musallin* by eight noble qualities, and again, nowhere is fighting or martyrdom mentioned.[412] In short, basic common sense shows that Wilders's claim that paradise is for those who die while ensuring others suffer is wholly alien to Islam.

---

411. Qur'an 23:2–12. (Emphasis added.)

412. Qur'an 70:23–36.

ALLEGATION 48

Islam and Democracy are Incompatible

Wilders references a Pew survey on how Muslims in Egypt view government to allege that Islam and democracy are incompatible.[413]

REFERENCE: Pew Research Center.

RESPONSE: Wilders reference to the Pew data is a thinly veiled insult to Islam and Egyptian Muslims, saying that their preference for democracy is "negated by the people's widespread support for Islamic customs that undermine a democratic society."[414] Wilders's claim that Islamic customs undermine a democratic society is provided—not surprisingly—without reference. His unqualified opinion aside, as already stated numerous times, I do not address what Muslims today may or may not think as that is outside this book's scope. Likewise, if Wilders objects to this, I refer him back to his own statement that the majority of Muslims are moderate and he has no problem with Muslims. I address here once more his problem with Islam.

The fact is that Islam and democracy are perfectly compatible because Islam empowers the people to adopt the system of rule that suits them. The Qur'an prescribes two principles of governance—present in successful democracies as well—and leaves the rest to the people to decide: first, *'adl* (absolute justice),[415] and second, *mushawarah* (consulta-

413. Wilders, *Marked for Death*, 65–66.

414. Wilders, *Marked for Death*, 65.

415. Qur'an 4:59.

tion).[416] Indeed, *mushawarah* contains within it the notion of representative government that the West terms "democracy."

By this easy to understand definition, the United States government is ostensibly an "Islamic" government because the United States Constitution is based on justice and we elect members to congress to collaborate, consult, and pass legislation. Our American government is not without its flaws—I don't think anyone would argue that—but my point is instead about the constitutional and justice based principles upon which our government stands.

The thoroughly discussed Charter of Medina is a prime example of a government established—by Prophet Muhammad[sa] himself—on the tenets of justice and mutual consultation. So long as a government meets the requirements of absolute justice and consultation, Islam makes no objection.[417] Obviously, a theocracy violates both absolute justice and ignores mutual consultation because it enforces a state religion and does not care for the voices of minorities and the marginalized. The Charter of Medina, instead, obliged Prophet Muhammad[sa] to mutual consultation and specifically declared that all citizens of the State of Medina were equals—regardless of religious affiliation. Thus, Islam—as Prophet Muhammad[sa] taught and practiced—cannot and does not support a theocracy.

Whatever point Wilders attempts from his Pew reference, it is not a point founded in Islamic teachings. Instead, he cannot present even a single Qur'anic verse that condemns democracy or requires theocracy. As long as absolute justice and mutual consultation are employed—just as Prophet Muhammad[sa] employed in the Charter of Medina—Islam

---

416. Qur'an 42:39.

417. Mirza Tahir Ahmad, *Islam's Response to Contemporary Issues* (Tilford: Islam International Publications, Ltd., 2007), 224.

gives people the power to develop the form of government they choose.[418] This simply reflects the freedom Islam affords humanity.

---

418. It is worth nothing that, due to Islam's requirements of absolute justice and mutual consultation, by definition Islam rejects theocratic, communist, dictatorial, and fascist rule. Such forms of government inherently are unjust and dismiss consultation.

ALLEGATION 49

Islam Is Not a Religion but a Theocratic Political Ideology

Wilders, citing known anti-Islam personalities, alleges that "Islam is not a religion but a political ideology"[419] that "differs little from...National Socialism and communism."[420]

REFERENCE: Nonie Darwish, Hugh Fitzgerald, J.M. Roberts.

RESPONSE: Wilders cites Professor Howard Kainz's review of ex-Muslim and Islamophobe Nonie Darwish's book, *Cruel and Unusual Punishment*. Darwish argues that "Islam fails four major tests that religions should fulfill," which I list here and reply to in turn. Before I do, however, I point out the obvious: this is the wildest criticism Wilders levies against Islam in his chapter. No serious thinker, scholar, or theologian—for or against Islam—has ever argued that Islam is not a religion. They leave that to the likes of Nonie Darwish, whose credentials are absent, and Hugh Fitzgerald, who is altogether absent (as we shall soon see).

Darwish claims a religion should meet these tests:

"1. Adherence to the religion must be a personal choice."

---

419. Wilders, *Marked for Death*, 67.

420. Ibid., 69.

Indeed; religion should be a personal choice. God commands in the Holy Qur'an, "There should be no compulsion in religion."[421] Islam prescribes no worldly punishment for apostasy or blasphemy and categorically forbids religious compulsion—facts I have established repeatedly throughout this book. Islam passes Darwish's own first metric.

"2. No religion should demand that those who leave it be killed."

I agree with Darwish's second test. As noted in my chapter 1, Islam prescribes no worldly punishment for apostasy—and in fact specifically condemns forcing belief upon people. Thus, Islam passes this second metric.

"3. A religion must never mandate the killing and subjugation of those who choose not to belong."

See test 2. Thus, Islam passes Darwish's third metric.

"4. A religion must be in accord with basic human rights."

The human rights enshrined in the Qur'an are superior to those in the Universal Declaration of Human Rights (UDHR). In fact, the former president of the United Nations General Assembly, Sir Zafrulla Khan, makes this very argument. In his seminal work, *Islam and Human Rights*, he compares the UDHR and the Holy Qur'an, proving the latter's superiority.[422] Likewise, Prophet Muhammad established advanced rules of war that spared civilians, children, women, elderly, monks, property, trees, and animals—rules that even modern societies today have not

---

421. Qur'an 2:257.

422. Sir Muhammad Zafrulla Khan, *Islam and Human Rights*.
   http://www.alislam.org/library/books/Islam-HR.pdf.

uniformly accepted. Thus, Islam passes Darwish's fourth and final metric.

Having addressed these points, I now come to their author. Not only is Darwish another hard-line Islamophobe like Wilders, one who imputes the actions of misguided Muslims to Islam, she possesses no qualifications to establish the above criteria to determine what is and is not a religion. She is neither an academic nor a theologian.[423] I am not surprised, however, that Wilders cites someone with equally deficient credentials as himself.

Wilders also cites the highly enigmatic and problematic "Hugh Fitzgerald." SpencerWatch.com, an Islamophobia watchdog site that focuses on hatemonger Robert Spencer's anti-Islam propaganda, asks, "Who is Hugh Fitzgerald?" It posits that this person was most likely a figment of Robert Spencer's fanatical imagination.[424] This online character's hate speech was egregious, beyond that of even Spencer, which has led some commentators to suggest he was a fictitious persona who provided Spencer cover to say what he could not say himself. Although Fitzgerald was supposedly Spencer's website's vice president, Spencer made countless public appearances with numerous anti-Islam personalities but has never been pictured with Fitzgerald. Indeed, there are no pictures of Fitzgerald at all, nor is he listed as vice president on the David Horowitz Freedom Center's tax return Form 990. In November 2010, Spencer "released" Fitzgerald, penning a tribute to the hatemonger and citing financial constraints as the reason for their parting.[425]

---

423. Better than Howard Kainz's 880-word, uncritical appraisal of her book is the 1877-word review by SUNY Buffalo Professor Jim Holstun, "Nonie Darwish and the al-Bureij Massacre"—which, according to Islamophobia watchdog Loon Watch, "lays bare Nonie's excessive Islamophobia, as well as her contradictions and lies." Accessed June 4, 2012. http://electronicintifada.net/content/nonie-darwish-and-al-bureij-massacre/7586.

424. See http://spencerwatch.com/who-is-hugh-fitzgerald/. Accessed August 12, 2012.

425. See http://www.Jihadwatch.org/2010/11/a-tribute-to-hugh-fitzgerald.html. Accessed August 12, 2012.

It is ridiculous for Wilders to cite individuals with zero academic credentials on Islam—and the height of absurdity to cite a person who does not even exist. Needless to say, Wilders's allegation that Islam is not a religion is as baseless as are his qualifications to speak on Islam.

ALLEGATION 50

Islam Requires That Prayer Be Enforced on Muslims

Wilders previously cites known anti-Islam personalities to bolster his opinion. Here, he takes a turn to the other extreme and cites known extremists to claim that Islam requires that prayer be enforced.[426]

REFERENCE: Abul Ala Maududi; Nonie Darwish

RESPONSE: Now Wilders cites known terrorist Mullah Abul Ala Maududi, whose Jamaat e Islaami terrorist party has been convicted of war crimes, rape, and murder. Wilders's (research team's) ability to dig up the most extreme personalities to justify his sordid view of Islam never ceases to amaze. His Holiness Hadhrat Mirza Tahir Ahmad[rm], fourth khalifa of the Ahmadiyya Muslim Community, wrote an eye-opening book entitled *Murder in the Name of Allah* in the early 1960s rebutting Maududi's warped philosophy. Maududi is well known as the father of modern-day "Islamic" terrorism. Wilders, instead, hails Maududi as some scholar, ignoring the fact that like Wilders, Maududi had no credentials to speak on Islam. But perhaps this similarity is exactly why Wilders is so attracted to Maududi's propaganda.

Hadhrat Mirza Tahir Ahmad[rm] reports, "Maulana Maududi, as we have seen, was neither an historian nor a religious scholar. He was essentially a journalist and he had the two basic qualities of a journalist: a good command of the Urdu language and the ability to write quickly."[427]

---

426. Wilders, *Marked for Death*, 70.

427. Mirza Tahir Ahmad, *Murder in the Name of Allah* (Islam International Publications, Ltd., 2001), 28.

In another place, Hadhrat Mirza Tahir Ahmad[rm] compares Oriental-
ists and Maududi—which, when read, sounds like a comparison of Wilders and Maududi:

> The snide remarks of the orientalists about the Prophet of Islam
> are as unsurprising as they are hurtful. They are sometimes made
> out of ignorance, but mostly out of malice. The hostility towards
> Islam colors the objectivity of even the most balanced historian.
> But most hurtful of all are the writings of Muslims who claim de-
> voutly to follow the Prophet, yet present him, either through ig-
> norance or arrogance, as a barbarian who wielded the sword to
> convert and conquer.[428]

Suggesting that Maududi speaks for Islam is akin to claiming Nathan
Bedford Forrest, the first Grand Wizard of the Ku Klux Klan, speaks for
Christianity. Thus, as a man with zero credentials on Islam, Maududi has
equally zero authority to speak on Islamic teachings—yet Wilders
shamelessly cites him as a scholar.

To address Wilders's allegation: the truth is that Islam does not
compel prayer. It is, of course, obligatory on all adult Muslims, but the
decision to pray rests with each believer, as he or she must choose to
worship God of his or her own volition to earn His pleasure. Again, the
Qur'an states, "There should be no compulsion in religion."[429]

Many Muslims do not pray because they have fallen away from the
true, beautiful teachings of Islam. They no longer know the God of Islam, His Prophet, or His Word. It is not through force, but through
peaceful exposition of Islam that Muslims will return to prayer. And this
was the mission of Hadhrat Mirza Ghulam Ahmad[as] of Qadian, the
promised messiah. Addressing this dilemma, he writes:

---

428. Ibid., 14–15.

429. Qur'an 2:257.

Prayer is a wonderful thing. It is pity that those who pray are not aware of the true manner of prayer, nor are they acquainted with the ways of the acceptance of prayer. The truth is that the very reality of prayer has become strange. There are some who deny the effectiveness of prayer altogether.[430]

Wilders then cites Nonie Darwish, who complains, "What a Muslim says in his prayers and time of prayers is not a choice for a Muslim who must recite what is ordered at specific times."[431] So let me get this right: Darwish's criticism is that a *religion* prescribes prayer? Not only is her allegation laughable, but also, it is incorrect. While the Islamic prayer prescribes certain words to be prayed at certain windows of time, these prayers are not the only prayers, and such times are not the only "specific times" a person may pray. Allah hears all who pray to Him, however a person chooses to pray, and in whatever language that person chooses to pray.

What Darwish describes is entirely foreign to Islam. Likewise, what Wilders alleges about prayer in Islam is not an allegation against Islam only, but another reflection of his objection to the idea of worshiping a Creator—an objection he has as an atheist or agnostic. I challenge either Wilders or Darwish to cite a single verse of the Qur'an or a single hadith that compels prayer or offers some worldly punishment for those who do not pray. Seek as they might, both will come up empty.

---

430. *Al-Hakm* 7, no. 8 (February 28, 1903), 1–3.

431. Wilders, *Marked for Death*, 68.

ALLEGATION 51

Islam Seeks to Establish a Caliphate to Conquer the World

Wilders writes, "Indeed, Islam's most important goal, its ultimate ambition, is the establishment of a worldly state, a global political empire: the Caliphate, to whose authority all of mankind—Muslims and non-Muslims alike—are subjected."[432] Wilders again makes a similar unreferenced allegation subsequently in his chapter 5 and again in chapter 8.[433]

REFERENCE: None.

RESPONSE: The Arabic word *khalifa* (caliph) refers to the successor of a prophet. Similar to the pope in Catholicism, the khalifa is responsible for continuing the task of reformation and moral training that the prophet leaves behind after his demise, and for being a symbol of unity. Accordingly, Prophet Muhammad[sa] prophesized the advent of khilafat after his passing, and its reestablishment in the latter days:

> Prophethood shall remain among you as long as Allah shall will. He will bring about its end and follow it with khilafat on the precepts of prophethood for as long as He shall will and then bring about its end. A tyrannical monarchy will then follow and will remain as long as Allah shall will and then come to an end. There will follow thereafter monarchical despotism to last as long as Al-

---

432. Wilders, *Marked for Death*, 70, 78.

433. Ibid., 78.

lah shall will and come to an end upon His decree. There will then emerge khilafat on precept of prophethood.[434]

In the same prophecy, Prophet Muhammad[sa] laid down a timeline of future events: monarchy and tyrannical rule would follow khilafat, only for khilafat to be reinstituted in the latter days on the precept of prophethood. Upon Prophet Muhammad's[sa] demise in 632 CE, the "rightly guided" khalifas—the first four khalifas succeeding Prophet Muhammad[sa]—assumed leadership of the Muslim *ummah*, one after another. As Wilders fails to mention any specific incidence of these khalifas to support the contention that khilafat is working toward world domination, I can only challenge Wilders to produce a single incidence supporting his claim. Criticism of the caliphates *following* the "rightly guided" caliphate, while somewhat legitimate, has no bearing on Islam, as Prophet Muhammad[sa] himself proactively disassociated himself from them in the prophecy above.

In his Chapter 5, Wilders lists a few organizations that are allegedly working to reestablish the caliphate.[435] But the plot thickens. As with his allegation in his chapter 4, Wilders deliberately fails to list the only Islamic organization that has already reestablished the caliphate. Not a decade or two old, the Ahmadiyya Muslim Community's caliphate was established in 1908. The Community's membership is in the tens of millions and spans over two hundred countries—all united under one khalifa.

And here's the best part: Wilders cannot plead ignorance to this fact or to this khalifa's existence. Wilders well knows of the Ahmadiyya Muslim Community—and its caliphate. Prior to his book's publication, Wilders wrote to the Dutch government specifically about the Ahmadiyya Muslim Community and its fifth khalifa—His Holiness Hadhrat

---

434. Masnad Ahmad bin Hanbal, Mishkat, Chap. Al-Anzar Wal Tahzir.

435. Wilders, *Marked for Death*, 77.

Mirza Masroor Ahmad[aba].[436] Yet, according to his book, he is ignorant to a worldwide khilafat that has existed for more than a century. Instead, Wilders chooses to deliberately (or deceptively) ignore the example of the Ahmadiyya Muslim Khilafat.

Even when faced with bitter persecution, the Ahmadiyya Muslim Khilafat requires Ahmadi Muslims to be steadfast, categorically rejecting all forms of religious violence, political supremacy, dictatorship, or authoritarian rule. The Ahmadiyya Muslim Khilafat champions the cause of the dispossessed through international humanitarian efforts, service, and dialogue. Yet Wilders ignores this single caliphate in existence altogether, hoping instead his readers will succumb to fearmongering about a caliphate that does not exist, and of whose potential existence no evidence is available.

In fact, during a recent tour of the Far East, His Holiness the khalifa of Islam once again remarked:

> Khilafat has no relation to government or politics. When [Islam] Ahmadiyyat spreads far and wide the Khilafat will play no role in government and will never interfere with matters of State. We have no political ambitions or desires. We believe entirely in a separation of religion and matters of State.[437]

Thus, the only khilafat that actually exists in the world has made it painstakingly clear that the khilafat is entirely separate from matters of state. Yet Wilders keeps these facts censored from his readers.

---

436. See http://www.themuslimtimes.org/2011/11/countries/netherlands/dutch-government-defends-ahmadiyya-muslim-jamaat-from-false-allegations. Accessed August 12, 2012.

437. "True Khilafat Compatible with Democracy," *Al Islam eGazette* (November 2013). http://www.alislam.org/egazette/egazette/november-2013-egazette-true-khilafat-compatible-with-democracy/.

In his Chapter 8, Wilders alleges that the 9/11 terrorists were following commands from some sort of caliphate.[438] Per Wilders's protocol, a baseless allegation is levied, no reference is provided, and Wilders sits back and assumes he has presented an argument. To what "Caliphate" is Wilders referring? We are left only to guess, because Wilders provides us nothing substantive to which we can reply. Yet, this is ostensibly Wilders's argument—that his opinion alone of whom the Al Qaeda terrorists served is proof enough that some sort of caliphate exists. What remarkable research!

The fact remains that Wilders proffers no evidence of some political caliphate seeking to dominate the world. On the contrary, the spiritual khilafat that actually exists is censored from Wilders's readers, despite his own previous admission and acknowledgement of its existence.

---

438. Wilders, *Marked for Death*, 127.

Conclusion

Wilders transitions from attacking Islamic history in his Chapter 3 to attacking Islamic teachings as they apply to the contemporary world in Chapter 4. He makes repeated attempts to suggest that Islam is misogynistic, incompatible with modern legal codes, and is an inherent political threat. In doing so, Wilders offers little substance in argument but instead offers a plethora of opinionated and biased findings.

In Chapter 5, Wilders attempts once again to expose alleged Islamic anti-Semitism, regales us with his understanding of jihad, and introduces his readers to a bizarre and alien to Islam concept called *taqiyya*, all the while again grossly misrepresenting several important events in Islamic history.

Chapter 5

Wilders Lies to Himself

"LIBERTY! FREEDOM! DEMOCRACY! True anyhow no matter how many liars use those words."

— LANGSTON HUGHES

In this Chapter, a man who admits Muslims are moderate, once again focuses on pitting Muslims and Jews against each other with allegations of Islamic anti-Semitism. He puts forth wholly incorrect statements about jihad and thoroughly confuses several crucial events in Islamic history.

Earlier in my book, I forewarned you that Wilders attempts to make an argument around the concept of taqiyya, in which—as Wilders alleges—Muslims are allowed to lie to gain some advantage over non-Muslims. In this Chapter, Wilders spends extensive time building up this house of cards. I knock it down with facts and common sense.

Wilders interestingly begins his Chapter 5 discussing his interest in Australia, praising Dutch navigator Willem Janszoon's "discovery" of Australia in 1606—

as if a million or more Aborigines did not live there for roughly 40,000 years prior. I expected he might mention the horrific genocide of Australian Aborigines that followed European colonialism, during which some estimate the Aborigine population decreased a shocking 90 percent in just over a century. Not surprisingly Wilders ignores it altogether. It seems Wilders only objects to Muslims (whom he describes as moderate) immigrating to Europe, not devastating mass genocide caused by European expansion into foreign lands. He continues his tirade of screaming for freedom and democracy as if he has some patent on the concepts.

Overall, Wilders's Chapters five and six are the last two Chapters in which he presents new allegations that fall within *EXTREMIST*'s scope. After that, he largely repeats himself and complains some more about Muslims (while still claiming most of them are moderate). In short, you're in the home stretch.

ALLEGATION 52

Islam Wages Jihad to Forcibly Conquer the World

Wilders writes, "That is the crux of Islam: it is an ideology of global war. It advocates the incorporation of the non-Islamic *Dar al Harb*, or 'House of War,' into the *Dar al Islam*, or 'House of Submission,' so that the former will cease to exist and the whole world, united under Muslim rule, will become *Dar al-Salam*, the 'House of Peace.'"[439]

REFERENCE: Abul Ala Maududi.

RESPONSE: Once again the extremist politician Wilders cites the extremist Mullah Maududi—i.e. the father of terrorism. With this allegation, Wilders does nothing more than expose his own grotesque ignorance to the purpose and meaning of the word *jihad*. The Qur'an uses the word thirty-four times to express the idea of struggling to the utmost to refine oneself,[440] to improve society,[441] or to defend the freedom of conscience.[442] Accordingly, Prophet Muhammad[sa] has, for example, used the word when referring to serving one's parents,[443] refining

---

439. Wilders, *Marked for Death*, 78, 84.

440. Qur'an 2:219; 3:143; 4:96; 5:36, 5:55; 8:73, 8:75, 8:76; 9:16, 9:19, 9:20, 9:24, 9:41, 9:44, 9:79, 9:81, 9:86, 9:88; 16:111 22:79; 25:53; 29:7, 29:70; 47:32; 49:16; 60:2; 61:12.

441. Qur'an 2:219; 3:143; 4:96; 5:36, 5:55; 8:73, 8:75, 8:76; 9:16, 9:19, 9:20, 9:24, 9:41, 9:44, 9:73, 9:79, 9:81, 9:86, 9:88; 16:111; 22:79; 25:53; 29:7, 29:70; 47:32; 49:16; 60:2; 61:12.

442. Qur'an 3:143; 4:96; 5:36, 5:55; 8:73, 8:75, 8:76; 9:16, 9:19, 9:20, 9:24, 9:41, 9:44, 9:73, 9:81, 9:86, 9:88; 16:111; 29:7, 29:70; 47:32; 49:16; 60:2; 61:12; 66:10.

443. "A man came to the Prophet asking his permission to take part in Jihad. The Prophet asked him, 'Are your parents alive?' He replied in the affirmative. The Prophet

---

one's character,[444] performing the hajj pilgrimage,[445] and defensive war for freedom of conscience.[446] Prophet Muhammad[sa] also, after returning from battle, declared the jihad of refining oneself to be superior to jihad to defend the freedom of conscience: "We are returning from the lesser Jihad to the greater Jihad."[447] The following ahadith elaborate on these facts:

> Imam Ja'far as-Sadiq[ra] said: "The Prophet[sa] of God dispatched a contingent of the army (to the battlefront). Upon their (successful) return, he[sa] said: 'Blessed are those who have performed the minor Jihad and have yet to perform the major Jihad.' When asked, 'What is the major Jihad?' the Prophet[sa] replied: 'The Jihad of the self'."[448]
>
> Hadhrat Abu Dharr[ra] asked Prophet Muhammad[sa], "Which struggle is the best?" The Holy Prophet[sa] replied, "To struggle against one's own self and lusts."[449]

---

said to him, 'Then exert yourself in their service.'" Sahih Jami' Bukhari, vol. 4, Book 52, #248.

444. Imam Ja'far as-Sadiq[ra] said: "The Prophet[sa] of God dispatched a contingent of the army (to the battlefront). Upon their (successful) return, he[sa] said: 'Blessed are those who have performed the minor Jihad and have yet to perform the major Jihad.' When asked, 'What is the major Jihad?' the Prophet[sa] replied: 'The Jihad of the self'." Al-Majlisi, Bihar al-Anwar, vol. 19, p. 182, #31; Hadhrat Abu Dharr[ra] asked Prophet Muhammad[sa], "'Which struggle is the best?' The Holy Prophet[sa] replied, 'To struggle against one's own self and lusts.'" Bihar al-Anwar, vol. 67, p. 62.

445. "A man came to the Prophet and said, 'O Allah's Apostle! I have enlisted in the army for such-and-such Ghazwa, and my wife is leaving for Hajj.' Allah's Apostle said, 'Go back and perform Hajj with your wife.'" Sahih Jami' Bukhari, vol. 4, Book 52, #295; "The Prophet was asked by his wives about the Jihad and he replied, 'The best Jihad (for you) is (the performance of) Hajj.'" Sahih Jami' Bukhari, vol. 4, Book 52, #128.

446. Qur'an 22:40–42.

447. "Kashful-Mahjub" by Ali bin Osman Hajveri pg. 213; "Al-Kashsbaaf" part 3 pg. 173 under commentary of Qur'an 22:78.

448. Al-Majlisi, Bihar al-Anwar, vol. 19, p. 182, #31.

449. Bihar al-Anwar, vol. 67, p. 62.

Contrary to Wilders's position, the Qur'an: prohibits fighting against any peaceful group,[450] repeatedly underscores the importance of freedom of conscience,[451] and permits fighting only to uphold the freedom of conscience and defend oneself against an aggressor.[452] The Qur'an, as mentioned earlier, also states that no single religion can monopolize salvation[453] and endorses ecumenism.[454] Wilders continues to demean the Qur'an while praising the Bible despite biblical verses that call for blasphemers to be put to death.[455]

Instead of relying on the Qur'an and ahadith, Wilders relies on Mullah Abul Ala Maududi, founder of Pakistan's extreme right-wing religio-political party Jamaat e Islami. No doubt influenced by the philosophies of medieval clerics, Maududi divided the world into two "houses" and preached violence against non-Muslims and also against Muslims he disagrees with. But not only do Maududi's views contradict the Qur'an, I remind my readers once again how vociferously Prophet Muhammad[sa] condemned such clerics:

> Their clerics will be the worst creatures under the heaven. Discord will rise from them and will come right back to them.[456]

---

450. Qur'an 60:9.

451. Qur'an 2:5, 257, 273; 3:21, 86–92; 4:56, 80–81, 138; 5:91–93, 99–100; 6:67, 105–108, 112–113, 150; 10:100–101, 109; 11:29; 13:41; 16:83; 17:54–55; 18:30; 21:42; 22:18, 68; 24:55; 25:32, 42–44; 27:108–110, 92–93; 29:19; 36:8, 17–18, 31; 39:40–42; 42:7–8, 48–49; 43:8; 50:46; 51:57; 64:9–13; 67:26–27; 76:30; 84:7; 88:22–25; 109:2–7.

452. Qur'an 2:191; 22:40–42.

453. Qur'an 2:63, 112–114; 3:114–116; 5:67, 70; 7:160; 22:69.

454. Qur'an 3:65.

455. II Chronicles 15:13. "All who would not seek the LORD, the God of Isra'el, were to be put to death, whether small or great, man or woman."

456. Al-Baihaqi as quoted in al-Mishkat Kitab-ul 'Ilm, chap. 3, p. 38 and Kanzul 'Ummal, chap. 6, p. 43.

In my Ummah an era of fear will come, and people will turn to their clerics for guidance, but will find them as monkeys and swine.[457]

[A time will come when] there will be nothing left of knowledge. People will make the ignorant their leaders and will seek guidance from them in matters of religion. These leaders will issue *fatwas* without any knowledge. They will themselves be misguided and will lead others astray.[458]

As already mentioned, Hadhrat Mirza Tahir Ahmad[rm], fourth khalifa of the Ahmadiyya Muslim Community, thoroughly debunked Maududi's worldview in *Murder in the Name of Allah*. Commenting on the general corrupt nature of many Muslim clerics, Hadhrat Mirza Ghulam Ahmad[as], the promised messiah and founder of the Ahmadiyya Muslim Community, wrote more than a century ago (indeed, even before Maududi's birth):

When these clerics meet present day rulers, they bow down as if ready to prostrate; but among their own kind they insist repeatedly that this country is *dar-ul-harb*... They adhere so strongly to their doctrine of *Jihad*—which is completely misguided and entirely contradicts the teachings of the Holy Qur'an and *Hadith*— that they label as anti-Christ and advocate the murder of anyone who objects... They should remember that their understanding of *Jihad* is not at all correct, and that human sympathy is its first casualty. Their belief, that *Jihad* should be lawful today because it was permitted in early Islam, is totally incorrect...their reasoning is baseless. Under no circumstance did our Holy Prophet[sa] raise

---

457. Kanzul 'Ummal, vol. 7, 190.

458. Mishkat, Kitab ul-Ilm, chap. 3, p. 38.

the sword against anyone unless they had first raised the sword—mercilessly killing innocent, pious men, women and children with such brutality that reading about these events even today brings tears to our eyes."[459]

Wilders unfortunately ignores these clear condemnations of violence in the name of Islam. He ignores that Islam only permits fighting in self-defense—never as an offensive attack. Instead, Wilders quotes Professor Bernard Lewis to argue that Lewis considers Islam a totalitarian ideology.[460] Contrary to Wilders's wishes, however, Lewis suggests that the concept of suicide bombing is a twentieth-century invention having no basis in Islam,[461] and that those Muslims who endorse terrorism—like Maududi—are unaware of their own religion:[462]

> At no time did the classical jurists offer any approval or legitimacy to what we nowadays call terrorism. Nor indeed is there any evidence of the use of terrorism as it is practiced nowadays.[463] The fanatical warrior offering his victims the choice of the Koran or the sword is not only untrue, it is impossible" and that "generally speaking, Muslim tolerance of unbelievers was far better than anything available in Christendom...[464]

Thus, Wilders not only presents a wholly incorrect understanding of jihad, but the "Islamic scholar" he cites is none other than a debunked

---

459. Mirza Ghulam Ahmad, *British Government and Jihad* (1900), 8–9.

460. Wilders, *Marked For Death*, 79).

461. Bernard Lewis and Buntzie Ellis Churchill, *Islam: The Religion and the People* (Wharton School Publishing, 2008), 153.

462. Ibid., 145–50.

463. Ibid., 151.

464. Ibid., 156.

ignoramus and the modern founder of terrorism, Maududi. As I have repeated time and time again, I defend Islam, the Qur'an, Prophet Muhammad[sa], and the rightly guided khalifas, not extremists professing to act in Islam's name. Finally, even the professor whom Wilders quotes does not lean in Wilders's favor—but refutes him altogether.

ALLEGATION 53

Taqiyya ("Lying") is an Islamic Duty

Wilders writes, "Muhammad and his followers gained many of their victories through deception. The Islamic principle of *taqiyya*—lying for the sake of Allah—allows a believer to conceal his true intentions in order to advance the cause of Islam. Islam has used *taqiyya* since the seventh century to confound and confuse unbelievers. In Islamic jurisprudence, the use of *taqiyya* is regarded as a virtue and a religious duty."[465]

Considering how frequently Wilders has lied and deceived his readers in his polemic, he has some nerve accusing anyone else of lying—especially someone as truthful and noble as Prophet Muhammad[sa], who never once told a lie. Wilders then proceeds with several other "applications" of taqiyya that Islam allegedly encourages. Each of his allegations are as baseless as the one listed above.

REFERENCE: Qur'an 16:105 (in fact, Wilders meant to cite 16:107). Sahih Jami' Bukhari, vol. 7, Book 67, #427; Sahih Jami' Bukhari, vol. 6, Book 60, #138.

RESPONSE: As in much of his work, Wilders has borrowed this anti-Islam conspiracy theory from post-9/11 anti-Islam bigots. In order to rouse anti-Muslim sentiment, he employs just what he accuses all Muslims of—deceit and lies. The concept of taqiyya has no basis in Islam. But before addressing this concept and the verse in question—a verse Wilders could not even correctly cite—I draw your attention to three things.

---

465. Wilders, *Marked For Death*, 87.

First, this particular argument is structured as the ultimate propaganda argument. It basically says, "You are wrong, so even if you prove you are right, you are lying and therefore wrong." In other words, this argument does not prove anything against Islam—it baselessly assumes everything against Islam. Like a fixed sporting event, it determines the winner before the game is played. I find this tactic abhorrent in practical life, and any true seeker after truth should find it likewise.

Second, consider that even Prophet Muhammad's[sa] bitterest enemies, such as Abu Jahl,[466] Abu Sufyan,[467] and Umaiyya and his wife[468] all acknowledged that Prophet Muhammad[sa] never lied. In fact, when Prophet Muhammad[sa] first announced his prophethood to the Meccans, he asked them to acknowledge his truthfulness—which the entire community did.[469] Prophet Muhammad's[sa] attachment to truth was so strict that he instructed his followers to joke only if there was no lie in the joke.[470] Furthermore, the Holy Qur'an considers speaking truth, not lying, as a religious duty,[471] and emphasizes observing truth and justice in every circumstance—even when testifying against oneself.[472]

I now ask you to recall the incident I cited earlier in my book—when the Meccans demanded to know if Prophet Muhammad[sa] was *that* person who spoke against their idols. Under that threat of death, Prophet Muhammad[sa] spoke only the truth and did not delay in the slightest. When the time was ripe to engage in alleged taqiyya and therefore "advance the cause of Islam," through lies as Wilders defines it, Prophet Muhammad[sa] instead unhesitatingly told nothing but the truth. Thus,

---

466. *Dala'ilan Nabuwwatae li Baihaqi* (Beirut: Darul Kutab al-'Ilmiyya), 198

467. Sahih Jami' Bukhari, vol. 4, Book 52, #191.

468. Sahih Jami' Bukhari, vol. 4, Book 56, #826.

469. Sahih Jami' Muslim, Book 1, #406.

470. Sahih Sunan At-Tirmidhi, *Book of Righteousness*, #1990.

471. Qur'an 2:9–21; 4:70, 136; 5:9; 9:119; 33:36; 61:3–4.

472. Qur'an 4:136.

Prophet Muhammad's[sa] noble example in the face of mortal danger and the testimony of his bitterest enemies should be enough for any fair-minded person to recognize that lying has no place in Islam.

Third, while Wilders describes taqiyya as a "religious duty in Islamic jurisprudence," the word *taqiyya* does not even appear even once in the Qur'an or ahadith of Prophet Muhammad[sa]. Indeed, it appears nowhere in any ancient authentic Islamic jurisprudence. Wilders censors this fact from his readers. How Islam can be held accountable for a concept that does not exist in Islamic jurisprudence is beyond me. With this important context, I proceed to refute Wilders's specific allegations.

First, Wilders cites Qur'an 16:105, which reads, "As for those who do not believe in the Signs of Allah, surely, Allah will not guide them, and they shall have a grievous punishment." This verse has nothing to do with making any sort of declaration. If this is in fact what Wilders meant to cite, then I have nothing more to say than that this verse does nothing to substantiate Wilders's allegation. It does not even deal with relevant subject matter.

I realized, however, that Wilders may have meant to cite 16:107. That verse reads, "Whoso disbelieves in Allah after he has believed—save him who is *forced* thereto while his heart finds peace in the faith—but such as open their breasts to disbelief, on them is Allah's wrath; and they shall have a severe punishment."[473] The crucial word is *uk'riha* (forced). Its trilateral root, *kāf rā hā*, appears forty-one times in the Qur'an. It connotes hatred toward a thing, hardship, or coercion.

A subsequent verse[474] defines those who are "forced" as those who, due to their faith, emigrate from their homes, thereafter engaging in rigorous preaching. Then, if they cannot bear ensuing persecution, they can recant their faith. This is the "lie" the Holy Qur'an permits—to recant

---

473. Qur'an 16:107.

474. Qur'an 16:111.

under extreme coercion and hardship. This is a far cry from the fabrication of lying to gain some tactical advantage that Wilders paints this as.

Furthermore, even when faced with the most hostile circumstances in Mecca, Muslims did not hide their faith and continued to bear extreme persecution for twelve or thirteen years. If taqiyya were an Islamic injunction, then the Meccan era would have been the best time to use it. Yet, Wilders is unable to cite a single example where this so-called Islamic teaching was employed, in Mecca or otherwise. Moreover, because Wilders repeatedly holds the Bible superior to the Qur'an, I am eager to hear his justification for why the Bible justifies taqiyya.[475]

It is also necessary to relate a few Qur'anic verses that demonstrate how vociferously Islam condemns lying. The Qur'an declares, "And confound not truth with falsehood, nor hide the truth knowingly."[476] And, "Falsehood cannot approach it either from before or from behind it. It is a revelation from the Wise, the Praiseworthy."[477] Likewise:

> O ye who believe! Be strict in observing justice, and be witnesses for Allah, *even though it be against yourselves* or against parents and kindred. Whether he be rich or poor, Allah is more regardful of them both than you are. Therefore follow not low desires so that you may be able to act equitably. *And if you conceal the truth or evade it, then remember that Allah is well aware of what you do.*[478]

Thus, these (and countless other verses) demonstrate beyond a shadow of a doubt that lying has no refuge in Islam. Wilders cites none of these examples.

---

475. Genesis 12:12–13; Judges 3:20–22, 5:24–26; Corinthians 9:19–22.

476. Qur'an 2:43.

477. Qur'an 41:43.

478. Qur'an 4:136. (Emphasis added.)

Instead, Wilders quotes the following hadith: "If I take an oath and later find something else better than that, then I do what is better and expiate my oath." To answer Wilders's allegation, I first provide the reader something important that Wilders repeatedly does not—the full hadith:

We were in the company of Abu Musa Al-Ash'ari and there were friendly relations between us and this tribe of Jarm. Abu Musa was presented with a dish containing chicken. Among the people there was sitting a red-faced man who did not come near the food. Abu Musa said (to him), "Come on (and eat), for I have seen Allah's Apostle eating of it (i.e. chicken)." He said, "I have seen it eating something (dirty) and since then I have disliked it, and have taken an oath that I shall not eat it." Abu Musa said, "Come on, I will tell you (or narrate to you). Once I went to Allah's Apostle with a group of Al-Ash'ariyin, and met him while he was angry, distributing some camels of Rakat. We asked for mounts but he took an oath that he would not give us any mounts, and added, 'I have nothing to mount you on.' In the meantime some camels of booty were brought to Allah's Apostle and he asked twice, 'Where are Al-Ash'ariyin?' So he gave us five white camels with big humps. We stayed for a short while (after we had covered a little distance), and then I said to my companions, 'Allah's Apostle has forgotten his oath. By Allah, if we do not remind Allah's Apostle of his oath, we will never be successful.' So we returned to the Prophet and said, 'O Allah's Apostle! We asked you for mounts, but you took an oath that you would not give us any mounts; we think that you have forgotten your oath.' He said, 'It is Allah Who has given you mounts. By Allah,

277

and Allah willing, if I take an oath and later find something else better than that, then I do what is better and expiate my oath.'"[479]

First, regarding oaths in court, Prophet Muhammad[sa] said, "If someone swears a false oath near this pulpit of mine, he will take his seat in the Fire."[480] Again, he said, "Shall I inform you about the greatest of major sins? They are three: to associate partners with Allah, to disobey your parents, and to bear false witness (or he said) to speak falsely."[481] The Holy Qur'an corroborates the essence of these statements.[482]

Second, a substantive difference exists between an oath of allegiance and the regular pledges one makes on a daily basis—and the hadith that Wilders cites clearly refers to the latter. Whereas regular pledges cannot be broken, superior pledges can replace them. Recall that even Abu Sufyan could not relate to Heracles Caesar a single oath that Prophet Muhammad[sa] had ever violated. In the full narration that Wilders deceitfully omits, this premise is clear.

Hadhrat Abu Musa[ra] is trying to convince a man who has taken an oath never to eat chicken to eat the chicken he was served. In fact, this hadith clearly demonstrates a point counter to what Wilders attempts to prove—that is, the importance of keeping an oath under all circumstances. The fear of breaking one was so engraved on the hearts of Muslims that this man refused to touch the chicken because of his oath, even though eating chicken is halal in Islam. Abu Musa cited Prophet Muhammad's[sa] example of how he had at one point pledged not to give any camels to a group of Al-Ash'ariyin. When circumstances changed and he had possession of more camels, however, Prophet Muhammad[sa] distributed the camels among them.

---

479. Sahih Jami' Bukhari, vol. 7, Book 67, #427.

480. Sahih Jami' Al-Muwatta, vol. 36, Book 8, #10.

481. Sahih Jami' Muslim, Book 1, #158.

482. Qur'an 3:77–78; 16:92–93.

Finally, it is crucial to recognize the premise upon which Prophet Muhammad[sa] changed his position—he found "something better." Better for whom? Certainly not for himself: he found a method by which he could help others more effectively. In giving the Al-Ash'ariyin the camels, Prophet Muhammad[sa] violated no one's rights, committed no injustice, and deceived no one. On the contrary, he changed his position because he realized the change would allow him to more effectively help those in need. Prophet Muhammad's[sa] act was no different from that of a person who pledges $1 to charity, receives unexpected funds, and therefore increases the pledge—the oath—to $100. Can such a person be called a liar? According to Wilders—yes.

It is clear that the only lying going on here is that of Wilders when he makes his allegation. As far as Islam is concerned, lying has no place and no refuge.

ALLEGATION 54

Isra' and Miraj Were Physical Experiences

Wilders fails to properly describe the *isra'* and *miraj* and fabricates new elements not recorded anywhere in Islamic history. He writes, "Islam's theological claim to [Jerusalem] stems from a Koranic verse and various Islamic traditions relating that Muhammad once travelled from Mecca seated on *Buraq*, a winged horse with a woman's face, which took him to the *Masjid al-Aqsa*, or "the Farthest Mosque." From there, Muhammad ascended into heaven for an audience with Allah before the *Buraq* returned him to Mecca. The next morning, Muhammad told the Meccans he had taken a long journey on a winged horse with a woman's face. Unsurprisingly, the Meccans said he was crazy and complained about the absurd story to Abu Bakr, later the first Caliph, who simply replied that if Muhammad said it was true, it had to be true."[483]

The only thing absurd is Wilders's incessant misrepresentation of even basic historical facts.

REFERENCE: None.

RESPONSE: Wilders commits countless errors in this concocted allegation. First he conflates the accounts of these two events in Prophet Muhammad's[sa] life—the *isra'* ("journey to the distant mosque") and the *miraj* (journey to the heavens). These events have been described in the Qur'an in two separate places. Chapter 53 speaks exclusively of the *miraj* while Chapter 17 mentions the *isra'* without reference to the journey of the *miraj*.

---

483. Geert Wilders, *Marked for Death*, 78.

The two events are also temporally distinct. The *miraj* occurred much earlier than the *isra'*. The five daily prayers—sanctioned during the *miraj*—were instituted in the fifth year of Prophet Muhammad's[sa] prophethood. The *isra'*, on the other hand, took place in the eleventh year.[484] Some Christian writers are of the opinion that it occurred even later—in the twelfth.[485] Regardless, these events did not happen one immediately after the other as Wilders incorrectly claims.

For some time after the death of his wife Hadhrat Khadija[ra], Prophet Muhammad[sa] lived at the house of his cousin, Umme Hani[ra]. This is where he experienced the *isra'*. Incidentally, Umme Hani[ra] is the first person with whom Prophet Muhammad[sa] shared his experience. At least seven different hadith collectors have given her account of the incident. In all accounts, not a single reference exists to substantiate Prophet Muhammad's[sa] physical ascent to heaven or the skies. On the contrary, on the authority of four different reporters, the narration ends with the words "then he [i.e., the Prophet] woke up." The accounts do consistently narrate Prophet Muhammad's[sa] journey to Jerusalem and back the same night. If the two events—the journey to Jerusalem and the one to the heavens—took place simultaneously, it is impossible that Umme Hani could have missed the seemingly more important part of the journey—in which Prophet Muhammad[sa] is even reported to have met God.

Having established that Wilders conflates two separate events, I emphasize that neither event is to be understood literally but instead as extraordinary spiritual visions. As proof, first consider that the Qur'an states that not Prophet Muhammad's[sa] eyes, but his "heart," experienced the *miraj*.[486] During the *miraj*, the Qur'an again says that Prophet Muhammad[sa] "saw" God with his heart.[487] In fact, Prophet Muhammad[sa]

---

484. Az-Zurqani, *Zurqani*, vol. 1, 306.

485. Muir, *Life of Mahomet*, 121.

486. Sahih Jami' Muslim, Chap. 78, Book 1, #334–336.

487. Qur'an 53:12.

considered it the "greatest lie" against Allah if anyone alleged that he had seen Allah with his naked eye.[488]

Second, while not a single Qur'anic verse mentions Prophet Muhammad's[sa] physical ascension, the Qur'an actually affirms the opposite. The Qur'an records Prophet Muhammad's[sa] reply—in the same Chapter that mentions the *isra'*—to the Meccans when they mocked him and asked him to ascend to the heavens and bring down a book as proof of his truth. The Qur'an commands Prophet Muhammad[sa] to say, "I am not but a man *sent as a* Messenger."[489] God directed Prophet Muhammad[sa] to convey to the Meccans that as a human being, such feats were impossible for him as they are outside the laws of nature, and God does not break His laws of nature. (The Qur'an also rejects the notion of miracles that require breaking the laws of nature—miracles are simply the revealing of hitherto unknown natural laws, not the breaking of natural laws.[490])

Third, Prophet Muhammad's[sa] wife, Hadhrat Ayesha[ra], said, "The Prophet's body remained where it was but God removed his spirit by night."[491] This is yet another unambiguous testimony that no physical ascension or movement occurred.

Fourth, the hadith indicates that Prophet Muhammad[sa] did not move during either event: "The Prophet then woke while he was in the Sacred Mosque (at Mecca)."[492] Likewise, "[I experienced the vision] while I was in a state between that of one sleeping and one awake."[493] Thus, Wilders's claim that Prophet Muhammad[sa] experienced some sort

---

488. Sahih Jami' Muslim, Chap. 78, Book 1, #337–339.

489. Qur'an 17:94.

490. Qur'an 17:78; 33:63; 35:44; 48:16, 24.

491. Guillaume, *Life of Muhammad*, 183.

492. Sahih Jami' Bukhari, vol. 9, Book 93, #608.

493. Sahih Jami' Bukhari, 59:6.

of physical journey finds no support in the Qur'an or ahadith—both of which testify to precisely the opposite fact.

Wilders also, without any reference, describes *Buraq* as a "winged horse with a woman's face" and seems to find this amusing. It *is* amusing. This description reflects Wilders's wild imagination, because no such description is found in the ahadith and certainly not in the Qur'an. *Buraq* has been described in the ahadith as a white animal between the size of a mule and a donkey with far-reaching steps—but not as a physical creature.[494] Furthermore, the *miraj*'s import was to demonstrate the spiritual supremacy of Prophet Muhammad's[sa] stature over all human-kind and all creation as he "entered" a realm where even the Angel Gabriel could not. Again, this is a matter of spiritual elevation and nearness to God—not something Wilders can possibly claim to appreciate from his atheist perspective.

It is necessary to establish, again, that if Wilders finds fault with these spiritual experiences, then he must also find fault with Prophet Moses[as] seeing the burning bush and speaking to God on Mount Sinai. Likewise, Wilders must also object to the angel that appeared to Prophet Abraham[as] and his wife Hadhrat Sarah[as] to inform them of the birth of Prophet Isaac[as]. Further, Wilders must also object to the experience of Mary, mother of Jesus[as] upon the visit from Angel Gabriel to inform her about the birth of Christ. Wilders must also object to Christ's[as] claim that Satan tempted him. Thus, Wilders only reaffirms that his argument is not against Islam, but against religion in general. This should not be a surprise to anyone.

Finally, the *isra'* contained a hidden prophecy that Prophet Muhammad[sa] would emigrate from Mecca and be successful in Medina. Indeed, just a year after the vision of *isra'*, he emigrated to Medina and ultimately peacefully conquered Mecca. All of these facts are quite

---

494. Sahih Jami' Bukhari ,vol. 5, Book 58, #227.

clear—but hidden from Wilders because he is too busy fabricating allegations rather than trying to uncover the truth.

Conclusion

Fabricated meanings of jihad, fabricated concepts such as taqiyya, and fabricated renderings of well-established historical events summarize Wilders's efforts in his Chapter 5. It is unremarkable that Wilders does not cite any of his sources yet makes each of these outlandish allegations with full certitude. Wilders further incorrectly cites the Qur'anic verse when claiming the taqiyya argument and censors the full hadith from his readers, perhaps hoping they take him at his word. Indeed, the only evidence of taqiyya that Wilders provides is that of his own deceitful example.

As I proceed to discuss his Chapter 6, you will soon see that Wilders's arguments beyond his Chapter 6 consist largely of his complaints against modern acts of terrorism (and a regurgitation of arguments I've already refuted), which are outside *EXTREMIST*'s scope.

Wilders—A Slave to His Own Hatred

"Islam was the first religion that preached and practiced democracy."

— SAROJINI NAIDU

Chapter 6 is Wilders's proverbial last stand. With the exception of a few new allegations in his Chapters 7 through 13, everything thereafter is mere repetition—or complaint against certain extremist Muslims.

It is particularly confusing that Wilders spends so much time complaining about extremist Muslims for two reasons. First, no legitimate Muslim organization endorses the behaviors of these extremist organizations. If anything, Wilders merely repeats what numerous Muslim organizations have been condemning for years before him.

Second, Wilders claims he considers the vast majority of Muslims peaceful—that instead, his complaint is against Islam. If Wilders were sincere in his position, he would not have spent the lion's share of the second half of his book complaining about Muslims. His hypocrisy is perhaps the most telling aspect of his character.

In his Chapter 6, Wilders raises objections to Islam's interactions with non-Muslims, revisits some new allegations about the roles and rights of women in Islam, and even alleges that Islam endorses slavery. Wilders does a slightly better job in this Chapter of offering references for his allegations—but I emphasize: *slightly*. Several of his allegations still have no references, and one allegation even remarkably gives the Christian Broadcasting Network as a source on Islam.

In short, it is painfully obvious throughout his book that Wilders has let his hatred get the best of him and that hatred has brought out the worst of him. Wilders has literally become a slave to his own hatred.

ALLEGATION 55

Muhammad^sa Endorsed Female Genital Mutilation

Wilders alleges that Prophet Muhammad^sa endorsed female genital mutilation. He writes, "[Female genital mutilation (FGM)] involves cutting out the clitoris, was sanctioned by Muhammad, though he thoughtfully ordered Muslims not to cut off the *whole* clitoris. 'Do not cut severely as that is better for a woman and more desirable for a husband,' he said."[495] He further asserts that Muslims throughout history used this to torture their slaves.[496] Wilders repeats this allegation in Chapter 10.[497] I respond to both allegations here.

REFERENCE: Abu Dawud 41:5251.

RESPONSE: This is another example where Wilders's lack of any training in Islamic sciences is evident. Extremists ascribing to Islam and anti-Islam extremists may passionately hate each other—but both agree on much. One such myth both espouse is the fabrication that Islam endorses female genital mutilation, also known as FGM or infibulations. Most often, FGM supporters cite the Hadith recorded by Imam Abu Dawud[498]—Wilders is no different in his claim. The Hadith reads, "A woman used to perform circumcision in Medina. The Prophet said to her: Do not cut severely as that is better for a woman and more desirable for a husband."

---

495. Wilders, *Marked for Death*, 102.

496. Ibid.

497. Ibid., 163.

498. Sahih Sunan Abu Dawud 41:5251.

Before even delving into this Hadith, it is important to note that the vast majority of the Muslim world condemns FGM, and always has throughout history. FGM existed long before Islam and it sadly persists today as a cultural tradition that traverses religious lines. For example, in Ethiopia, Muslims, Christians, and Jews have all practiced FGM—though no faith endorses the act. I demonstrate with facts here that nothing in Islam endorses or promotes this barbaric act.

First, I once again remind the reader that Islamic jurisprudence requires that the Qur'an be taken as primary authority on all Islamic matters. Upon referring to the Qur'an, we discover that nothing in the Qur'an substantiates the argument that Islam or Prophet Muhammad[sa] endorsed FGM. On the contrary, the Qur'an implores, "...it is not lawful for you to inherit women against their will..."[499] Extremists and Wilders both ignore the Qur'an altogether and focuses only on the single Abu Dawud Hadith. But herein lies a second problem.

Had FGM proponents researched this Hadith, they would have discovered that this is the one and only attributed Hadith mentioning FGM. Thus, no possibility exists for corroboration or substantiation. More significantly, this Hadith is widely regarded as a weak tradition amongst Islamic scholars throughout history. Imam Abu Dawud, the very collector of this Hadith, himself declared the narration dubious, noting, "Its chain of transmitters is not strong. Besides, it is reported not as a direct quote attributed to the Prophet[sa] ... This Hadith is poor in authenticity."[500] In short, not a single authority links this alleged Hadith back to Prophet Muhammad[sa].

Thus, when we realize that the Qur'an does not in any way endorse FGM, that no corroboration for this Hadith exists, and that not a single narrator relates this Hadith to the time of Prophet Muhammad[sa] or as

---

499. Qur'an 4:20

500. Sahih Sunan Abu Dawud, XIII, 125–26.

having emanated from his mouth, it becomes clear that only a fool would accept this Hadith as true. Enter extremists and Islamophobes.

In fact, countless classical Islamic scholars after Imam Abu Dawud also dismissed the authenticity of this Hadith. Among them are the Egyptian scholar Ibn-e-Hajar al-Asqalani, widely regarded in the Sunni world for his knowledge of Ahadith;[501] Yusuf ibn Abdallah al-Barr,[502] another great Sunni scholar of Andalusia Spain; and the more recent Muhammad ash-Shawkani of Yemen.[503]

So why haven't Muslim scholars condemned FGM without exception? Well, they have, repeatedly, without exception. But the inability to listen to reason and logic is just another attribute extremists and Wilders share.

As with historical Islamic scholars, the present offers no shortage of Muslim scholars who condemn FGM. In 2005 a dean of Al-Azhar University of Cairo declared infibulations a criminal act.[504] An International Islamic Conference held in Cairo the following year in 2006 converged specifically to condemn infibulations.[505] Following in the footsteps of al-'Asqalani, Sheikh Ali Gomaa of Egypt issued a fatwa in 2007 against

---

501. Ibn Hajar's *Talkhis al-habir fi takhrij Ahadith ar-Rafi'i al-Kabir.*

502. "It is based on the authority of a transmitter whose report cannot be admitted as evidence", from *At-Tamhid lima fil-Muwatta minal-Ma`ani wal-Asanid* (Shams al-Haq al-Azhim Abadi's *Awn al- ma'bood fi sharh Sunan Abu Dawud*, XIV, 124). Al-Barr further states, "Those who consider (female) circumcision a *sunna*, use as evidence this *Hadith* of Abu al-Malih, which is based solely on the evidence of Hajjaj ibn-e-Artaa, who cannot be admitted as an authority when he is the sole transmitter. The consensus of Muslim scholars shows that circumcision is for men" (*Al-Tamhid lima fil-Muwatta min al-Ma`ani wal-Asanid*, XXI, 59).

503. "In addition to the fact that the *Hadith* is not valid as reference, it does not give any evidence to prove the case in question" (*Nayl al-Awtar*, Vol. I, pg. 139).

504. See http://www.ghanaweb.com/GhanaHomePage/NewsArchive/artikel.php?ID=77396 (Last Visited on August 12, 2012).

505. See http://news.bbc.co.uk/2/hi/6176340.stm (Last Visited on August 12, 2012).

infibulations.[506] In 2008 another East African country saw Somali Islamic scholars in Kenya call for an end to infibulations.[507] Then in January of 2010, 35 Islamic scholars in the West Coast African country of Mauritania banned infibulations.[508] The Muslim world and Muslim scholars have spoken loud and clear—FGM has nothing to do with Islam, and Islam has nothing to do with FGM.

As a final note, history well records that Prophet Muhammad[sa] answered detailed questions about personal hygiene for men and women. This included the proper way for each gender to clean themselves after using the facilities and after sexual intercourse; and for women—after menstruation. Furthermore, in maintaining the religious covenant Prophet Abraham[as] made with God to circumcise male children, Prophet Muhammad[sa] and Islam also admonished Muslims to circumcise male children. Every opportunity existed for at least one historical record to testify that Prophet Muhammad[sa] endorsed, let alone advocated, FGM. Yet, on this alleged Islamic practice, history is silent. For Islamophobes and extremists to yet insist that Islam endorses this barbaric act, without a shred of evidence, is by definition fabrication and propaganda.

Wilders's allegation that Islam somehow supports FGM is nonsense. Islam is clear that FGM is nothing more than a barbaric act of terrorism. It is a crime and those who engage in this crime must be held accountable—without exception.

Wilders also suggests, without reference, that such practices were used to torture slaves into submission. This allegation is likewise false

---

506. See http://www.medindia.net/news/Egyptian-Clerics-Say-Female-Circumcision-UnIslamic-23055-1.htm (Last Visited on August 12, 2012).

507. See
http://www.intactnetwork.net/intact/cp/files/1297081681_Islamic%20Scholars%20Find%20No%20Rel igious%20Justification%20for%20FGMC.pdf (Last Visited on August 12, 2012).

508. See http://news.bbc.co.uk/2/hi/africa/8464671.stm (Last Visited on August 12, 2012).

and the next section discusses the topic of Islam and slavery in extensive detail. Regarding Wilders's allegation that Prophet Muhammad[sa] endorsed infibulations, however, the facts and history clearly state otherwise.

ALLEGATION 56

Muhammad^{sa} Endorsed Slavery

Wilders writes, "Islam does not and *cannot* apologize for slavery, nor can it abolish the institution, because the Koran allows the faithful to enslave their enemies... Thus, admitting slavery is morally wrong would be tantamount to acknowledging the fallibility of the Koran, which is impossible since Allah himself supposedly wrote it."[509]

REFERENCE: Qur'an 33:51.

RESPONSE: For the same reason no religion can apologize for slavery, Islam cannot apologize for slavery; slavery is not solely an institution of religion. The institutions that Islam promotes are found in the Qur'an. Had the Qur'an itself been given the gift of speech, it could not simply apologize on behalf of those who have ignored its teachings. But if it could speak, it would loudly declare, "And what should make thee know what the steep ascent is? *It is* the freeing of a slave."[510]

This verse implements the scheme that would ultimately end slavery. The "ascent" is the striving for higher spirituality, which requires the freeing of a slave. Despite this clear incentive, Wilders objects that though the Qur'an promotes the freeing of slaves, it does not unequivocally say that slavery is outright abolished.

Wilders claims that because Islam and the Qur'an never flat-out declare, "Slavery shall stop immediately," Prophet Muhammad^{sa} therefore "en-

---

509. Wilders, *Marked for Death*, 106, 108.
510. Qur'an 90:13–14.

dorsed slavery." This line of argumentation is a result of ignorance and a lack of reflection on Islam's unprecedented teachings to abolish slavery—which it successfully did. Slavery's eventual re-emergence in the Muslim world long after Prophet Muhammad[sa] died was in spite of Islam, not because of it. That re-emergence only reflected the spiritual and moral decay some Muslims had (and have) succumb to. Regardless, those Muslims who later employed—and those extremists who to this day employ slavery as we understand slavery today—act contrary to Islamic teachings. Nothing in Islam justifies their criminal actions.

Islam employed an effective process to end slavery rather than issue an empty declaration alone. Islam submits, thus, that while society can pass rules and regulations, it is both unwise and impossible to force the mind to accept what the heart does not. In other words, Islam recognizes that racism, prejudice, and bigotry do not just disappear simply because a law is passed. Such diseases ingrain themselves into society—a fact supported with statistics below. Racism and prejudice must be extracted thoroughly if a society has a hope of permanently eliminating them as opposed to merely covering them up.

First, slavery was rampant during pre-Islam Arabia (i.e. the society Wilders ignorantly calls "progressive" and "multi-cultural"). It should be no surprise, therefore, that slavery was rampant at Prophet Muhammad's[sa] advent. Prophet Muhammad[sa] sought to eliminate it under Islam's teaching of humanity's universal equality. To systemically abolish slavery, Prophet Muhammad[sa] first forbade that any free person be enslaved, thus stopping the slave trade from expanding.

Next, Prophet Muhammad[sa] firmly established that all humanity is equal—one could not accept Islam without embracing this principle. Thus, as slave owners accepted Islam, they unambiguously recognized that their slaves were their equals. These free Muslims naturally developed affection for their fellow human beings—slave or free. As a result of the compassion for humanity Islam infused in Muslims, slave owners freed their slaves of their own accord, thus shrinking the population of those yet in slavery.

Perhaps Wilders envisioned the Qur'an saying something like "Thou shalt not take another person into bondage." But instead of saying "don't do that"—a command that includes no guarantee of being obeyed—the Qur'an encourages performing a kind act to earn blessings. In this style, the Qur'an has given Muslims many reasons to free slaves and zero reasons to enslave free men and women.

The reasons to free a slave include the above-mentioned verse—a nod to those whose goals are to reach for the stars (i.e., the steep ascent). But the Qur'an has also mandated the freeing of slaves to expiate sins. The Qur'an requires the freeing of a slave as one stipulation to be absolved of involuntary manslaughter.[511] The Qur'an also states that a husband must free a slave should he insult his wife—and he must do so before he hopes to enjoy relations again.[512]

Now, if the freeing of a slave were so powerfully atoning that it could help redress accidental killings, would not one also recognize it as a blessed deed beyond that? And if a comparatively small thing like insulting one's wife requires the freeing of a slave for atonement, an inquisitive Muslim might ponder how many other "minor" sins might also be rectified by freeing a slave. The Qur'an has established a system that, *if followed*, is geared toward abolishing slavery at every opportunity.

Accordingly, Prophet Muhammad[sa] made it a habit to free slaves whenever an eclipse of the sun[513] or moon[514] occurred. No restitution for killing, no penance for name-calling, just the absence of sunlight or moonlight. Prophet Muhammad[sa] practically gave his followers *any* reason to free slaves. Upon his marriage to Hadhrat Khadija[ra], she willingly transferred all her property—and her slaves—to his name. As his first

---

511. Qur'an 4:93.

512. Qur'an 58:4.

513. Sahih Jami' Bukhari, Vol. 3, Book 46, #695

514. Ibid., #696.

order of business, Prophet Muhammad[sa] freed every slave given to him without demanding or hinting at the least compensation.

The classical hadith scholar, Imam Nawawi, has preserved several ahadith in his great work *Riyadus-Salihin*. These ahadith illustrate the calculated manner in which slaves were freed and further demonstrate that Islam endorsed the emancipation of all slaves. Imam Nawawi relates a narration of Hadhrat Abu Dharr[ra]:

> I asked the Prophet... "What is the best kind of manumission (of slaves)?" He replied, "The manumission of the most expensive slave and the most beloved by his master."[515]

What? No consideration for a slave master? Does this Prophet[sa]—whom Wilders would swear was the equivalent of the most sadistic Southern slaveholder (not that Wilders ever mentions American slavery)—proceed to force another slave owner to give up his best merchandise? I mention this hadith in particular because Wilders alleges, again without reference, that Muslims *only* considered elderly and destitute slaves for emancipation. Obviously, history records the exact opposite scenario.

Muslims had immense incentives to free slaves and immense obstacles to enslave anyone. The companion Hadhrat Abu Hurairah[ra] relates that the Prophet Muhammad[sa] said: "He who sets free a Muslim slave, Allah will deliver from the fire of Hell every limb of his body in return for every limb of the slave's body, even his private parts."[516]

I want to emphasize, additionally, that freeing slaves was secondarily about pleasing Allah, and primarily about recognizing the equality of all human beings. As I discuss later, Prophet Muhammad[sa] re-emphasized

---

515. Ibid., #694.

516. Imam Nawawi, "The Merit of Emancipation of Slaves (#1358)," Chapter 236 in *Riyadus-Salihin*. Original hadith found in Bukhari, Chapter 52 ("Book of Setting Free"), #2382.

the uncompromising equality of all humanity in his farewell address. Islam offers no refuge for those seeking to please Allah while abusing humanity.

But even if Wilders hypothetically concedes that Islam created an effective system to free slaves, what does Islam say about those living as slaves today—are they doomed to a life of servitude? Not in the least. Prophet Muhammad declared:

> Allah says, "I will be against three persons on the Day of Resurrection: 1. One who makes a covenant in My Name, but he proves treacherous. 2. *One who sells a free person (as a slave) and eats the price*, 3. And one who employs a laborer and gets the full work done by him but does not pay him his wages."[517]

Thus, Islam first categorically forbade selling slaves, effectively ensuring the slave trade would grind to a halt. Ibn 'Umar relates that "The Prophet[sa] forbade the selling of slaves or giving it as a present."[518]

Next, the Qur'an requires Muslim slave owners to free slaves if a slave could purchase freedom. If the slave could not, the slave owner must help: "And such as desire a deed of manumission in writing from among those whom your right hands possess, write it for them if you know any good in them; and give them out of the wealth of Allah which He has bestowed upon you."[519]

This teaching is paramount because it helped Arab society avoid a massive pitfall (from which American society still hasn't escaped even 150 years after its slavery was abolished). This Islamic teaching did not simply end slavery. It ended slavery *while* providing former slaves the means to be absorbed into society at a rate both the economy and work-

---

517. Sahih Jami' Bukhari, vol. 3, Book 30, #430. (Emphasis added.)

518. Sahih Jami' Bukhari, vol. 8, Book 80, #748.

519. Qur'an 24:34.

force could manage. The gravity of this teaching is profound: a slave could be freed upon simple request and nothing else. This is a far cry from promoting slavery, as Wilders deceptively ascribes to Islam.

Likewise, Islam has also taught that societies with slaves must treat them with respect. Far from the rampant injustices inherent in America's antebellum system of slavery, the Qur'an commanded equal rights with regard to capital punishment for all classes of society.[520] Prophet Muhammad[sa] himself stated, "Whoever kills his slave shall be put to death."[521] Thus, no slave master has the right to murder a slave and not be held accountable.

Contrast this teaching enacted fourteen hundred years ago with American law just a century and a half ago (which was allegedly based on biblical justification). Contrary to the Qur'an, American law allowed a slave master to kill a slave without consequence. For example, the Georgia Supreme Court held as a matter of public policy that killing a slave was not a felony because the Old Testament cursed Blacks and, therefore, the master and slave were "but fulfilling a divine appointment."[522]

And if Wilders argues that the New Testament removed these vicious teachings, I respond as I have before—that Jesus[as] in the New Testament did not abrogate Old Testament law.[523] In fact, the Georgia Supreme Court used this exact line of reasoning when delivering its verdict:

> Christ came not to remove the curse; but recognizing the relation of master and servant, he prescribed the rules which govern, and thus ordained [slavery] an institution of Christianity. It is the

---

520. Qur'an 2:179.

521. Ibn Majah; Sunan Abu Dawud, vol. 4, 652–54; Sunan an-Nasa'i, vol. 8, 20–21; Tirmidhi, vol. 4, 26.

522. David Sehat, *The Myth of American Religious Freedom* (2011), 82–83.

523. Matthew 5:17–18

crowning glory of this age and of this land, that our legislation has responded to the requirements of the New Testament in great part, and if left alone, the time is not distant when we, the slaveholders, will come fully up to the measure of our obligations as such, under the Christian dispensation.[524]

This approach to slavery was common. Virginia, Arkansas, and North Carolina (among others), legally and while citing the Bible, justified beating and murdering slaves without consequence.[525] Remarkably, this was precisely the attitude that pre-Islamic Arabs had had toward slaves. And again—I do not present these historical events to malign Jesus Christ[as]. Rather, I point out that even in recent history, governments and courts used Christianity to propagate slavery and kill slaves. Islam, on the contrary, had condemned and abolished such barbaric practices fourteen hundred years prior.

Compared to the form of slavery that Wilders's Dutch slave-trading forefathers had introduced, Islam commanded advanced and humanitarian rules of how to treat those yet in slavery. Indeed, these commandments demonstrated that the "slave" was less a slave and more a family member. Prophet Muhammad[sa] said concerning the treatment of slaves:

Your servants and slaves are your brothers and your stewards: Allah has placed them under your hands; whoso then has a brother under his hands, let him feed him out of what he feeds himself, and let him clothe him out of what he clothes himself; and compel them not to do work which will overpower them, and if ye do compel them (to any such work), then assist them in doing the same.[526]

524. David Sehat, *The Myth of American Religious Freedom* (2011), 82–83.

525. Ibid.

526. Sahih Jami' Bukhari, vol. 8, Book 73, #76.

Can this even be called slavery? Making a slave eat as you eat and dress as you dress? Help them with their hard labor? Such exemplary treatment does not even exist today in the most civilized of nations and most advanced jobs. Consider: what employee can say that he or she eats as the CEO eats, dresses as the CEO dresses, and lives as the CEO lives? The relationship that Islam prescribes here is not "slave/master" but employee/employer, with the "slaves" receiving better treatment than employees even in many advanced nations today.

Prophet Muhammad[sa] not only promoted the good treatment of slaves and their freedom, but he also warned against their mistreatment. Hadhrat Abu Masud al-Bad'ri relates:

> I was beating my slave with a whip when I heard a voice behind me: Understand, Abu Mas'ud; but I did not recognise the voice due to intense anger. He (Abu Mas'ud) reported: As he came near me (I found) that he was the Messenger of Allah (may peace be upon him) and he was saying: Bear in mind, Abu Mas'ud; bear in mind, Abu Mas'ud! He (Abu Mas'ud) said: I threw the whip from my hand. Thereupon he (the Holy Prophet) said: Bear in mind, Abu Mas'ud; verily Allah has more dominance upon you than you have upon your slave. I (then) said: I would never beat my servant in future.[527]

In another hadith Prophet Muhammad[sa] admonished, "Give food to the hungry, pay a visit to the sick and release (set free) the one in captivity (by paying his ransom)."[528]

Thus, Muslims were admonished to use their own funds to pay for the freedom of those enslaved. Emancipation and equal treatment of slaves resonated throughout Islamic history and even after Muslims be-

---

527. Sahih Jami' Muslim, Book 15, #4086.

528. Sahih Jami' Bukhari, vol. 7, Book 65, #286. (Emphasis added.)

came disunited and adrift. But these are not our words and opinions. Numerous well-known and respected Christian scholars and historians cannot help but admit that Muslims treated slaves with utmost compassion and equality. For example, historian Lerone Bennet Jr. writes:

> As a religious ethic, Islam was unusually effective in cutting across racial lines. All Moslems, whatever their color, were brothers in faith. "If a Negro slave is appointed to rule you," Mohammed said, "hear and obey him, though his head be like a dried grape." In this climate, a man could be a slave today and a prime minister tomorrow. An extraordinarily large number of Negroes played heroic roles in the rise and spread of Islam...there were...numerous black generals, administrators, and poets...race was not a crucial factor in the Islamic world.[529]

Indeed, Bennet was commenting on established history. Usama bin Zaid[ra] and Zaid bin Harr were former slaves that were raised to the status of generals in Muslim armies. Ata bin Abi Rabah, Ibn-e-Sireen, and Nafi' became renowned imams of ahadith and *fiqh* (jurisprudence); each rose to these great heights from slavery. Imam Ibn-e-Sireen, another former slave, is regarded to this day as a premier authority on dream interpretation. Likewise, Abdullah bin Mubarak is another brilliant imam of *fiqh* who was once a slave. Mujahid bin Jubair, Musa bin Akba, Muhammad bin Isaac were prolific scholars and historians who were once slaves and rose to unmatched heights—all because of Islam's strategy to eliminate slavery through a process of promoting compassion, not as some executive order.

Under Islam, these individual acts of emancipation were made communal by an inherent antislavery policy grown out of Islam's charitable systems of zakaat and charity. The Qur'an has encouraged such institu-

---

529. Lerone Bennett Jr., *Before the Mayflower: A History of Black America* (1969), 13.

tions by ordering that alms (some of which are made obligatory for Muslims) be applied toward specific goals, one of which is the emancipation of slaves.[530]

Moreover, Islam's commandment of kind and equal treatment and education of those yet in slavery ensured that when a person gained his physical freedom, he was already mentally free. When discussing late 20th century South African apartheid (which Wilders ignores was done by so-called Christians) Steve Biko profoundly stated "The most powerful weapon in the hands of the oppressor is the mind of the oppressed." Islam sought to ensure not just physical freedom, but mental freedom so that when a former slave was freed, he was empowered to work for himself, provide for himself, rely on himself, and not succumb to economic or mental slavery in the future.

With this important but certainly not exhaustive context and correct history of Islam's view of slavery, I can properly address the verse Wilders quotes that he claims supports slavery (33:51). This verse offers nothing to support his wild allegation. It states, "O Prophet, We have made lawful to thee thy wives whom thou hast paid their dowries, and those whom thy right hand possesses from among those whom Allah has given thee as gains of war."[531]

In other words, Wilders equates prisoners captured during wartime with average citizens enslaved against their will. The Qur'an is clear that POWs cannot be held against their will once a war ends,[532] whereas slaves generally have no fixed period of "employment." (Earlier, I also discussed at length the magnanimous manners Muslims showed to POWs and encourage the reader to refer to that discussion as necessary.)

Furthermore, nothing in the Qur'an concerning POWs suggests that they must work. If Wilders takes issue with the idea of a Muslim nation

530. Qur'an 9:60.

531. Qur'an 33:51.

532. Qur'an 47:5.

at war taking POWs and making them work, let him also take issue with all other nations who go to war, capture enemy combatants, and force them to perform hard labor. Let him be just as vocal about America's decision to hold Afghan POWs in Guantanamo Bay without due process, trial, charges, or any plan to release them—all acts that are required by American and international law.

Islam enacted a plan to stop the growth of slavery and then slowly eliminate it altogether. This Islamic method encouraged Muslims to treat their slaves equally, encouraged the education of slaves, and then encouraged their freedom. Freed slaves were then empowered to become productive members of society. Yes, some Muslims have brutalized slaves, but they did so contrary to Islam. Islam offers such extremists no refuge. As I have demonstrated, Islam is clearly aligned against slavery. Even when Europe began the transatlantic slave trade, Muslims largely opposed it. For example, *The Report of the Commission of Inquiry, Sierra Leone* reports:

> About six years before, the Sherief [sic] of Mecca had sent a letter to the King of Fulas for circulation through all these "Mandingo" tribes, strictly prohibiting the selling of slaves—and which later was also promulgated among Yorubas, Fulanis and other neighboring tribes. The slave traffic was declared to be contrary to the teachings of Muhammad (on whom be peace) which pronounce the most fearful denunciations of Allah's wrath in the hereafter against those who persist in the traffic with the European nations.[533]

Some Muslims did reengage in slavery—but even non-Muslim historians admit that its levels cannot be compared with those of American or European slavery. As Thomas R. R. Cobb writes:

---

533. Sultan A. Latif, *Slavery: The African American Psychic Trauma* (1994), 125.

The treatment of slaves in British India was generally mild. The slave is a favorite and confidential servant rather than an abject drudge...[owners] contribute to insure good treatment to the slave. The food and raiment allowed them were scanty, but fully equal to that of the free laborers of that class.[534]

Eminent historian Ina Corinne Brown likewise adds that "domestic slaves [of Muslims] were treated more or less as members of the family, often attained to positions of importance, and tended to be absorbed into the general population."[535]

Christian pastor and historian Edward Wilmot Blydon writes, "Christian travelers, with every wish to think otherwise, have remarked that the Negro who accepts Mohammedanism acquires at once a sense of the dignity of human nature not commonly found even among those who have been brought to accept Christianity."[536] Pastor Blydon then adds, "Wherever the Negro is found in Christian lands...he is slow and unprogressive...there is no Christian community of Negroes anywhere which is self-reliant and independent. On the other hand, there are numerous Negro Mohammeden communities and states in Africa which are self-reliant, independent, [and] dominant."[537]

He again argued, as a Christian pastor, that Islam's emphasis on universal brotherhood, education, and racial tolerance provided a benefit to former slaves that the Christian behaviors of enslavement, declaration of racial superiority, and restrictions on reading even the Bible could not offer.[538] Pastor Blydon made these remarks in 1887, at the height of the

---

534. Thomas R. R. Cobb, *An Inquiry into the Law of Negro Slavery in the United States of America* (1858), iv.

535. Ina Corinne Brown, *Story of the American Negro* (1934), 20.

536. Edward Wilmot Blydon, *Christianity, Islam, and the Negro Race* (1887), 11.

537. Ibid., 12.

538. Ibid., 18–33.

post-Civil War fallout from slaves who were emancipated (in the sweeping manner Wilders finds appropriate) yet denied the tools to reach their full potential. Pastor Blydon foresaw the reality: that the influx of slaves into society, combined with the rancor many still harbored against Black Americans, would prove destructive. Yet, this is the method Wilders would demand out of Islam. In doing so, Wilders shamelessly ignores the wisdom Prophet Muhammad[sa] employed in building love for slaves as equal human beings, educating them, helping them earn money, and then freeing them.

And, in fact, more than a century later, we see that Pastor Blydon was quite accurate in his assessment. Wilders argues that slavery should have been abolished immediately—without the aforementioned process that changes the hearts (and then minds) to recognize the equality of people. Fortunately, history affords us examples of both methods (and their consequences). The United States practiced slavery for centuries before abolishing slavery outright as Wilders endorses. The pre-Islamic Arabs practiced slavery for centuries before Islam gradually eliminated it over a period of a few decades.

Below I further analyze the results of the American approach Wilders prefers (the allegedly "Christian" strategy): immediately and without first transforming a society—keeping in mind that Islam implemented a transformation of hearts and minds, both of slave owners and former slaves.

First, history records no slave revolts under Islam or civil wars resulting from Muslims freeing slaves. Contrast this with the violence and numerous slave rebellions before the Civil War, the countless KKK bombings of Black churches after the American Civil War—and, of course, the bloodbath of the Civil War itself.

Next, contrast the above testimony that former slaves were raised to the status of generals, poets, scholars, and imams in Islam, with the following statistics that show the intense governmental and social discrimination Black Americans suffer to this day in twenty-first-century America:

Black Americans represent 13.6 percent of America's population,[539] yet a disproportionate 40 percent of incarcerated Americans are Black—a significantly higher proportion than of any other racial demographic.[540] In 2009, Black Americans comprised nearly 30 percent of all arrests.[541] More than one in five (22 percent) of Black Americans live under the poverty line—also significantly higher than any other racial demographic.[542] Likewise, in 2009, the average Black American annual family income was $38,409, while the average White American annual family income was $62,545.[543] Black children suffer from low birth weight twice as often as any other demographic[544] and have nearly a 33 percent higher rate of infant mortality than those in second place (Native Americans).[545] In 2010, 19.8 percent of Black Americans held college degrees compared to 30.3 percent of White Americans.[546] Black students have historically scored lower than any other demographic on the SAT[547] and the ACT.[548] Despite lower

539. US Bureau of the Census, *The Black Population: 2010* (2010 Census Briefs), September, 2011. http://www.census.gov/prod/cen2010/briefs/c2010br-06.pdf.

540. Prison Policy Initiative, "The Sentencing Project: Facts about Prisons and Prisoners." http://prisonpolicy.org/scans/prison_facts.pdf.

541. US Bureau of the Census, "Table 325. Arrests by Race: 2009." http://www.census.gov/compendia/statab/2012/tables/12s0325.pdf.

542. National Center for Education Statistics, *Status and Trends in the Education of Blacks*. http://nces.ed.gov/pubs2003/2003034.pdf, 12.

543. US Bureau of the Census, "Table 695. Money Income of Families—Number and Distribution by Race and Hispanic Origin: 2009," http://www.census.gov/compendia/statab/2012/tables/12s0695.pdf.

544. National Center for Education Statistics, *Education of Blacks*, 15.

545 Ibid., 19.

546. US Bureau of the Census, "Table 229. Educational Attainment by Race and Hispanic Origin: 1970 to 2010," http://www.census.gov/compendia/statab/2012/tables/12s0229.pdf.

rates of drug use, Black Americans suffer a 2.8 to 5.5[549] times higher rate of drug arrest and charges than White Americans; and up to 11.3 times higher in some states.[550]

This is the consequence, 150 years later, of mercilessly enslaving millions, stripping them of their identities, and then "freeing" them without any means of self-reliance, funds, education, mental freedom, or a plan for the future. Most harmful, however, was that the outright emancipation of American slaves did nothing to change the hearts of their Christian former owners. As a result, proslavery terrorist organizations like the Ku Klux Klan emerged after the Civil War, and at their peak in the 1920s included one of every thirteen White Americans—a shocking four million people.

The fair conclusion is that Prophet Muhammad's method to end slavery was not only practical, but also effective and long lasting. As a result, slavery ended quickly, and racial harmony flourished for millennia to come. On the contrary, American history demonstrates that Wilders's demand on Islam is ignorant and counterproductive. His allegation that Islam promotes slavery is unfounded and deceitful.

547. National Center for Education Statistics, *Education of Blacks*, 63.

548. Ibid., 65.

549. Human Rights Watch, *Decades of Disparity: Drug Arrests and Race in the United States*, 2009. http://www.hrw.org/sites/default/files/reports/us0309web_1.pdf.

550. US Bureau of the Census, *The Black Population*; Prison Policy Initiative, "Facts about Prisons and Prisoners;" National Center for Education Statistics, *Education of Blacks*.

ALLEGATION 57

Islam Endorses Concubines

Having thoroughly addressed Islam and slavery, I turn to Wilders's unqualified statement that Islam condones sex with slave girls. He writes,
"...the Koran condones sex slavery by granting men sexual access to 'what
their right hands possess' (meaning female captives or slaves) and to 'the
slave girls whom Allah has given you as booty.'"[551]

REFERENCE: Qur'an 33:51, 23:6–7, 70:29–30.

RESPONSE: Perhaps Wilders is not aware that the Holy Qur'an has
condemned fornication and adultery.[552] Islam does not permit concubi-
nage, and fornication and adultery trigger the penalty of physical repri-
mand. [553] Hadhrat Abu Musa al-Ashari recalls that Prophet
Muhammad[sa] said, "Any man who has a slave-girl whom he teaches good
manners so that she has good manners and educates her in the best possible way and then frees her and marries her has two rewards."[554]

Wilders makes a weak case by again referring to 33:51 as well as
23:6–7 and 70:30–31 of the Qur'an, all of which use the expression
"those whom thy right hand possesses." As stated previously, one of the
meanings of this expression relates to POWs. But the Qur'an has also
stated that this term can be applied to slaves and servants:

---

551. Wilders, *Marked for Death*, 108.

552. Qur'an 5:6; 17:33; 25:69; 60:13.

553. Qur'an 24:3.

554. Sahih Jami' Bukhari, vol. 3, Book 46, #720.

And whoso of you cannot afford to marry free, believing women, *let him* marry what your right hands possess, namely, your believing handmaids. And Allah knows your faith best; you are *all* one from another; so marry them with the leave of their masters and give them their dowries according to what is fair, they being chaste, not committing fornication, nor taking secret paramours. And if, after they are married, they are guilty of lewdness, they shall have half the punishment prescribed for free women. This is for him among you who fears lest he should commit sin. And that you restrain yourselves is better for you; and Allah is Most Forgiving, Merciful.[555]

Thus, Islam has allowed for mutually consenting marriages between masters and slaves—a union that would automatically lead to the end of the master-slave relationship. We also see yet another warning against illicit sexual affairs. Likewise, former slaves have been given a degree of leniency with regard to indiscretions they might commit, acknowledging that such people may likely have been brought up in a non-Islamic environment. Among the worst of these indiscretions is adultery, and Wilders should take special note that the punishment would then be *half* of the standard punishment for adultery.

The verse in question further states, "you are all one from another," which means that despite being from different social classes, all believing Muslims are equal. No Arab slave master before Islam would have had the gall to reject tradition. No Arab noble would have ever conceived of marrying a slave. But with Islam, the Arabs realized that all people are created equal. Prophet Muhammad[sa] said:

Let none of you call out to his slave saying, "My slave boy!" or "My slave girl!" nor let a slave call out to his master saying, "My

---

555. Qur'an 4:26.

310

Lord!" but let the master call out to the slave saying, "My young man!" or "My young woman!" and let the slave call out to the master as "My chief!" for, verily, ye are all slaves, and your Lord is Allah, the Almighty.[556]

Prophet Muhammad[sa] inspired a new way of thinking in Arab society and redefined the relationship between master and servant—so much so that he led by example and himself married a former slave, a matter I address in the next section. Indeed, as discussed in the previous section regarding Islam's effective method to abolish slavery, this act was yet another means to demonstrate that all people are equal.

---

556. Sunan Masnad Ahmad, chap. 9.

ALLEGATION 58

Mary[ra] the Copt Was Muhammad's[sa] Slave, Not His Wife

Wilders writes, "Muhammad...was a slave trader who owned many slaves, including female concubines such as Mary the Copt."[557]

REFERENCE: None.

RESPONSE: I have already established that Prophet Muhammad condemned slavery and immediately freed every slave that came into his authority. Prophet Muhammad[sa] was married to a slave girl in 7 AH (629 CE) by the name of Mariah[ra], i.e. "Mary the Copt." She did not, contrary to Wilders's belief, remain a slave afterward. Having explained the rules of engagement—that slaves must be freed before marrying—no reason exists (indeed, Wilders presents none) to think that Hadhrat Mariah[ra] remained enslaved after her marriage to Prophet Muhammad[sa]. History well records Hadhrat Mariah[ra] was his wife, not a concubine.

The king of Egypt arranged the marriage. He sent Mariah[ra], who was a Coptic Christian, to Arabia specifically as an "offering" to the new "king" of Arabia—i.e., Prophet Muhammad[sa]. This was a time in history when nations and tribes used marriage to form cultural and political bonds—a tradition that goes back to the time of King Solomon[as] and Sheba. Furthermore, that a descendent of Ishmael would marry a woman from Egypt kept with tradition.

---

557. Wilders, *Marked for Death*, 109.

The Arabs, who considered themselves Ishmael's[as] descendants even before the dawn of Islam (and other nations were aware of this claim), are themselves the direct result of Egyptian-Ishmaelite relations. Biblical history records that Prophet Abraham married an Egyptian woman[558] and that his son Prophet Ishmael also married a woman from Egypt.[559] So Prophet Muhammad[sa] marrying this Egyptian was in the same spirit as that tradition. Otherwise, how could the Christian king of Egypt be unaware of this fact when he sent this "Hagarish" servant girl to this Ishmaelite out of Arabia who claimed to be a prophet in the tradition of biblical prophets? Hadhrat Abu Hurairah[ra] said:

> I have loved the Banu Tamim people since I heard the Messenger of Allah say three things about them. I heard him say, "They will be the strongest community against the anti-Christ." When their charitable donations came in, the Messenger of Allah said, "This is the charitable offerings of our people." Aisha had a slave-girl from them and he told her, "Set her free. She is one of the descendants of Ishmael."[560]

As such, Muslims today all share respect for this former Egyptian slave, Mariah[ra]. Like Prophet Muhammad's[sa] other wives, Muslims also honor Mariah[ra] with the moniker "mother of the faithful." Prophet Muhammad[sa] married women whom society considered less worthy and gave them an honored status—an action the Qur'an endorses: "And marry widows from among you, and your male slaves and female slaves who are fit for marriage. If they be poor, Allah will grant them means out of His bounty; and Allah is Bountiful, All-Knowing."[561]

---

558. Genesis 16:3.
559. Genesis 21:21.
560. Sahih Jami' Bukhari, chap. 52, #2405.
561. Qur'an 24:33.

Prophet Muhammad[sa] also married former POWs. Two widows, Hadhrat Jawairiyah[ra] and Hadhrat Safiyyah[ra], were former POWs who married Prophet Muhammad[sa] *after* having been freed, and *after* having voluntarily accepted Islam. This is a general rule of thumb in Islam:

> And marry not idolatrous women until they believe, even a believing bondwoman is better than an idolatress, although she may appeal to you. And give not *believing women* in marriage to idolaters until they believe; *even* a believing slave is better than an idolater, although he may appeal to you. These call to the Fire, but Allah calls to Heaven and to forgiveness by His command. And He makes His Signs clear to the people that they may remember.[562]

Thus, it should be no surprise that Wilders's unsupported allegations regarding Mary[ra] the Copt do not stand up to the facts of history. Mary[ra] was not a concubine, but Prophet Muhammad's[sa] honored wife.

---

562. Qur'an 2:222.

ALLEGATION 59

A Muslim Man's Child Must Be Raised Muslim Despite His Wife

Wilders writes, "...according to Islamic law, when a Muslim man marries a non-Muslim woman (the opposite is forbidden), the children have to be raised as Muslims."[563] To boot, he cites the Christian Broadcasting Network as his authority for this.

REFERENCE: Christian Broadcasting Network.

RESPONSE: This merits a short response because I fail to see the substance behind Wilders's objection. Muslim men are encouraged to marry Muslim women first and foremost,[564] and they are allowed to marry "People of the Book"—namely, Christians and Jews.[565] Why then should Wilders find it so outrageous that one of the ideals desired in a Muslim marriage is that children born therein should be raised as Muslims? Does he raise this objection out of sympathy for the miniscule number of Christian and Jewish mothers who marry Muslim men? And why does Wilders not raise similar objections to Orthodox Jews who only consider other Orthodox Jews as "marriage material?" The same objection could be applied to devout Catholics. Yet Wilders is silent on these matters.

---

563. Wilders, *Marked for Death*, 96.

564. Qur'an 5:6.

565. Qur'an 2:222.

Moreover, I have already spoken at length on Islam's emphasis on religious freedom, and those same principles apply here. I know that Wilders would much rather have children not raised in any religious tradition at all. Thus, this argument is really just another pointless complaint against religion in general, more than specifically against Islam. It is also remarkable that Wilders deemed it wise to cite a fundamentalist Christian television station as an allegedly credible source for Islamic research. Therefore, this entire allegation is based on the unqualified opinion of an extremely right-wing Christian television network—and we know how much extreme wing television networks of any worldview know about worldviews they disagree with.

ALLEGATION 60

Islam Oppresses Dhimmis and Demands Jizya or Death

Wilders writes, "Islam offers most *kafirs* a simple choice: convert to Islam or die. For Jews and Christians—the so-called "people of the book"—there is a third option: they are allowed to accept the humiliating status of dhimmitude—the status of permanent humiliation, degradation, and insecurity—[it] led to the asphyxiation of Christian and Jewish life in the Islamic world, consigning Islamic society to poverty and backwardness, forcing it to constantly conquer new lands in order to capture more economically productive dhimmis. Reliant on forced *jizya* payments from ever dwindling numbers of dhimmis, Islamic rule was parasitic and economically disastrous. [...] Dhimmis who chose not to flee Islamic rule faced a wide range of incentives to convert to Islam. Some converted to end their own persecution and to eliminate the risk of themselves or their families being randomly enslaved or killed. [...] Dhimmis also converted to escape the crushing tax burden imposed on non-Muslims."[566]

Wilders repeats this allegation in Chapter 7 of his book.[567] Wilders also takes issue with Umar, second khalifa of Prophet Muhammad, claiming that he demanded jizya under penalty of death.[568] In his Chap-

---

566. Wilders, *Marked for Death*, 95–97.

567. Ibid., 112–15.

568. Ibid., 95.

ter 9, Wilders repeats this allegation once more but applies it to the broader Muslim world.[569]

REFERENCE: Wilders offers no Islamic reference regarding his allegation of dhimmi subjugation. He submits Qur'an 9:29 to support his allegation that Islam demands jizya under penalty of death.

RESPONSE: I address these two allegations together—regarding dhimmis and jizya—because the two concepts are so closely related.

I begin with a proper explanation of what exactly a dhimmi is. *Dhimmi* is a historical term referring to non-Muslim subjects of a Muslim state.[570] The word literally means "one whose responsibility is taken" or "people with whom a covenant or compact has been made."[571] The word describes citizens of a Muslim state afforded security over their persons, property, and religious practice in return for a tax (the jizya). Historically, when empires won battles and wars, common people were subjugated, looted, and forced to work as laborers and serve in the military. Islam did away with such practices by affording all non-Muslim subjects the special dhimmi status.[572]

History records that dhimmis had a special place in Medina. Prophet Muhammad[sa] said, "If anyone wrongs a man with whom a covenant has been made [i.e., a dhimmi], or curtails any right of his, or imposes on him more than he can bear, or takes anything from him without his ready agreement, *I shall be his adversary* on the Day of Resurrection."[573]

---

569. Ibid., 153.

570. Juan Eduardo Campo, ed., "dhimmi," in *Encyclopedia of Islam* (Infobase Publishing, 2010), 194–95.

571. Edward William Lane, *Arabic-English Lexicon* (London: Willams & Norgate, 1863), 975–76.

572. H. Patrick Glenn, *Legal Traditions of the World* (Oxford University Press, 2007), 218–19.

573. Sahih Sunan Abu Dawud, #3052. (Emphasis added.)

Prophet Muhammad[sa] also made it clear that protecting the lives and honor of dhimmis was the responsibility of the Muslims, and failing in this regard would incur God's wrath: "Whoever killed a *Mu'ahid* (a person who is granted the pledge of protection by the Muslims, i.e. a dhimmi) shall not smell the fragrance of Paradise though its fragrance can be smelt at a distance of forty years (of traveling)."[574] At the conquest of Mecca, Prophet Muhammad[sa] had the upper hand against those who had persecuted him for more than two decades. He could have silenced his enemies forever. Instead, he turned to the Meccans and asked:

> "O' Quraish! How do you think I would treat you?" They replied: "We expect nothing but good from you as you are a noble and kind brother to us and the son of a noble and kind brother as well." The Prophet said, "I say to you what the Prophet Joseph said to his brothers: 'No blame against you! You are free.'"[575]

Even before the conquest of Mecca, the Charter of Medina—discussed extensively earlier in this book—set the precedent for the treatment of *mua'ahids* (dhimmis are those non-Muslim subjects who become subjects after a war. If there is no war and there is a negotiated settlement, then they are called *mua'ahids*). When Prophet Muhammad[sa] was popularly appointed Medina's ruler, he entered into a pact with the Jewish communities of Medina. Through this pact, he granted equal political rights to non-Muslims. They were ensured complete freedom of religion. They were not required to take part in the religious wars of the Muslims, but they were required to fight a common enemy of the state. Even as the head of state, Prophet Muhammad[sa] afforded non-Muslims the same social status he afforded Muslims. For example, "once a funeral procession passed before Prophet Muhammad[sa] and he stood up [out of re-

---

574. Sahih Jami' Bukhari, vol. 9, Book 83, #49.

575. Zadul-Ma'ad, vol. I, 424.

spect]. He was told that he [the dead man] was a Jew. Upon this he remarked: 'Was he not a human being or did he not have a soul?'"[576]

After the Prophet Muhammad's[sa] demise, non-Muslim inhabitants of the fast-expanding Islamic empire enjoyed the same dignified treatment.[577] When Hadhrat Umar[ra], second khalifa of Prophet Muhammad[sa], conquered Jerusalem, he entered into a pact with all inhabitants of the city, declaring:

> In the name of Allah, the most Gracious, most Beneficent. This is a covenant of peace granted by the slave of Allah, the commander of the faithful 'Umar to the people of Jerusalem. They are granted protection for their lives, their property, their churches, and their Crosses, in whatever condition they are. All of them are granted the same protection. No one will dwell in their churches, nor will they be destroyed and nothing will be reduced of their belongings. Nothing shall be taken from their Crosses or their property. There will be no compulsion on them regarding their religion, nor will any one of them be troubled.[578]

A dhimmi assassinated Hadhrat Umar[ra] in 644 CE. Rather than lashing out against dhimmis, at his deathbed, Hadhrat Umar[ra] specifically ordered:

> I urge him (i.e. the new Caliph) to take care of those non-Muslims who are under the protection of Allah and His Messenger in that he should observe the convention agreed upon with

---

576. Sahih Jami' Muslim, Book 4, #2098.

577. Glenn, *Legal Traditions,* 219.

578. Tarikh at-Tabari, 2/308.

them, and fight on their behalf (to secure their safety) and he should not over-tax them beyond their capability.[579]

Wilders continues, ranting extensively about how Jews and Christians suffered greatly under Muslim regimes and faced intense taxation. Wilders provides no citations from the Holy Qur'an or any of the six major ahadith sources. Yet, the example we see from Hadhrat Umar[ra] specifically condemns taxing dhimmis beyond what they can bear. Instead, though a dhimmi assassinated their leader the Khalifa, Muslims were commanded to care for dhimmis, fight for dhimmis, and to keep dhimmis safe.

Indeed, Hadhrat Umar's[ra] example was founded in Prophet Muhammad's[sa] noble teaching regarding Christians who live under Muslim rule. In a famous letter that Prophet Muhammad[sa] wrote to the Christians of Saint Catherine's Monastery at Sinai, he ensured that no Muslim was ever permitted to wrong or oppress a Christian:

This is a message from Muhammad ibn Abdullah as a covenant to those who adopt Christianity near and far—we are with them. Verily I, the servants, the helpers, and my followers defend them, because Christians are my citizens; and by God I hold out against anything that displeases them. No compulsion is to be on them. Neither are their judges to be removed from their jobs nor their monks from their monasteries. No one is to destroy a house of their religion, to damage it, or to carry anything from it to the Muslims' houses. Should anyone take any of these, he would spoil God's covenant and disobey His Prophet. Verily, they are my allies and have my secure charter against all that they hate. No one is to force them to travel or to oblige them to fight. The Muslims are to fight for them. If a female Christian is married to a Muslim,

---

579. Sahih Jami' Bukhari, vol. 4, Book 52, #287.

it is not to take place without her approval. She is not to be prevented from visiting her church to pray. Their churches are to be respected. They are neither to be prevented from repairing them nor the sacredness of their covenants. No one of the nation (Muslims) is to disobey the covenant until the Last Day (end of the world).[580]

In short, Prophet Muhammad[sa] gave his written promise that all Christians are to have complete freedom and equality under Muslim rule. Wilders, instead, ignores this entirely and censors it from his readers.

Wilders furthermore claims that Islamic societies in general were poverty stricken, backward, and forced to "wage Jihad" into new lands to conquer them to maintain their economic viability. Paradoxically, he then claims some non-Muslims converted to Islam to join Islam's wealthy class. These wealthy classes that somehow also existed in the poverty-stricken Muslim nations are never specifically identified, but Wilders does offer the origin of his source for this comment.

Wilders's source is Bat Ye'or, Jewish author and self-appointed expert on the history of dhimmitude in the Muslim world. Ye'or has never taught on the university level and is not an academic. Even then, instead of quoting from one of her books, Wilders quotes from an interview she had with John W. Whitehead. I am not here to deny that Muslims committed injustices at some point during their rule. Rather, I contest whether Islam may be blamed for such injustices. As I've shown from Prophet Muhammad's[sa] example, Islam demands equality for all citizens.

Yet Wilders continues and next alleges that Hadhrat Umar[ra] forced taxation on non-Muslim populations under penalty of death. To support his assertion, he cites the Qur'an 9:29:

---

580. Prophet Muhammad, "Prophet Muhammad's Letter to St. Catherine's Monastery at Sinai," in ZMD Corporation, *Muslim History: 570–1950 C.E.*, trans. Dr. A. Zahoor and Dr. Z. Haq (Gaithersburg, MD), 167.

> Fight those from among the People of the Book who believe not in Allah, nor in the Last Day, nor hold as unlawful what Allah and His Messenger have declared to be unlawful, nor follow the true religion, until they pay the tax with *their own* hand and acknowledge their subjection.[581]

Nowhere does this verse suggest that death is a penalty for not paying taxes. I cannot tell you how Wilders arrived at such a conclusion. I can tell you that the Qur'an has mentioned the use of the death penalty elsewhere for reasons unrelated to tax evasion:

> And kill not the soul which Allah has forbidden except for just cause. And whoso is killed wrongfully, We have surely given his heir authority to demand retaliation, but let him not exceed the prescribed bounds in slaying; for therein he is helped by law.[582]

As mentioned earlier, the Qur'an has reserved the death penalty for murder and treason. Some jurists, though a minority, have argued that those who commit severe acts of violence that shock the conscience (such as rape or torture) may also receive the death penalty. Tax avoidance, however, does not even remotely approach any of these situations.

Hadhrat Umar[ra], second khalifa of Prophet Muhammad[sa], never sentenced a non-Muslim to death for not paying his taxes, and I challenge Wilders to cite such an incident. The verse he quotes does not support his allegation; neither has Wilders provided any references from ahadith or Islamic books of history to support his wild accusation. Wilders also states that, short of death, defaulters can be tortured—again without reference.

---

581. Qur'an 9:29.
582. Qur'an 17:34.

Wilders then alleges that Muslim immigrants to Western nations consider themselves "divinely entitled" to the welfare payments they receive in these countries. Quoting the following verse, Wilders baselessly claims that Muslims consider the Western nations their dhimmis and such welfare payment the jizya.[583]

Fight those from among the People of the Book who believe not in Allah, nor in the Last Day, nor hold as unlawful what Allah and His Messenger have declared to be unlawful, nor follow the true religion, *until they pay the tax considering a favor and acknowledge their subjection.*[584]

Reading this verse plainly demonstrates that it has no connection with Wilders's allegation. Wilders, like his Orientalist predecessors and Islamophobe compatriots, plays on the West's general ignorance of Arabic—especially Qur'anic—terminology. If it sounds incredible that the man who would save the West from Islam does not know basic Arabic, keep reading.

Having established that Islam required Muslims to protected dhimmis with equal and just treatment, I transition to Wilders's allegations regarding jizya. Remember, the term dhimmi literally means "protected." If no such protection existed, such minority communities could potentially be exploited. The jizya tax was the only tax imposed on non-Muslims; it was typically lower than taxes on the Muslims of that state and was paid by fewer people. The term *jizya* comes from same Arabic root as *jaza'*, which means "reward" and "compensation." So, according to Sharia or Islamic law, this money was returned to the minorities. The jizya tax, like other taxes, creates accountability on the part of the government to do right by its citizens—not unlike governments that deal with immigration and minority communities. In Christian-ruled Sicily,

---

583. Wilders, *Marked for Death*, 153.

584. Qur'an 9:29.

324

for example, the Christian officials had such a tax for minorities—and they too called it "jizya."

Thus, non-Muslims paid jizya as free citizens of the Muslim state in return for the protection of their civil and political liberties. Aside from this, Wilders also hides the fact that Muslims were also taxed. As I've pointed out, the tax levied on Muslims was often heavier than the jizya. Additionally, Muslims were obligated to perform military service, from which all non-Muslims were exempt.[585]

Jizya served as the sole citizen tax to assure protection from all foreign attacks. Thus, if protection could not be promised, then jizya was impermissible. In *The Preaching of Islam*, Thomas Arnold records a statement of the Muslim general Khalid bin Waleed: "In a treaty made by Khalid with some town in the neighborhood of *Hirah*, he writes; 'If we protect you, then *Jizya* is due to us; but if we do not, then it is not.'"[586]

Abu Ubaida was a famous Muslim commander of Syria. When he entered the city of Hims, he made a pact with its non-Muslim inhabitants and collected the jizya as agreed. When the Muslims learned of a massive advance toward the city by the Roman emperor Heraclius, they felt they would not be able to protect its citizens. Consequently, Abu Ubaida ordered all the dues taken as jizya to be returned to the people of the city. He said to them, "We are not able to defend you anymore and now you have complete authority over your matters."[587] Al-Azdi records Abu Ubaida's statement as follows:

---

585. See http://www.alislam.org/quran/tafseer/?page=922&region=E1&CR. Accessed August 12, 2012.

586. Thomas Walker Arnold, *The Preaching of Islam: A History of the Propagation of the Muslim Faith* (2007) 61.

587. William N. Lees, *Futuh ash-Sham ed.* (Culcutta: Baptist Mission, 1854), 1/162.

We have returned your wealth back to you because we detest taking your wealth and then failing to protect your land. We are moving to another area and have called upon our brethren, and then we will fight our enemy. If Allah helps us defeat them we shall fulfill our covenant with you except that you yourselves do not like it then.[588]

This remarkable testimony is absent in Wilders's "research." Likewise, Abu Ubaida specifically declares that the Muslims shall fulfill their covenant *unless the Christians prefer otherwise.* This clearly demonstrates that the dhimmis were not in any way forcibly oppressed but instead lovingly embraced. The response that the people of Hims gave to the Muslims further substantiates this fact:

Verily your rule and justice is dearer to us than the tyranny and oppression in which we used to live.[589] May God again make you ruler over us and may God's curse be upon the Byzantines who used to rule over us. By the Lord, had it been they, they would have never returned us anything; instead they would have seized all they could from our possessions.[590]

Thus, contrary to the fabricated, fantastic stories Wilders concocts, these so-called "oppressed" dhimmis openly declared their desire to live under Muslim rule for the simple reason that life was just and fair under Muslim rule. The famous French political thinker, Montesquieu, also highlights the fair treatment of non-Muslim citizens in Muslim lands:

---

588. Ibid. 137–38.

589. Ibid., 1/162.

590. Ibid., 138.

It was this excess of taxes that occasioned the prodigious facility with which the Mahometans carried on their conquests. Instead of a continual series of extortions devised by the subtle avarice of the Greek emperors, the people were subjected to a simple tribute which was paid and collected with ease.[591]

Professor Bernard Lewis, whom Wilders quotes elsewhere in his book, observes that dhimmis welcomed the change from Byzantine to Arab rule. They "found the new yoke far lighter than the old, both in taxation and in other matters, and that some even among the Christians of Syria and Egypt preferred the rule of Islam to that of Byzantines."[592]

Moreover, the jizya was not forcefully collected. It was a tax paid willingly as a favor for the protection of the state. Hadhrat Mirza Bashiruddin Mahmud Ahmad[ra], second khalifa of the Ahmadiyya Muslim Community, notes:

The expression "with their own hand" is used here in a figurative sense, signifying (1) that Jizya should not be forcibly taken from the People of the Book but that they should pay it with their own hand i.e. they should agree to pay it willingly...; or (2) that they should pay it out of hand i.e. in ready money and not in the form of deferred payment; or (3) that they should pay it considering it as a favor from Muslims, the word, *yad* (hand) also meaning a favor.[593]

As previously noted, the jizya not only protected dhimmis, it also exempted them from serving in the military. Thus, as justice would hold,

---

591. Charles de Secondat, *The Spirit of Laws*, Book 13.

592. Bernard Lewis, *What Went Wrong? Western Impact and Middle Eastern Response* (2002), 57.

593. See http://www.alislam.org/quran/tafseer/?page=922&region=E1&CR. Accessed August 12, 2012.

the Muslim state exempted from jizya those dhimmis who chose to serve in the military. What more clear correlation can I present to demonstrate the true purpose of jizya and the true protected rights of a dhimmi? Perhaps Sir Thomas Arnold's elaboration might help:

> When any Christian people served in the Muslim army, they were exempted from the payment of this tax. Such was the case with the tribe of al-Jurajima, a Christian tribe in the neighborhood of Antioch who made peace with the Muslims, promising to be their allies and fight on their side in battle, on condition that they should not be called upon to pay jizya and should receive their proper share of the booty. When the Arab conquests were pushed to the north of Persia in A.H. 22, a similar agreement was made with a frontier tribe, which was exempted from the payment of jizya in consideration of military service. We find similar instances of remission of jizya in the case of Christians who served in the army or navy under the Turkish rule. For example, the inhabitants of Megaris, a community of Albanian Christians were exempted from the payment of this tax on condition that they furnished a body of armed men to guard the passes over Mounts Cithaeron and Geranea... The Christians who served as pioneers of the advance-guard of the Turkish army, repairing the roads and bridges, were likewise exempt from tribute and received grants of land quit of all taxation; and the Christian inhabitants of Hydra paid no direct taxes to the Sultan, but furnished instead a contingent of 250 able-bodied seamen to the Turkish fleet, who were supported out of the local treasury.[594]

The state is primarily responsible for protecting its citizens. In Islam, the state is also required to cater to the welfare of all its citizens. Besides oth-

---

594. Arnold, *The Preaching of Islam*, 61–62.

er infrastructure, this requires the establishment and maintenance of armed forces, a working judicial system, and civil service. It would be unfair to ask only the Muslims to fund the state and exempt the non-Muslim citizens—equal in status otherwise; hence the jizya tax.

Furthermore, only working men paid this tax. Women and children, the elderly, the unemployed, and the sick or disabled were all exempt. But while non-Muslim women were exempt from the jizya, Muslim women were required to pay the zakaat regardless of whether or not they worked. Sir Thomas Arnold notes:

> The tax was to be levied only on able-bodied males, and not on women or children. The poor who were dependent for their livelihood on alms and the aged poor who were incapable of work were also specially excepted, as also the blind, the lame, the incurables and the insane, unless they happened to be men of wealth; this same condition applied to priests and monks, who were exempt if dependent on the arms of the rich, but had to pay it if they were well-to-do and lived in comfort.[595]

Since the Qur'an instructs that the jizya be voluntarily given, early Muslim rulers specifically forbade punishment on nonpayment—quite contrary to what Wilders alleges about death and torture. Sir Thomas Arnold writes, "The collectors of the *jizya* were particularly instructed to show leniency, and refrain from all harsh treatment or the infliction of corporal punishment, in case of non-payment."[596]

In reality, the jizya tax was an agreement between those non-Muslims who *chose* to live in Muslim lands and under the Muslim government. The dhimmis recognized that they were under the protection of the Muslim state—and history records that they willingly chose that lifestyle

595. Ibid., 60.
596. Ibid.

because it was based on absolute justice. The reader will note that the historical testimony I present to substantiate these facts is from Muslim and non-Muslim scholars. Wilders ignores them both and instead concocts his own fairy tales.

Wilders instead cites an anti-Islam website to claim that non-Muslims "always lost their court cases to Muslims" in these allegedly oppressive Muslim nations unless such people converted to Islam. History, however, once again records to the contrary. The Spanish Almorvids, for example, are a living testimony to the integrity and compassion with which Muslims treated Jews and Christians. Historian Gwendolyn Hall writes at length:

> Some Spanish historians have emphasized the unacknowledged debt Renaissance Europe owed to Moorish Spain. In 1899, Francisco Codera, citing an early chronicle in Arabic, argued against racist interpretations of the Almoravids' rule in Spain. The chronicler wrote:
>
>> The Almoravids were a country people, religious and honest...Their reign was tranquil, and was untroubled by any revolt, either in the cities, or in the countryside...Their days were happy, prosperous, and tranquil, and during their time, abundant and cheap goods were such that for a half-ducat, one could have four loads of flour, and the other grains were neither bought nor sold. There was no tribute, no tax, or contribution for the government except the charity tax and the tithe. Prosperity constantly grew; the population rose, and everyone could freely attend to their own affairs. Their reign was free of deceit, fraud, and revolt, *and they were loved by everyone.*
>
> Even after its overthrow, other chroniclers of Islamic Spain praised the rule of the Almoravids. They wrote that learning was cherished, literacy was wide-spread, scholars were

subsidized, capital punishment was abolished, and their gold coins were so pure and of such reliable weight that they assured prosperity and stimulated trade throughout the Mediterranean world. Christians and Jews were tolerated within their realms. When the Christians rose up in revolt, they were not executed but were exiled to Morocco instead. *The Almoravids were criticized, however, for being excessively influenced by their women.* When the Moors ruled Western Islam, a great variety of trade goods passed abundantly within this vast region. Horses and cattle, hides, leather goods, skins, dried fruits, arts and crafts, tools, swords, and other weapons, ivory, onyx, grain, gold, silver, copper, precious gems, textiles, tapestries, pottery, salt, and kola nuts were widely traded. The coins of the Almoravids, were minted mainly from gold coming from Galam in the upper Senegal River, which arrived via long-established camel caravan routes across the Sahara. Knowledge as well as technology moved across the Sahara in all directions. Some Renaissance and post-Renaissance European music, including notation of pitch and rhythm, probably was transmitted from Moorish Spain.[597]

This is the history of Islam in Europe as it pertains to how Muslims ruled and treated those of other faiths. The only criticism found was that these Muslims were "excessively influenced by their women." At a time when the West drowns in misogyny demonstrated by rising rape and domestic violence cases, unequal pay based on gender, and an imbalance of female representation in the political sphere, perhaps the West could learn a thing or two from the Almoravid Muslims and ensure that women become "excessively" influential.

---

597. Gwendolyn Midlo Hall, *Slavery and African Ethnicities in the Americas: Restoring the Links* (2005), 6.

In closing, I present the following as an embodiment of the true spirit of jizya and dhimmitude:

> Once, Hadhrat Umar[ra], second khalifa of Prophet Muhammad[sa], met an old Jew begging on the street. Hadhrat Umar[ra] said to him, "Old man! We have not done justice to you. In your youth we took jizya from you and have left you to fend for yourself in your old age." Holding him by the hand, he led him to his own house, and preparing food with his own hands fed him and issued orders to the treasurer of the Bait-ul-Maal [treasury] that the old man and all others like him, should be regularly allotted a daily allowance which should suffice for them and their dependents.[598]

This is the reality of jizya and of the rights of dhimmis—personal attention from the khalifa himself, (the same khalifa Wilders earlier warns of as a threat). History well records the unmatched respect and justice Islam established for non-Muslim citizens. Indeed, this level of respect and justice is unprecedented in world history. Unfortunately, Wilders chooses to censor this history from his readers.

As Muslims, we hold fast to the word of our beloved Master Prophet Muhammad[sa] regarding dhimmis; i.e., the protected: "By God, Christians are my citizens and I hold fast against all that displeases them." Thus, I encourage Wilders to drop his anti-Islam hatemongering. Instead, he should follow Prophet Muhammad's[sa] noble example of compassion and pluralism to the minority number of Muslims residing in his country.

---

598. Kitabul-Khiraj, 1/139.

Conclusion

Chapter 6 boils down to two major allegations; Islam endorses slavery and promotes mistreatment of non-Muslims (i.e., dhimmis) in a Muslim-ruled land—each of these allegations are baseless. I responded with more detail to refute these than any other allegation in this book. While I did not specifically plan this, it reflects how important it is to recognize the immense emphasis Islam has placed on interfaith, interracial, and international harmony.

The reasons for Wilders's allegations about female genital mutilation, concubines, and marriage to slaves are equally obscure—and I have thoroughly responded to each appropriately. As mentioned, this Chapter of his book is, for all intents and purposes, Wilders's last stand. It is his final substantive attempt to malign Islam with new allegations. From Chapter 7 through Chapter 13, his last, Wilders presents only two new allegations within *EXTREMIST*'s scope.

Chapter 7

No New Allegations

"The Church also has a high regard for the Muslims... Over the centuries many quarrels and dissensions have arisen between Christians and Muslims. The sacred Council now pleads with all to forget the past, and urges that a sincere effort be made to achieve mutual understanding; for the benefit of all men, let them together preserve and promote peace, liberty, social justice and moral values."

— THE SECOND VATICAN COUNCIL
OCTOBER 28, 1965

Wilders spends Chapter 7 fabricating Islamic history in the thousand years after Prophet Muhammad's[sa] demise. He baselessly compares the Qur'an to Hitler's *Mein Kampf* and childishly refers to women who wear a niqab (face covering) as "mummies."

While yet defending Judeo-Christian and European culture, Wilders seems to forget that Rebekkah of the

Old Testament also wore a face veil.[599] In assuming European culture is anti-veil, Wilders also forgets that the French female icon, Saint Thérèse of Lisieux, proudly wore the veil after being inspired by veil-wearing biblical figure Veronica—who wiped Jesus's forehead with hers. Furthermore, Wilders forgets that Dutch empresses, such as "Holder of the Royal Authority" Dowager Queen Dorothea zu Brandenburg of Denmark, are proudly portrayed wearing the allegedly oppressive veil. Thus, Wilders demonstrates his ignorance of Islam, the Bible, and his own European culture.

In short, Geert Wilders presents no new allegations within *EXTREMIST*'s scope not already addressed. Therefore, I move on to the next chapter.

---

599. Genesis 24:64–65.

Chapter 8

No New Allegations

"The more one reflects on the history of Muhammad and of early Islam, the more one is amazed at the vastness of his achievement. It is my hope that this study of his life may contribute to a fresh appraisal and appreciation of one of the greatest of the sons of Adam."

— MONTGOMERY WATT

Wilders spends his Chapter 8 blaming Islam for 9/11, rehashing the allegation that Islam permits Muslims to lie (again without reference), and complains about individual contemporary Muslims with whom he disagrees.

Again Wilders presents no new allegations within *EXTREMIST*'s scope not already addressed. Therefore, I move on to the next chapter.

Chapter 9

No New Allegations

"If ever any man on this earth has found God; if ever any man has devoted his life for the sake of God with a pure and holy zeal then, without doubt, and most certainly that man was the Holy Prophet of Arabia."

— MAJOR A. LEANORD

Wilders spends Chapter 9 complaining about Muslim immigrants in Europe and social clashes. He attempts to blame Islam for these clashes without any actual evidence. His recent intolerant tirade against Moroccans—even Dutch born citizens of Moroccan ancestry—is just another example that his bigotry against anyone not exactly like him grows. This is, of course, no surprise. The biased and bigoted arguments Wilders employs are no different than the propaganda extremists in America use to categorically demonize Latino Americans, Black Americans, and Muslim Americans.

Wilders presents no new allegations within *EXTREMIST*'s scope not already addressed. Therefore, I move on to the next chapter.

Chapter 10

No New Allegations

"[I]t was the West, not Islam, which forbade the open
discussion of religious matters. At the time of the Crusades,
Europe seemed obsessed by a craving for intellectual conformity
and punished its deviants with a zeal that has been unique in
the history of religion. The witch-hunts of the inquisitors and
the persecution of Protestants by the Catholics and vice versa
were inspired by abtruse theoligical opinions which in both
Judaism and Islam were seen as private and optional matters.
Neither Judaism nor Islam share the Christian conception of
heresy, which raises human ideas about the divine to an
unacceptably high level and almost makes them a form of
idolatry. The period of the Crusades, when the fictional
Mahound was established, was also a time of the great strain
and denial in Europe. This is graphically expressed in the
phobia about Islam."

— KAREN ARMSTRONG

Wilders spends chapter 10 reviving his fabricated description and unreferenced understanding of Sharia
law, claims that Islam (not Muslims) is waging an

offensive to conquer Europe, and expresses annoyance that even the US State Department does not have a high opinion of his bigotry and intolerance.

Wilders presents no new allegations within *EX-TREMIST*'s scope not already addressed. Therefore, I move on to the next chapter.

Chapter 11

Wilders Grasps at Straws

"Without education, you are not going anywhere in this world."

— MALCOLM X

In Chapter 11 Wilders, the man with no actual higher education, praises himself as a hero for starting his right-wing political party, complains about cultural relativism and how it is allegedly destroying Western culture, and reemphasizes how much greater Western culture is than Islamic culture. His incessant repetition that Western culture is monolithic and that Islamic culture is its monolithic opposite stands only to prove his ignorance of human diversity. Likewise, it demonstrates his raging xenophobia and ethnocentrism.

In this chapter, Wilders's claim that Islam has always been archaic is the only substantive allegation he makes within this book's scope, which I address below.

ALLEGATION 61

Islamic Civilization Is and Always Has Been Archaic

Wilders writes, "...we must reject all forms of cultural relativism. Let's say it frankly: our civilized Western culture is far superior to the barbaric culture of Islam. Western nations should add an amendment to our constitutions stating that our societies are based on Judeo-Christian and humanist values. In other words, we owe nothing to Islam."[600] With these final allegations, Wilders is literally grasping at straws to find *something* problematic with Islam. Unfortunately for him, history proves him wrong yet again.

REFERENCE: None.

RESPONSE: I do not intend to engage in a "which civilization is better" debate. By what standard do we judge? Which time frame? Do we account for crime rates? Rapes? Murder? Inventions? Nobel Prizes? What weight do we place on each positive characteristic? And who may judge? The questions are limitless, and so are the answers.

Rather, I respond to the allegation that Islamic civilization is backward and that "the West" owes Islam nothing. Such a statement is nothing more than one of ignorance and arrogance.

The Qur'an, more than 140 times, highlights knowledge as a distinguishing characteristic of believers. Prophet Muhammad[sa] declared, "Seeking knowledge is a duty upon every Muslim."[601] Prophet Muhammad[sa] himself was an arbiter, arbitrator, businessman, cobbler, council-

---

600. Geert Wilders, *Marked for Death*, 178, 213.

601. Ibn-e-Majah, chap. 1, #224.

man, economist, general, hygienist, king, legislator, liberator, orator, philanthropist, philosopher, preacher, skilled cavalier, soldier, statesman, swordsman, treasurer, teacher—all the while unlettered.

Prophet Muhammad's[sa] example left an incredible impact on the Muslim *ummah*. Due to the stress he placed on pursuit of knowledge, Islamic history has borne a vast number of intellectual giants—many of whom we have mentioned throughout this book. These giants are such whose genius "the West" benefits from today. The prophet's followers have made advancements in agriculture, anthropology, architecture, arts, astronomy, biology, cartography, chemistry, coinage, cosmology, culture, diplomacy, economics, education, engineering, finance, geodesy, geography, geology, government, hermeneutics, history, industry, literature, law, mathematics, medicine, music, navigation, philosophy, physics, poetry, politics, psychology, sociology, and technology. While the list below is not exhaustive, it provides a glimpse into the vast arena of Muslim scholarship. This list is available from even a cursory Internet search and is one of the easier set of facts to find. It is remarkable that Wilders even makes the allegation he does. (Please note that * denotes a polymath.)

Hadhrat ibn-e-Abbas[ra], Akbar the Great,* al-Amidi, Malik ibn-e-Anas, ibn-e-Arabi, Nana Asma'u, al-Astrulabi, al-Athir, Hadhrat Ayesha[ra], al-Azraqi, Al-Baghdadi, ibn Bajjah,* Rabiah of Basra, al-Battani, ibn Battuta, Bayhaqi, Ulugh Beg, al-Biruni,* Al-Bitruji, al-Bukhari, al-Buzjani, Katib Chelebi,* Abu Dawud, ad-Dimishqi, al-Din,* ad-Dinawari, ad-Durr, Erzurumi, al-Farabi,* al-Farghani, ibn-e-Firnas,* al-Ghafiqi, al-Ghazali,* al-Hajjaj, al-Halabi, ibn-e-Hanbal, Abu Hanifa, Ibn-e-Hisham, al-Haytham,* ibn-e-Hayyan,* ibn-e-Hazm, Hadhrat Salim Mawla Abu-Hudhayfah (ra), al-Humaydi, ibn-e-Ibrahim, al-Idrisi,* Ibn-e-Ishaq, al-Ishbili, Hadhrat Muadh bin Jabal[ra], al-Jahiz,* al-Jahshiyari, Zubaidah bint Jafar, al-Jazari,* al-Jurjani, Hadhrat Ubayy ibn Kab, al-Udar al-Karimah, al-Kashi, Ibn-e-Kathir, Abul Khair, ibn-e-Khaldun,* Zafrulla Khan, al-Kharkhi, al-

Khawarizmi,* al-Khayyam,* al-Khazini,* al-Kindi,* Ali Kuşçu, al-Latif, al-Maghribi, ibn-e-Majah, Abdul Malik, al-Mardini, al-Marrakushi, Hadhrat Abdullah ibn Masud, al-Masudi,* al-Misri, ibn Mubarak,* Sitt al-Mulk, al-Muqaddasi,* the Banu Musa, Walladah bint Mustakfi, Ibrahim Muteferrika,* Rabi'ah bint Mu'awwadh, an-Nabati, an-Nafis,* Sayyida Nafisa, an-Nasa'i, an-Nuwairi, an-Nawawi, al-Qalasadi, Hadhrat Fatima bint Qays^{ra}, ibn-e-Qutayba,* Radiyah Begum, al-Razi,* Razia Sultanah of India, Rumi, ibn-e-Rushd,* Abdus Salaam, Shaghab, ash-Shatir,* Fathullah Shirazi, ibn-e-Sina,* ash-Sufi, as-Sulayhi, ash-Suli, ash-Suyuti,* at-Tabari, at-Tabarani, Hassan bin Thabit, at-Tirmidhi, ibn-e-Tufail,* at-Tusi,* Abu Ubaida, Maryam bint-e-Uthman, ibn-e-Yunus, ibn-e-Zubair, ibn-e-Zuhr,* and az-Zahrawi.*

This list is by no means comprehensive. Muslims established the world's first universities centuries before Judeo-Christian Europe even conceived such ideas. In fact, a Muslim female scholar named Fatima al-Fihri founded Al-Karaouine University in 859 AD. Not only does this fact demolish Wilders's earlier accusation that Islam oppresses women, but it also demonstrates that Islam raised the status of women to such an extent that a Muslim woman pioneered one of world history's most crucial social developments—public universities. Thus, Guinness World Records has officially recorded Al-Karaouine University as the world's oldest existing educational institution, while UNESCO has recognized it as the world's oldest university.[602]

To be fair, I don't blame Wilders for not appreciating the invention of the University; seeing as how he's never actually attended one. Thus, I'll concede this point—when it comes to Islam's emphasis on the virtue

---

602. UNESCO, "Medina of Fez," accessed September 27, 2013. http://whc.unesco.org/en/list/170/.

of attaining higher education, Wilders indeed owes Islam nothing, as he's never actually attained higher education.

Islam aside, it hurts one's head to try to rationalize how Wilders can attribute Western intellectualism to "Judeo-Christian" culture. Aside from its debt to the Islamic world, Western civilization is the product of the Renaissance, the Scientific Revolution, and the Age of Enlightenment—phenomena whose essence mandated the near wholesale rejection of prevailing Judeo-Christian thought.

Whose culture was shared during the conquest of South America or the transatlantic slave trade? When Galileo was condemned for "heresy"? When blasphemous books were burned, when women were denied their basic civil rights until the twentieth century, when thousands upon thousands of witches were burned or hanged in Europe? The Holocaust? History records that each of these worldwide atrocities—in some cases genocides—were largely due to the mob's reading of the Bible.[603] Even today, the "intellectual" descendants of those uncompromising Bible advocates decry evolution as a pseudoscience—just as they did back then.

Yes, some cultures today who happen to comprise of Muslims are barbaric and backward, and Muslims the world over reject them as un-Islamic and inhumane. Islamic history rejects them because history is clear that Muslim empires during Prophet Muhammad's[sa] time, during the time of the rightly guided khalifas, and even the Almoravids fostered education, pluralism, and multiculturalism. Wilders's allegations against "Islamic culture" are as unfounded as any of his prior allegations. His insistence that Western nations amend their constitutions to "recognize" their Judeo-Christian and humanist values ignorantly and rather immaturely paints all Jews, Christians, and humanists as one monolithic group.

---

603. Exodus 22:18; Deuteronomy 18:10–11; Galatians 5:19–20; Revelation 21:8.

Let's say it frankly: Wilders would be better served if he simply studied European history and the Golden Age from actual scholars and stopped wasting his time on anti-Islam websites. Henry David Thoreau says it best, "It is never too late to give up your prejudices." For the sake of those Wilders discriminates and persecutes, I hope he at least gives up his prejudices against Islam's teaching on attaining higher education. It is never too late to attain knowledge from universities, even if a female Islamic scholar invented them.

Conclusion

Chapter 11 again shows Wilders's xenophobia and raging ethnocentrism. As I neared the conclusion of Wilders's book, I discovered his increasing calls for recognizing Western superiority over Islamic teachings.

While a rigorous debate about the alleged only way to govern a society is outside this book's scope, I ask you to reflect on how intolerant Wilders is to any viewpoint not his own. His ideology is dangerous. Europe, and the world, has already suffered enough at the hands of politicians who did not tolerate the other. Wilders's fear of an "archaic" Islamic culture is misplaced and baseless.

In his Chapter 12, Wilders repeats his claim of Western supremacy by praising himself for exposing Islam's alleged threat in his childish documentary, *Fitna*. I address this documentary next.

Chapter 12

Wilders—
Lost in the Wilderness

"I have prophesied about the faith of Mohammad that it would be acceptable the Europe of tomorrow as it is beginning to be acceptable to the Europe of today."

— SIR GEORGE BERNARD SHAW

By chapter 12, Wilders is entirely lost in the wilderness of his own hatred and ignorance. Perhaps as yet another means to pat himself on the back, Wilders alleges that his *Fitna* documentary, made with the assistance of "Koran experts," exposes the "Islamic threat."[604] He alleges *Fitna* is his attempt at becoming an inspiration in history. In reality, this film reaffirms a theme prevalent throughout his book—Wilders's hatred has left him unable to separate fact from fiction.

---

604. Wilders, *Marked for Death*, 187.

As Sir Shaw rightly points out, Islam will continue to gain popularity because of its vitality, service to humanity, and pluralism. Wilders and his ilk simply do not stand a chance against progressiveness and tolerance.

This is Wilders's final allegation within *EXTREMIST*'s scope. His belief that *Fitna* actually served any legitimate scholarship purpose is laughable at best and sad in every way. In short, Wilders is entirely lost on how to admit he is wrong.

ALLEGATION 62

Wilders's *Fitna* "Documentary" Exposes the Islamic Threat

Regarding *Fitna*, the only matter that confuses me is Wilders's belief that he accomplished anything of merit. *Fitna* only succeeds in exposing Wilders's own ignorance, arrogance, and hatred for anyone unlike him.

REFERENCE: Various Qur'anic verses and various incidents of Muslim backlash against *Fitna*.

RESPONSE: *Fitna* is a short film roughly fifteen minutes long. Wilders naively assumes that citing a few Qur'anic verses along with footage of rogue Muslims presents a damning indictment of Islam's alleged extremist roots. YouTube it and watch it for yourself just to get a feel for how ridiculous it is. No legitimate academic intellectual is interviewed; neither is the credibility of the "Koran experts" questioned—let alone the fact that the practice of cutting and pasting verses leaves the Bible, not the Qur'an, open to attack.

For example, the Bible orders capital punishment—sometimes by stoning—for disobedience to one's parents,[605] for being unchaste,[606] for false prophecy,[607] for blasphemy,[608] or for those worshipping other

---

605. Exodus 21:17; Deuteronomy 21:18–21.

606. Deuteronomy 22:21–25; Leviticus 20:100.

607. Deuteronomy 13:5.

608. Leviticus 24:16.

gods.[609] Again, should Wilders argue that these teachings are relegated to the Old Testament, New Testament verses can also be considered alarming.[610] Jesus Christ[as] himself says that nothing of the Old Testament is abrogated—a fact that American supreme courts championed even during the nineteenth century.[611] Moreover, Jesus Christ[as] himself alludes to the validity of stoning for disobedience to parents.[612] Maybe Wilders could make another documentary placing such verses alongside footage of the National Liberation Front of Tripura, the Lord's Resistance Army, Anders Breivik, the Hutaree Christian militia, Warriors of the Boer Nation, the Aryan Nation, the Irish Republican Army, the Ku Klux Klan, or various violent antiabortion groups?

As to the "Koran experts"—consider, for example, that *Fitna* cites Qur'an 8:61, a detailed explanation of how Muslims should prepare for battle should the situation arise. These "experts," however, fail to mention—or simply do not know—that the verses preceding and following 8:61 emphasize diplomacy and an undying inclination to peace. Only if all means of diplomacy fail is 8:61 applicable as a final means of self-defense (never preemptive or offensive attack). In fact, 8:61 actually commands Muslims to live in peace and fight only to preserve the state—not to spread or compel religion. Thus, 8:61 champions a secular cause based on absolute justice.

The "experts" also found Qur'an 8:40 to promote terrorism: "And fight them until there is no persecution and religion is wholly to Allah. But if they desist, then surely Allah is Watchful of what they do." What does Wilders find offensive about establishing religious freedom and stopping persecution?

---

609. Deuteronomy 13:2–10.

610. Matthew 10:21, 34; Luke 22:36.

611. Matthew 5:17–18; 23:1–4.

612. Matthew 15:1–9.

Fitna also shows footage of churches being destroyed but conveniently forgets to cite Qur'an 22:41, which commands Muslims to protect all houses of worship from attack—mentioning churches specifically—*even before* protecting a mosque. No Qur'anic verse accompanies clips of mullahs calling for death sentences for adulterers, apostates, and LGBTs—because no such Qur'anic verses exist. Perhaps Wilders forgot that it is the *Bible*, not the Qur'an, which prescribes death for an adulterer and LGBT[613] as well as an apostate.[614] Moreover, Pilgrims cited the Bible to validate their conquests of Native Americans.[615] Should the Dutch then ban the Bible as well?

Fitna also does not cite the written covenant that Prophet Muhammad[sa] made with Christians at Saint Catherine's Monastery, in which he promises to protect them and fight on their behalf should anyone attack them—among several other guarantees. Unfortunately for Wilders, I have cited this important letter earlier in this book because this is what history actually records. I request Wilders to inform his readers what exactly about "verily [Christians] are my allies and have my secure charter against all that they hate" creates *Fitna*? This written covenant is the authority Wilders should have cited—not pseudointellectuals with a severe anti-Islamic bias.

Wilders next depicts mullahs calling for the deaths of Jews and attempts to blame the Qur'an for their behavior. As I have already demonstrated, Wilders fails to realize (or rather, fails to admit) nothing in the Qur'an even slightly advocates or endorses anti-Semitism. This is a fact that world-leading Christian scholars such as Dr. Philip Jenkins unreservedly declare. Rather, the Qur'an simply clarifies that those who violate the sanctity of the Sabbath—that is, only those Jews who malign the message of their own Prophet Moses[as]—fall into the category of

---

613. Leviticus 20:10, 13.

614. Deuteronomy 13:6–18.

615. Psalms 2:8; Romans 13:2.

"apes."[616] Lest we forget that Jesus Christ[as] called such people swine—so, in reality, the Qur'an only agrees with what Christians already believe about those *particular* individuals who violate the Sabbath.[617] And, if Islam promotes anti-Semitism, why did the Jews find peace in Medina during Prophet Muhammad's[sa] reign or in Moorish Spain? Recall that it was only after the Christians conquered Spain that Jews were persecuted. Likewise, it was only after Hitler, a self-described Christian, came to power that Jews suffered the Holocaust. A reference to mullahs accompanies every single verse *Fitna* dubs "extreme," as if mullahs have any Islamic authority. Wilders does not tell his viewers that Islam has no clergy. He does not refer to how Prophet Muhammad[sa] or his companions understood and practiced Islam.

Indeed, the mullahs Wilders cites to validate his claims are the very same miscreants Prophet Muhammad[sa] completely dissociated himself from, declaring the clergy of the latter days as "the worst of creatures on earth...fitna will initiate from them and return to them."[618] *Fitna* would have been a fitting title for the documentary if Wilders had identified the real culprit—the mullah.

---

616. Qur'an 2:66; 7:167.

617. Matthew 7:6.

618. Kanzul Aamaal, vol. 6, 43; *Mishkat* Kitabul 'Ilm.

Conclusion

In chapter 12, I arrived at and refuted Wilders's final allegation within this book's scope. Needless to say, his final allegation was as meritless and ignorant as every preceding allegation.

In his chapter 13 Wilders's once again attempts to establish himself and "his" Western culture as superior to all others; namely, to Islam. While he makes no new allegations, Wilders demonizes tolerance and pluralism, to which I felt compelled to respond.

Chapter 13

No New Allegations

"The secret of freedom lies in educating people, whereas the secret of tyranny is in keeping them ignorant."

— MAXIMILIEN ROBESPIERRE

Wilders spends his chapter 13 addressing his readers on how to "finally" defeat Islam. Instead, he does an excellent job of yet again keeping his readers ignorant to everything I have uncovered in my book.

First, Wilders demands free speech that involves "repealing all hate speech laws."[619] He demands recognition that "Western culture is far superior to the barbaric culture of Islam" (again ignorantly assuming that Western culture and Islamic culture are each completely monolithic).[620] He demands a cessation of all "Islamic immigration" to the West.[621] And finally, he calls

---

619. Wilders, *Marked for Death*, 213.

620. Ibid., 213.

621. Ibid.

upon his followers to "cherish their national identity" as "a Western spirit."[622] In short, Wilders makes a great argument for why I titled my response to him *EXTREMIST*. Little difference exists between Wilders's extreme anti-Islam demands, and the extreme anti-West demands of those like the Taliban or Al Qaeda.

Rather than comment on how ridiculous Wilders's demands are, I prefer to show the reader how similar are his demands to recognize his culture's superiority, to exclusively protect his culture's identity, and to demonize those not of his particular culture to those of another European politician some seventy-five years prior. Just like Wilders, this earlier politician declared:

> The most precious thing that exists the whole world over is our own people. And for these people, and with these people, I shall struggle and I shall fight, and never slacken, and never tire, and never falter, and never doubt. [...] What we must fight for is to safeguard the existence and reproduction of our race and our people, the sustenance of our children and the purity of our blood, the freedom and independence of the fatherland, so that our people may mature for the fulfillment [sic] of the mission allotted it by the creator of the universe. Every thought and every idea, every doctrine and all knowledge, must serve this purpose. And every-

---

622. Ibid., 215.

thing must be examined from this point of view and used or rejected according to its utility.[623]

The above statement's author is none other than one of history's most intolerant, bigoted, and hate-filled men—Adolf Hitler. How horrifying is it that Wilders's call to protect his culture, his national identity, and his Western spirit and to instead annihilate Islam is uncannily similar to Hitler's call to protect his culture and destroy all others? Wilders is following the same intolerant path—blaming all Europe's problems on Muslims and demonizing Muslims—that Hitler followed with Jews. May Europe and the world learn from history and stop Wilders and his hate-filled propaganda now.

As far as new allegations go, in his chapter 13 Geert Wilders presents no new allegations within *EXTREMIST*'s scope not already addressed. Therefore, I move on to my conclusion.

---

623. Hitler, *Mein Kampf*, vol. 1, chap. 8.

Conclusion to *EXTREMIST*

"There is a lesson in this story for the pro-Jihad Mullahs. The growth of such horrible doctrines among the Muslims has done lasting injury to the cause of Islam and created an abhorrence for it in the hearts of other nations. How could the religion be from God, whose teachings needed the flash of the sword to get an entrance into the human heart? The true religion is that which on account of its inherent property and power and its convincing arguments is more powerful than the keenest sword, not that which depends upon steel for its existence."

— THE MESSIAH, MIRZA GHULAM AHMAD[AS]

I wrote *EXTREMIST* because a Dutch politician with a high school diploma and no training in Islamic jurisprudence, Qur'anic hermeneutics, hadith interpretation, Arabic, or Islamic history concocted unsupported, unreferenced—and many previously unheard-of—allegations against Prophet Muhammad[sa], Islam, the *khulafa-e-rashidin*[ra], and the companions[ra]. Likewise, I wanted to show by example, education, and fact that the narrative of terrorism some extremists ascribing to Islam espouse is not a narrative Islam even slightly endorses.

Throughout this book, I have methodically responded to every one of Wilders's meritless allegations. In total, Wilders raised several hundred allegations, which I have condensed into sixty-two. Of these, nearly half offered no references but only Wilders's weightless opinion. It merits describing yet again: Wilders's opinion is that of a man with no knowledge of any Islamic science, no knowledge of even the most rudimentary Arabic, no knowledge of Islamic history, and comes from a man who does not even rise to the level of college dropout.

I furthermore reject the notion some extremists hold that Islam is somehow above criticism—it is not. Islam welcomes criticism, open dialogue, debate, discussion, and scrutiny. This is the fundamental reason why the Qur'an commands Muslims on literally hundreds of occasions to reflect, ponder, and investigate. As a Muslim, I readily and unhesitatingly state this fact: if Islam cannot stand under critical inquiry, then it is not worth its name. Those extremists who promote blasphemy laws are a cancer to all humanity—such laws are an affront to human decency. Islam can answer for itself and invites critical inquiry—it does not need barbaric blasphemy laws for protection.

And with that invitation to critical inquiry is an obligation for justice and honesty. Critical inquiry without justice and honesty is neither critical nor an inquiry. It is simply a shameless attempt at reinforcing a preconceived notion. Thus, common sense tells us that critical, referenced inquiry is one thing, and unsubstantiated, unreferenced propaganda is an entirely different phenomena.

Islam demands, just as the tenets of justice dictate, honesty, integrity, and civility in all dialogue. In *Marked for Death*, Wilders avoids each of these fundamental building blocks of a productive discussion. These tactics are abhorrent to civilized dialogue and freedom of conscience. Far from building bridges of understanding, such tactics create hatred and instill enmity for others through ignorance.

These tactics of hatred and enmity through ignorance are likewise the strategy that extremists ascribing to Islam promote. Thus, I likewise condemn such extremists just the same. They malign Islam, the Qur'an, and Prophet Muhammad[sa]—each of whom instead champions open and honest dialogue. Those extremists ascribing to Islam will ultimately destroy themselves. My hope and my struggle, however, is that we as humankind can work together to use education as a means to elevate these extremists out of their current pit of darkness and into an era of tolerance and light. We can work together to save the current generation and also future generations. But this struggle to elevate must be a unified one. This struggle becomes all the more difficult when anti-Islam extremists, such as Wilders, insist on giving mullahs and terrorists a platform and the unmerited claim of legitimacy.

Thus, just as I categorically condemn extremists ascribing to Islam, I make one final appeal to anti-Islam extremists like Wilders, and remind him of the three paths before him.

First, I invite him to respond to this rejoinder. If Wilders believes his worldview of Islam is based in fact, then he should have no difficulty in responding. And, just to be clear, "respond" requires the use of legitimate Islamic sources when criticizing Islam, citing the source for every allegation, and undertaking a more thorough study of Islam than can be summed up with "I have read the Koran several times."

If Wilders chooses not to respond, a second path remains available to him. Wilders can tacitly accept defeat by simply desisting from slandering Islam and Prophet Muhammad[sa] any further. This is not a request for censorship. Instead, this is a request for Wilders to recognize the plain truth that his view of Islam and Prophet Muhammad[sa] is factually incorrect, promotes extremism, empowers extremists, and increases hatred against Muslims. Therefore, Wilders should simply desist from propagating false information.

Should Wilders reject the first and second options, I remind him of the unfortunate third path he will have chosen. I do so by conveying once more the words of warning already conveyed to him in an open letter penned by His Holiness the khalifa of Islam, Hadhrat Mirza Masroor Ahmad[aba], fifth khalifa of the Ahmadiyya Muslim Community:

> We have no worldly power, nor will we ever use any worldly force. But the prayers of people whose hearts have been grieved are enough to shake the Heavens... Listen carefully—you, your party, and every other person like you will ultimately be destroyed.

Epilogue

"It has to start somewhere. It has to start sometime. What bet-ter place than here? What better time than now? All, hell, can't stop us now!"

— RAGE AGAINST THE MACHINE

I still remember the first death threat I ever received. It was, in fact, from an extremist ascribing to Islam. And, as such threats have continued, I've also received several threats of violence from some who ascribe to Christi-anity. I've received some of the most vulgar and igno-rant e-mails from atheists, Hindus, and Jews. Overall, I get more than my fair share. But what does this prove about each of those faiths or ideologies? And what does it prove about my expertise on any of those faiths or ideologies?

Nothing.

That is, nothing more than a reality of life that any child can tell you—some people are just bad people. People treat others badly for a variety of reasons—fear or ignorance, or maybe they just woke up on the wrong side of the bed. The true tragedy, however, is when the response is like that of Wilders—one that promotes more fear and ignorance and extremism. And that is precisely why my response to those who send me death threats is the opposite of his.

My response is to look for a way to build a bridge, to recognize the other person as a human being, and to find common ground. It is not to demonize 1.6 billion people. It is not to condemn a faith through which billions have found peace for centuries. And when I do respond directly to condemn an act, it is to that individual alone, not the countless more he or she often claims to stand for.

But this isn't rocket science, and I'm certainly no one special. This bridge-building is the example of the great teachers and prophets humanity has been blessed with—Buddha[as] and Krishna[as], Jesus[as] and Moses[as], Muhammad[sa] and Ahmad[as]. Receiving death threats doesn't make me an expert on extremism. It gives me an opportunity to combat that extremism with education, compassion, and love. It gives me an opportunity to win the hearts. This is an opportunity each of us has and must embrace if we truly wish to reconcile our differences.

And what better time to start than here and now?

This is precisely why I cited the Qur'an 12:8 at my book's onset, *"Surely, in Joseph and his brethren there are Signs for the inquirers.* Joseph was wronged, abused, and persecuted for years on end—though he had wronged no one, abused no one, and persecuted no one. Yet, his example of compassion to his brothers elevated his status and forged a strong alliance for peace and understanding. Prophet Muhammad[sa] cited none other than Prophet Joseph[as] when he offered forgiveness to all of Mecca for all those who wronged, abused, and persecuted him and his loved ones for years on end. And the result was a society dedicated to human equality, universal freedom of conscience, and progressive thinking.

Indeed, in Joseph and his brethren there are Signs for all inquirers—of all faiths and of no faith—who seek a path to reconciliation, societal advancement, and an end to war, distrust, and discord.

Thus, I implore you to write your own narratives of pluralism, tolerance, and service to humanity. We need not suffer under political propaganda that demands we fear one another. Let us rise above the intolerance and forge strong relationships based on personal experience, civility, and compassion. Let us write the narrative of a more peaceful, tolerant, pluralistic, and loving world. Let us look past the injustices against us and find ways to become more than merely just to others. Let us have the courage to be compassionate. That is the best way to combat extremism. By reading *EXTREMIST*, which responds to that extremism with education, you've already begun your journey. United against intolerance, all hell can't stop us.

And to non-Muslims, I make this special request that I cannot stress enough: befriend a Muslim. Befriend a Muslim coworker, a neighbor, your doctor, or your cabdriver. And if you feel uncomfortable doing so, that's all the more reason to step outside your comfort zone. Muslims are ingrained in every part of society and are determined to build a more beautiful world with all people. Let us discard fear of one another and work together to write our brighter, future narrative.

I began this book citing Prophet Muhammad's[sa] guidance on life, and it seems appropriate to end it with his dying words. He exhorted in his farewell sermon: "Do treat women well and be kind to them for they are your partners and committed helpers," and, "All mankind is from Adam and Eve, an Arab has no superiority over a non-Arab nor a non-Arab has any superiority over an Arab; also a white has no superiority over black nor a black has any superiority over white." This is the true Islam taught by the right kind of Muslim, the greatest Muslim, and the man whom Muslims consider God's greatest creation. His is the narrative I invite humanity to study, for indeed, "Muhammad[sa] was the walking Qur'an."

Thank you for reading *EXTREMIST: A Response to Geert Wilders & Terrorists Everywhere*. I hope you enjoyed it and find it worth sharing. We've got a long journey ahead of us, and our narrative for tolerance is our fuel. Let us use education and dialogue for a brighter, more successful future. Let us have the courage to be compassionate.

Together, we can cure extremism.

The ~~End~~ Beginning

Bibliography

Abbas, Imam Ibn. *Al Marefat Wal Tareekh LeAbi* Yousuf Yaqoob Baab Ikrama Mola.

Aboul-Enein, H. Yousuf and Sherifa Zuhur. *Islamic Rulings on Warfare.* Darby, PA: Diane Publishing Co.

Ahmad, Mirza Bashir. *The Life and Character of the Seal of Prophets.* 3 vols. Islam International Publications Ltd., 2011.

Ahmad, Mirza Bashiruddin Mahmood. *Life of Muhammad.* Islam International Publications Ltd., 2005.

Ahmad, Mirza Bashiruddin Mahmood. *The Introduction to the Study of the Holy Qur'an.* Guildford: Islam International Publications Ltd., 1996.

Ahmad, Mirza Ghulam. *Barahin-e-Ahmadiyya.* 5 vols. 1908.

Ahmad, Mirza Ghulam. *British Government and Jihad.* 1900.

Ahmad, Mirza Tahir. *Islam's Response to Contemporary Issues.* Tilford: Islam International Publications, Ltd., 2007.

Ahmad, Mirza Tahir. *Murder in the Name of Allah.* Islam International Publications, Ltd., 2001.

Ahmad, Mirza Tahir. "Ask Islam." November 17, 1983. http://www2.alislam.org/askislam/mp3/MEI_19841117_08.mp3. Accessed August 15, 2012.

Ahmed, Zubair. "'Hindu Terrorism' debate grips India." November 21, 2008. http://news.bbc.co.uk/2/hi/7739541.stm. Accessed May 26, 2012.

Al Alal Wal Mutanahiyya. Vol. 1.

Al-Ḥajjāj, Al-Minhāju bi-Sharḥi Ṣaḥīḥ Muslim bin. *Kitābul-Masājid wa Mawāḍi'iṣ-Ṣalāh, Bābu Sujūdit-Tilāwah, Dāru Ibni Hazam.* First. 2002.

Al-Baihaqi. *al-Mishkat Kitab-ul 'Ilm.*

Al-Barr, Imam. *Al-Tamhid lima fil-Muwatta min al-Ma`ani wal-Asanid.* Vol. 21.

Al-Bayhaqi, Imam. *Shu`ab al-Imaan.*

Al-Hakm. 7, no. 8. (February 28, 1903).

Al-Majlisi, Imam. *Bihar al-Anwar.* Vols. 19 and 67.

Al-Mishkat, *Kitab ul-Ilm.*

Anti-Defamation League. ADL. March 25, 2011. http://www.adl.org/main_Extremism/sioa.htm (accessed August 15, 2012).

Aquinas, Saint Thomas. *Letter on the Treatment of the Jews.*

Aquinas, Saint Thomas. Summa Theologiae: A Concise Translation. Edited by Timothy McDermott. Westminster, MD: Christian Classics, 1997.

Arnold, Thomas Walker. *The Preaching of Islam: A History of the Propagation of the Muslim Faith.* 2007.

Ar-Rāzī, Imām Muḥammad bin 'Umar bin Al-Ḥusain Fakhr-ud-Dīn. *At-Tafsīrul-Kabīr.* Second. Vol. 23. Beirut, 2004.

At-Tabari, Imam Abu Ja'far Muhammad ibn Jarir. *Tarikh al-umam wa al-mamloo'k.* Vol. 4. Beirut: Dar al-fikr, 1979.

Al-Tibiyan wat Tabayyen, vol. 2,

Augustine, Saint. *The Confessions of Saint Augustine.* Translated by Edward Bouverie Pusey. Vol. 12.

Az-Zahabi, Imam. *Siyar A`la'ma'l-nubala'.* Vol. 2. Beirut: Mu'assasatu'l-risala'h, 1992.

Az-Zarqānī, Muḥammad bin 'Abdul-Bāqī. *Sharḥul-'Allāmatiz-Zarqānī 'alal-Mawāhibil-Ladunniyyah.* Vol. 2. Beirut, 1996.

Az-Zurqani, Muhammad. *Zurqani.* Vol. 1.

BBC News. "Call to end female circumcision." November 24, 2006. http://news.bbc.co.uk/2/hi/6176340.stm. Accessed August 15, 2012.

Bengalee, Sufi Mutiur Rahman. *The Life of Muhammad.* Kessinger Publishing, 2010.

Besant, Annie. *The Life and Teachings of Mohammad.* Madras, 1932.

Bisset-Smith, G. T. First. Edinburgh: William Green and Sons, 1902.

Blydon, Edward Wilmot. *Christianity, Islam, and the Negro Race.* 1887.

Borne, E. G. The Northmen, Columbus and Cabot, 985–1503: *The Voyages of the Northmen and The Voyages of Columbus and John Cabot.* 1906.

Brown, Ina Corinne. *Story of the American Negro.* 1934.

Bukhari, Imam. *Sahih Jami' Bukhari.* Cairo: n.d.

Calvin, John. 1931.

Campo, Juan Eduardo. *Encyclopedia of Islam.* Infobase Publishing, 2010.

Chaplinsky v. State of New Hampshire, 315 U.S. 568 (1942)

Charles de Secondat, baron de Montesquieu. *The Spirit of Laws.* Vol. 13.

Charter of Medina. "The Constitution Society." http://www.constitution.org/cons/medina/macharter.htm.

Churchill, Bernard Lewis and Buntzie Ellis. Islam: *The Religion and the People.* Wharton Publishing, 2008.

Cobb, Thomas R. R. *An Inquiry into the Law of Negro Slavery in the United States of America.* 1858.

"Dārul-Iḥyā'it-Turāthil-'Arabī." Beirut, 2003.

Dala'ilan Nabuwwata li Baihaqi. Beirut: Darul Kutab al-'Ilmiyya.

Dawud, Imam Abu. *Sunan Abu Dawud.*

Davenport, Frances Gardiner. European Treaties Bearing on the History of the United States and its Dependencies to 1648. Vol. 1. Washington: Carnegie Institution of Washington, 1917.

Denyer, Simon and Rama Lakshmi. "Hindu terrorism charges force India to reflect on prejudices against Muslims." The Washington Post, March 14, 2011. http://www.washingtonpost.com/wp-dyn/content/article/2011/03/12/AR2011031202421.html. Accessed May 26, 2012.

Dutch News. "Christians can't vote for Wilders, say vicars." February 25, 2010. http://www.dutchnews.nl/news/archives/2010/02/christians_cant_vote_for_wilde.php. Accessed August 15, 2012.

Evans, Richard J. The Feminists: *Women's Emancipation Movements in Europe, America and Australasia, 1840–1920. Stockholm:* Helsingborg: LiberForlag, 1979.

Falk, Gerhard. *The Jew in Christian Theology.* Jefferson, NC and London:, McFarland and Company, Inc., 2013.

Farid, Malik Ghulam. *Al-Tafsir ash-Saghir,* The Holy Qur'an 1-Volume Commentary. Tilford: Islam International Publications, Ltd., 2002.

Glenn, H. Patrick. *Legal Traditions of the World.* Oxford University Press, 2007.

Guillaume, Alfred. *Life of Muhammad: A Translation of Ibn-e-Ishaq's Sirat Rasul Allah .* Oxford University Press, 1955.

Hajar, Imam Ibn. *Talkhis al-habir fi takhrij aHadith al-Rafi'i al-Kabir.*

Hajveri, Ali bin Osman. *Kashful Mahjub.*

Hall, Gwendolyn Midlo. *Slavery and African Ethnicities in the Americas: Restoring the Links.* 2005.

Hanbal, Imam Masnad Ahmad bin. *al-Mishkat.*

Hanbal, Imam Masnad Ahmad bin. *Sahih Jami' Masnad Ahmad.*

Hart, Michael. *The 100: A Ranking of the Most Influential Persons in History.* 1978.

Hisham, Ibn. *Kitab Sirat Rasul Allah.*

Hitler, Adolf. *Mein Kampf.*

Holstun, Jim. "Nonie Darwish and the al-Bureij massacre." June 26, 2008. http://electronicintifada.net/content/nonie-darwish-and-al-bureij-massacre/7586. Accessed August 12, 2012.

Human Rights Watch. Decades of Disparity: Drug Arrests and Race in the United States. 2009. http://www.hrw.org/sites/default/files/reports/us0309web_1.pdf.

Imam al-Madkhal, Ibn 'Abd al-Barr. *Jami' Bayaan al-'Ilm, and al-Khatib.*

Irving, Washington. *Mahomet and His Successors.* Vol. 1. New York: Putnam's Sons, 1868.

Jenkins, Philip. *Laying Down the Sword: Why We Can't Ignore the Bible's Violent Verses.* Harper Collins, 2011.

John Chrysostom. *Eight Homilies Against the Jews* [Adversus Judeaus], vol. 98. Patrologia Greaca.

Justin Martyr. *Dialogue with Trypho.* Translated by Thomas B. Falls.

Kanzul 'Ummal.

Kathir, Ibn. *Al-Bidaayah wa an-Nihaayah.* Vol. 8. Al-jizah: Dar al-fikr al-`arabiy, 1933.

Kathir, ibn. *Long Commentary of the Holy Qur'an,* Tafsir. Vol. 3.

Khabriṣ-Ṣaḥīfah, *Bābu Dukhūlish-Sha'bi wa. Dārul-Kutubil-'Ilmiyyah.* First. Beirut, 1996.

Khan, Anwer Mahmood. *"Perception vs. Reality: Is Islam a Militant Religion? Response to Daniel Pipes Accusations."* The Muslim Sunrise 2 (Summer 2012): 27–30.

Khan, Sir Muhammad Zafrulla. *Islam and Human Rights.* Fifth. Islam International Publications, Ltd., 1999.

Khan, Sir Muhammad Zafrulla. *Fasting: The Fourth Pillar of Islam."* The Review of Religions (March 1994).

"Kitābu Tafsīril-Qur'ān, Sūratul-Qamar."

Kitabul Kharaj. Vol. 1.

Lamartine, Alphonse de. *Histoire de la Turquie.* Vol. 2. Paris, 1855.

Lane, Edward William. *Arabic-English Lexicon.* London: Williams & Norgate, 1863.

Lane, Edward W. and Stanley Lane-Poole. *An Arabic-English Lexicon.* Vol. 5. New York: Cosmo Classics, 2011.

Lane-Poole, Stanley. *Selections from the Quran and Hadith.* Lahore: Sind Sagar Academy.

Lane-Poole, Stanley *Studies in a Mosque.* 1883.

Latif, Sultan A. *Slavery: The African American Psychic Trauma.* 1994.

Lees, William N. Futuh ash-Sham ed. 1/162. Culcutta: *Baptist Mission,* 1854.

Lewis, Bernard. *What Went Wrong? Western Impact and Middle Eastern Response.* 2002.

Luther, Martin. *On the Jews and Their Lies: Luther's Works.* Translated by Martin H. Bertram. Philadelphia: Fortress Press, 1971.

Majah, Imam Ibn. *Sahih Jami' Ibn Majah.*

Majlis Khuddamul Ahmadiyya USA. *By the Dawn's Early Light: Short Stories by American Converts to Islam.* 2008.

Malik, Imam. *Sahih Jami' Al-Muwatta.* Vol. 21.

Meezaan al-Ai'tidal. Vol. 4.

Menka, Eunice. "Islam does not support female circumcision—Expert." March 15, 2005. http://www.ghanaweb.com/GhanaHomePage/NewsArchive/artikel.php?ID=77396. Accessed August 15, 2012.

Middle East Forum. *"Arab Liberals: Prosecute Clerics Who Promote Murder,"* The Middle East Quarterly (Winter 2005).

Muhammad, Abul-Qasim al-Hussein bin Mufaddal bin. Al-Mufradat.

Muir, Sir William. *The Life of Mahomet.* 1878. Reprint of the 1894 ed., New Delhi: Voice of India, 1992.

Muslim, Imam. *Sahih Jami' Muslim.*

Nawawi, Imam. *Gardens of the Righteous* (Riyadh ash-Salihin). Translated by Sir Muhammad Zafrulla Khan. Tilford: Islam International Publications, Ltd., 1996.

Nayl al-Awtar. Vol. 1.

National Center for Education Statistics. Status and Trends in the Education of Blacks. http://nces.ed.gov/pubs2003/2003034.pdf.

Neary, Lynn. *"Tamil Tigers: Suicide Bombing Innovators."* NPR, May 21, 2009. http://www.npr.org/templates/story/story.php?storyId=104391493. Accessed May 26, 2012.

NobelPrize.org. "Abdus Salam—Biographical." www.nobelprize.org/nobel_prizes/physics/laureates/1979/salam-bio.html. Accessed August 15, 2012.

Nu'Mani, Allama Shibli. *Sirat-Un-Nabi*. Vol. II.

PBS. "Muhammad: Legacy of a Prophet. Muhammand and...the Jews of Medina." http://www.pbs.org/muhammad/ma_jews.shtml. Accessed August 12, 2012.

Prison Policy Initiative. "The Sentencing Project: Facts about Prisons and Prisoners." http://prisonpolicy.org/scans/prison_facts.pdf.

PolitiFact.com. "Tim Kaine says Virginia women earn 79 cents to every $1 made by men." June 6, 2012. http://www.politifact.com/virginia/statements/2012/jun/15/tim-kaine/tim-kaine-says-virginia-women-earn-79-cents-every-/. Accessed August 15, 2012.

Population Council. "Islamic Scholars Find No Religious Justification for FGM/C." Frontiers in Reproductive Health (2008).

Interview by Stephen Sackur. "Geert Wilders on BBC Hardtalk." January 26, 2009. http://www.youtube.com/watch?v=o6cFKQNBH3s.

Savage, Heidi Hemming and Julie Hemming. Women Making America. Clotho Press, 2009.

Seerah-i Halabi. Vol. 1.

Sehat, David. The Myth of American Religious Freedom. 2011.

Shaw, Sir George Bernard. The Genuine Islam. Vol. 1. 1936.

Smith, Reverend Boswell. Muhammad and Muhammadism. 1946.

Southern Poverty Law Center. "Who We Are." http://www.splcenter.org/who-we-are.

Spencer Watch. "Who is Hugh Fitzgerald?" August 16, 2010. http://spencerwatch.com/who-is-hugh-fitzgerald/. Accessed August 12, 2012.

Sreeraman. "Egyptian Clerics Say Female Circumcision Un-Islamic." July 4, 2007. http://www.medindia.net/news/Egyptian-Clerics-Say-Female-Circumcision-UnIslamic-23055-1.htm. Accessed August 15, 2012.

State of California. "Criminal Consequences for Lewd Behavior." Cal. Pen. Code § 288.

Steinback, Robert. "The Anti-Muslim Inner Circle." Southern Poverty Law Center Intelligence Report, Summer 2011. http://www.splcenter.org/get-informed/intelligence-report/browse-all-issues/2011/summer/the-anti-muslim-inner-circle. Accessed August 15, 2012.

Sweeney, Annie. "Suspect Arrested in 2006 Slaying." Chicago Tribune, June 17, 2010. http://articles.chicagotribune.com/2010-06-17/news/ct-met-barber-cold-case-20100617_1_abdul-karim-slaying-barbershop. Accessed June 6, 2012.

Tafsir-ul Maalam-ut Tanzil.

Tarikh al-Tabari. Vol. 2.

Tehzeeb al-Tehzeeb. Vol. 11.

Thacher, John Boyd. Christopher Columbus. New York: Putnam's Sons, 1903.

The Catholic Encyclopedia: An International Reference of Work on the Constitution, Doctrine, Dicipline, and History of the Catholic Church. Vol. 3. New York: Robert Appleton Co.

Tirmidhi, Imam Muhammad ibn 'Isa. Sahih Sunan At-Tirmidhi.

Trevelyan, Bob. "Mauritania fatwa bans female genital mutilation." BBC News, January 18, 2010. http://news.bbc.co.uk/2/hi/africa/8464671.stm. Accessed August 15, 2012.

UNESCO Institute for Statistics. Adult and Youth Literacy. September 2011. http://www.uis.unesco.org/FactSheets/Documents/FS16-2011-Literacy-EN.pdf. Accessed August 15, 2012.

US Bureau of the Census. The Black Population: 2010 (2010 Census Briefs). September, 2011. http://www.census.gov/prod/cen2010/briefs/c2010br-06.pdf.

US Department of Education. Status and Trends in the Education of Blacks. National Center for Education Statistics, 2003.

Wasserstein, David J. "So, what did the Muslims do for the Jews? The JC Essay." The Jewish Chronicle Online, May 24, 2012. http://www.thejc.com/comment-and-debate/comment/68082/so-what-did-muslims-do-jews. Accessed August 12, 2012.

Wehr, Hans. A Dictionary of Modern Written Arabic . Fourth. Urbana: Spoken Language Services, 1994.

Wilders, Geert, Marked for Death: Islam's War Against the West and Me. Washington, D.C.: Regenery, Inc., 2012

Wilmore, Gayraud S. Black Religion and Black Radicalism. 2nd ed. 1983.

Zadul Ma'ad . Vol. 1.

About the Author

Qasim Rashid, Esq. holds a Bachelor's of Science in Marketing from the University of Illinois at Chicago and a *juris doctorate* from the University of Richmond School of Law. He's previously authored the critically acclaimed book, *The Wrong Kind of Muslim: An Untold Story of Persecution & Perseverance (2013)*.

Qasim is a frequent writer and lecturer on Islamic and human rights issues. He regularly speaks at various universities and houses of worship nationally and internationally. His work has appeared in *The New York Times, Washington Post, USA Today, CNN, Daily Beast, Huffington Post, NPR*, among several other national and international outlets. He likewise regularly interviews on FOX, NBC, CBS, BBC, Al Jazeera, and numerous local and regional radio programs.

Today, Qasim is a practicing attorney in Richmond, Virginia, where he resides with his wife and two children. He is an avid runner and *still* dreams of one day walking on another planet.